A THEORY OF EVERYONE

First edition
March 2021

Copyright © 2021
All rights reserved
Self-published

No part of this book may be reproduced, or stored in a retrieval system, or transmitted in any form or by any means, electronic, mechanical, photocopying, recording, or otherwise, without express written permission of the copyright owner.

Copper patina used on front cover by Caara Fritz Hunter (artafix.com)

From hunter-gatherers to civilisation

A Theory of Everyone

John Almeryn

Explaining modern human behaviour

Contents

Change and Continuity 1
Part One 43
Inherited Hierarchies 45
Levelling 92
Part Two 111
Our "Web" 113
Our "Self" 146
Modern Society and our Self and Web 180
Part Three 209
Simple Rules for Understanding Human Beings 213
Challenges and Provocation 226
Individual's Behaviours 249
Group Dynamics 263
Societal Dynamics 283
Social Media 309
Part Four 333
Emotions 335
Family & Parents 361
Core Needs 412
Modern Life 418

1
Change and Continuity

For the vast majority of our evolution, our hunter-gatherer ancestors lived in small tribes.

Now, we live in huge societies of millions of people, with national allegiances and complex social lives, spanning multiple groups.

This is a dramatic change in behaviour.

It happened less by choice, and more by the rumbling momentum of progress, or at least because, once the change started, it became impossible to stop.

On one hand, our large societies give us much greater security. They give us greater defence, and greater access to stable food supplies and amenities. Through our larger groups, we have worked together to build pyramids, map the globe, land a man on the moon, split the atom, and peer into the deepest depths of the universe.

Yet despite all this, part of us remains as hunter-gatherers. We still favour small social groups over large ones. When groups get too big, they tend to fragment into a number of smaller, tribe-sized ones. We like to explore, and move around, and don't like being too tied down. And, our lives can be shaped by a similar number of friends and family.

There is something deep within the various species on Earth that keeps them rooted to their behaviours. A leopard is unlikely to form social groups with other leopards. A bison is unlikely to leave the herd and live by themselves. They *could*, but such a change in behaviour would likely be uncomfortable, and less satisfying. The leopard would want to seek out its own territory, and the bison would miss living with other bison.

We still have much of our hunter-gatherer "programming". Our programming still wants everything it would get from a small tribe: belonging, security, definition, and the bonds of friends a family. We are born into the world with this programming, that expects to find something tribe-shaped, for which it is set up for.

However, the modern world we are born into is not tribe-shaped.

For example, instead of having all of our key social bonds in one place (in our tribe), they are now spread out across several groups, each with their own sub-culture and values. All the things that our programming wants, are now in different places, across our complex social lives of multiple groups, and often knotted in conflict.

Also, the world we are born into is unequal. Our programming expects something tribe-shaped, but then find there are some things more desirable, and some less. There are some things above the tribe, and some things below it. For example, there is great wealth and power out there to be amassed. With the chance of glory and adulation (or the desire to move "up" rather than "down"), then our programming, that is finely tuned to a tribe environment, gets a little out of balance and stretched.

People *can* amass fortunes, and it feels good to do so, at least whilst the going is good. And, if we don't do it, then someone else will. But, given our programming evolved without such things, we can find we are pulled in different directions, often wanting two incompatible things. For example, we can find it hard to feel completely fulfilled by comparative success alone.

Therefore, on average, living as a modern human is more difficult than it should be. Our modern world is different to the environment that our programming is set up for. Our social environment is more complex (and often a little muddled), and our societies are unequal. Some will see the good side of it, some the bad.

Our programming evolved over millions of years based on the environment around us: a tribe. That environment then fulfilled our programming. Hunter-gatherers are like a key that perfectly fits a lock, because the key and the lock were hewn in the same process. As modern humans, we are that same key, but we now face a huge range of new and different locks, some that we can open easily, and some that we can't.

Our modern societies can offer us greater joys, for example through success, but, perhaps, at times, it doesn't quite go to plan. Our various social groups, be they family, friends of colleagues, can become interlinked and occasionally muddled. The relationships that are supposed to fulfil us, as human beings, can sometimes become uncomfortable, and include unwanted conflict. And, the social mechanisms, that create smooth, harmonious hunter-gatherer tribes, can become confused, and act against themselves. These are no barrier to living a long, healthy, happy life overall, but it is just a little harder.

In contrast, living in a small hunter-gatherer tribe is when our programming fits our environment. Our ancient environment provided a square peg for a square hole, and a round peg for a round hole. We can't ever replicate this environment in the modern world, but we can understand how the difference between that environment, and the one we face, causes many of the behaviours we see around us.

This book proposes theories that explain people's behaviour. It comes not from the perspective of "I can't understand why someone behaved like that", but instead: "someone behaved like that, *why*". We often find others difficult to understand, irrational, of harbouring views that anger or frustrate us. They may feel the same way about us. We feel *we* are right, but they think they are.

Much of the focus of the book is exploring the impact that our modern social environment, and our unequal societies, have on the individual: from their self, to their bonds of friendship and family. At the end of the day, we are all just human beings facing unusual circumstances.

There are four parts to the book:

1. Levels;
2. Self & web;
3. Interactions; and
4. Our core.

Parts 1 and 2 describe many of the more fundamental reasons why behaviours and situations occur, and why "it is what it is". These parts cover three of the key aspects of living as a modern human: our complex hierarchies (levels); our spread-out social lives (webs); and our perceptions of ourself (self). Part 3 is more about our personal experiences, and is less theoretical and more tangible, looking at the types of experiences we have on a daily basis. Part 3 includes a discussion of social media. Part 4 looks at the core of the matter, including our own emotions, and our family and core needs.

A (very) brief history of us

Firstly, before we look at where we are, we have to understand where we've come from.

To reach where we are today, to be a modern human, has been less of a gradual change, and more of a roller-coaster ride, catapulting us forward.

1859

Before starting at the beginning, we can briefly consider 1859. This was a year that our understanding of our early history took a large step forwards: when Charles Darwin published *On the Origin of Species*.

The book was met with scepticism and opposition, but nevertheless sold out quickly on its first publishing run[1].

Darwin had written the book after travelling the world on the wooden ship HMS Beagle. A 22-year-old Darwin set sail as a passenger on the ship in 1831, leaving behind the crowded streets foggy London. The world was a changing place, and that was no more so than in England. The fog in Victorian London was air pollution from the first industrial revolution, that was in full swing at the time. Humans had learnt how to harness the energy from burning coal (which has greater energy density, and burns hotter than wood), and to use that energy to turn machines, that were engineered for mass manufacture.

The HMS Beagle crossed the Atlantic and spent a large amount of its voyage around South America. As a botanist, Darwin was cataloguing the flora and fauna he observed. He did this by hand, through beautiful sketches of the plants and wildlife around him (since there was no practical means of photography in the early 1800s).

Around the Galapagos islands, Darwin noticed differences in animals from one island to the next. Animals of similar species, separated by stretches of water, had noticeably different characteristics. He started to form the theory of evolution. He theorised that animals slowly adapt to their environment, and that animals separated on different islands were adapting in different ways. Over time, these adaptations led to large scale changes in a species.

Turning these theories on ourselves, Darwin theorised that humans evolved from apes. He wrote *On the Origin of Species*, and, when it was published in 1859, the wider world considered evolution for the first time.

We now largely believe this is true, and much evidence has been found, in fossils, that show our evolutionary journey. We understand that humans diverged from chimpanzees, around 4-6 million years ago, and became bipedal (stood up) for the first time.

2 million BC

Many, many species of humans used to exist. As we evolved over millions of years, various adaptions caused changes in how certain humans looked and behaved compared to others. At one point, there would have been many different species of human living side by side. Nevertheless, nature had its way, and the more successful species survived and expanded, and the others disappeared.

About 2 million years ago, Homo Erectus emerged. Homo Erectus was our predecessor, and of roughly similar size to ourselves. Roughly speaking, we can consider Homo Erectus as our "parent" species. From Homo Erectus, two "child" species evolved: Homo Sapiens (that's us), and Homo Neanderthalis (Neanderthals)[2].

Homo Erectus was the trailblazer. They started to develop more complex tools, and, significantly, they mastered fire, and used it for cooking.

The mastery of fire was an instigator for change. Cooked food is better in a number of ways. Cooking breaks down tough plant fibres and cell walls, meaning it takes less energy to chew. Cooking also breaks down the various proteins, carbohydrates and sugars, making them easier to digest. When we digest cooked food, we absorb more nutrition from it, compared to uncooked food[3].

This is why cooking smells good to us, and why cooking releases new, enjoyable flavours. Cooked food is more energy efficient, and our brains are still thinking like hunter-gatherers, subtly urging us towards more "advantageous" behaviours.

Cooking resulted in Homo Erectus having more energy available. That allowed their brains to expand (since brain activity is energy intensive). Then, they both had more energy, and greater intelligence. That greater intelligence allowed them to develop new tools, and use more complex language.

Cooking and brain size worked hand-in-hand to elevate our ancestors from just another species on planet Earth, to a highly intelligent and successful one. The path had been set.

200,000 BC

Homo Sapiens didn't arrive on the scene until relatively recently, about 200,000 years ago. Our brains were even bigger than Homo Erectus. With this increased intelligence came greater curiosity, improved use of tools, and we became so good at hunting that we could wipe out entire species around us. As a result, we were more prone to moving around, whether through inquisitiveness, or the desire, or need, for new hunting grounds.

Homo Sapiens migrated out of Africa about 100,000 years ago, and once we got a taste for exploration, we spread out over the entire globe. We got to Australia 50,000 years ago, the pacific islands 33,000 years ago and America 15,000 years ago. Our movements around the world were aided by land bridges no longer there. They were also aided by ice bridges. For much of this time the world was under the grip of an ice age, and the arctic extended as far south as northern Europe[2].

There is evidence to show that the world at the time was full of strange and giant beasts, and that the arrival of Homo Sapiens in an area generally coincided with their disappearance.

Our movements may seem fast, but it was actually fairly slow and gradual. We moved around more than Homo Erectus, or Neanderthals, but only a *little* bit more than them. For example you could walk from North Africa to Australia in about a year, assuming land bridges connected them[4]. So the fact it took Homo Sapiens 50,000 years represents a slow transition, with many generations making no inroads into exploration. However, it appears that our temperament was more biased towards exploring than some of our nearest kin, who were more static.

At one point, for many thousands of years, Homo Sapiens (us) lived alongside our "sibling" species, Neanderthals, in Europe, and alongside our "parent" species, Homo Erectus, in Asia. However, around 25-50,000 years ago, both Neanderthals and Homo Erectus became extinct, leaving just ourselves.

It is not conclusively known how and why Homo Sapiens became the only surviving species of human. Perhaps we have a dark secret, and we were responsible for their extinction.

However, there is evidence of peace and interbreeding amongst species, so it could be just circumstance, survivability, or the fact that we were spread further (so that if disaster occurred in one place, we'd survive in another).

10,000 BC

10,000 BC was when it all changed. Before that, for millions of years, the various species of human, Homo Sapiens included, lived in a very similar way: as hunter-gatherers. We would move around the ancient landscapes, picking fruit and berries, and hunting the local wildlife. We would set camp for the night, and spend the evening around a fire, cooking and telling stories, with our close tribe of friends and family.

Around 10,000 BC, in several different locations on Earth, for example Mesopotamia (modern day Syria) and China, we started farming. We settled down to one particular spot, and cultivated a plot of land for a particular crop. People gravitated towards this new technology. Those in these settlements had greater power and security, compared to the wandering hunter-gatherers. Soon, to not be a part of this changing world left small tribes vulnerable, and technologically inferior.

This was the stone age. We gave up our freedom and ability to roam, and instead lived in houses made of stone and mud. We became farmers, and worked together to grow crops and irrigate farmland: digging and maintaining the ditches and waterways.

With greater co-location, humans got their first taste of small society, with all its benefits and compromises.

Nevertheless, by all accounts this was a peaceful period for human beings. The towns and villages were small, bountiful, and remote, so there wasn't motivation for war, or group conflict. Life was also fairly straightforward, as people had relatively few possessions, and the ability to build their own houses, and therefore an element of self-determination (although less so than in the hunter-gatherer lifestyle we'd given up). The year revolved around the harvests, the warmth of summer, and the harshness of winter. Things stayed roughly similar for 7000 years, so there was stability and security. It was a period of co-operation, and learning to live together.

However, the population was slowly growing. Between 10,000 BC and 3,000 BC the population of humans on Earth grew many times, and small villages became towns, and then bigger still[5].

3000 BC

Around 3,000 BC, civilisations started to appear, and the bronze age began.

Vast collections of humans banded together, under single rule, and shared belief. They were based around the main rivers of the world, for example the Nile in Egypt, the Euphrates (and Tigris) in Mesopotamia, the Yellow River in China, and the Indus in India. The world became one of cities and empires, rulers and subordinates. and huge armies regularly went to war over power and resources.

Against all this, humans had lost their self-determination, and were now dependent on others, in the societies they found themselves in.

The ruling class grew in size and power, and started to interlink themselves with the belief systems. Rulers, feeling the power of being in charge of huge numbers of people, now claimed that they were on a par with the gods themselves, and a priestly class emerged, devoted to maintaining and spreading this message.

Mythology therefore became more important. It satisfied the egos of kings and queens, pharaohs and warlords. It reinforced their power, and it united large groups of disparate peoples, under a common culture.

The sky, with its unexplained and unreachable celestial objects, was an obvious basis for these common belief systems. As a result, mythology became intertwined with cosmology.

The priestly classes therefore became astronomers. They mapped the stars, and predicted the movements of the various dots of lights. They tried to explain it all, to the awe, fear, and amazement of the growing populations. Human's focus became less on the natural world around them, with its seasonal plants and wildlife, and instead on the sky above.

How different civilisations interpreted the sky above (the same sky that we look at today), can therefore provide a basis for discussing how humans changed over the next 5000 years.

Most civilisations in the bronze age tried to explain the universe in similar ways. Nearly all believed that the world was flat, with the sky above, and an underworld below. The sun was an important deity in each culture, and that deity would travel across the sky during the day, and through the underworld at night.

For example, the ancient Egyptians believed that the sun was the god Ra, who was depicted with the head of a falcon. Ra was the creator god, and he travelled across the sky on a solar-boat. At night, he travelled through the underworld (called Duat), and fought the god of chaos: Apophis, a giant serpent, who attempted to stop Ra on his journey. Every morning, when the sun rose, Ra was reborn[6].

The Mesopotamians believed that the sun was the god Utu. Utu had a long beard and long arms, and was the god of justice. He rode across the sky on a chariot, from where he saw everything going on below him. At the end of the day, he passed through a gateway in the West, and into the underworld (called Kur). Whilst in the underworld, he was the arbiter of the dead, until he rose again the next day, through a gateway in the East[7].

The Maya, whose civilisation first started to appear around 2000 BC, in the land-bridge that is modern day Mexico, also had similar beliefs. They believed that the sun was Kinich Ahua. When, at sunset, he disappeared into the ground, to a mellowing of light, and a reddening of the sky, it represented the death of the world. During the night, whilst Kinich Ahua was below them, beneath the deepest caves and sinkholes, he transformed into the Night Jaguar, for the long, arduous journey through the underworld. When he rose the next day, and light filled the sky once more, the world was reborn[8].

Each civilisation was trying to make sense of the strange objects in the sky, whilst also creating myths and stories that allowed people to unite. The moon, stars, and constellations all became a source of greater interest.

One dot of light: Venus, was particularly important to early civilisations. Given Venus' proximity to the sun (compared to Earth), we rarely get the chance to see it with the naked eye. It stays close to the sun in the sky, which means that most of the time it is either being drowned out by the light of the sun, or having followed the sun into the night. It is only visible every 9 months or so, when it is furthest from the sun, and only at either sunrise or sunset (as the Morning Star or Evening Star), when the brightness of the nearby sun isn't obscuring it[9].

Due to its infrequent, but regular, appearances, many early civilisations gave Venus special attention. Perhaps it elevated the status of priests who could accurately predict its arrival every 9 months. Perhaps it's infrequent arrivals could be used to signify special messages, depending on the whims of the leaders. Or, given it appears on a cycle of 9 months, which coincides with the length of a human pregnancy, perhaps they simply believed that it was delivering important messages of fertility, and was interlinked with human existence.

To the Mesopotamians, Venus was Inanna, who had a dual role as both the goddess of love and war, and therefore presided over both birth and death[10]. She became one of their most important gods. To the Egyptians Venus was two gods: Tioumoutiri and Ouait (most civilisations at the time didn't realise that the Morning Star and Evening Star were the same object). To the Maya, the Morning Star was Quetzalcoatl, a feathered snake, and a representation of the fertility of the earth, and the Evening Star was Tlaloc, who was depicted as humanoid, with fangs and a feathered headdress, and who was the god of rain.

People would watch for the arrival of Venus, who appeared only briefly every 9 months, at either sunrise or sunset. Venus' arrival would be a significant event, felt across entire civilisations (and the world).

Whilst the tiny dots of light in the sky (that we now know are stars and planets) moved with predictable precision, the humans of that era were still very much unaware of what the celestial bodies were, and truly believed them to be powerful deities.

Because of this, when an unexpected astronomical event occurred, such as an eclipse, it was met with fear and suspicion. It was interpreted as if it was a direct intervention from the gods. In each civilisation, the sun was seen as a bringer of life, and in a perpetual fight against the forces of death and destruction, who it battled through each night in the underworld, in order to be reborn at sunrise. There was no other logical reason why the sun disappeared each day. Most civilisations saw an eclipse as a fight between the sun and another mythical being, and if the sun lost, it would bring about the end of the world. As a result, when an eclipse happened, most civilisations banged drums, and performed ceremonies and ritual sacrifices, in order to aid their sun-god in its battle[11].

To live during the bronze age would have been a time of superstition and deeply held beliefs. Societies were fragile and experimental, and there was no historical precedent for how to run a civilisation, with its complex balance of law, economy, culture, defence, and personal rights. Many civilisations rose quickly, and fell just as fast.

It was a time of rapid change, and a time of mythology, against a world full of unknowns.

500 BC

Civilisation spread to other corners of the world, and as technology, knowledge, writing, and record keeping advanced, the myths and legends describing the sky above slowly started to contain greater understanding.

For example, around 500 BC, in the people in the Mediterranean, advances in our understanding of the sky started to occur.

These changes happened in iron-age Ancient Greece, with its city states of Athens and Sparta.

On May 28, 585 BC, an eclipse stopped a six-year war between the Medes and Lydians, fought in modern day Turkey. When the sun was covered, it was seen as an omen. The bloodshed was halted, weapons were put down, and both sides were reportedly anxious for a peace to be agreed, as willed by the gods[12].

Yet, 150 years later, Pericles showed his Greek Army that the eclipse was nothing more than a covering of the sun, by something bigger than his cloak[13].

This change in perception, of an event such as an eclipse, was aided by scientific advancement made at the time. Pythagoras was at the forefront of these.

Pythagoras was the first to propose that the Earth was spherical. By observing the phases of the moon (i.e. the different crescent shapes it makes at different times in the lunar cycle), he deduced that the moon must be spherical. From this, he reasoned that the Earth was spherical too[14].

Ancient Greece was a hot bed of philosophers, and, with each theory and argument, the world around us slowly started to unravel. For example, Aristotle, around 150 years later, added weight to the arguments (that the Earth was spherical) by inferring it from how different constellations are visible at different times throughout the year. Roughly 100 years after that, Greek astronomers calculated the circumference of the Earth.

The sun, the planets, and the stars all moved in intelligible, endless circular paths, but were becoming more explainable, and less of a source of myth and legend.

Nevertheless, astrology played a part in decision making for centuries to come. The celestial objects couldn't quite shed their mythological status, and many leaders throughout history would consult a fortune teller for a horoscope, when in need of advice and guidance.

1600s

In the 2000 years after Pythagoras, the world was a different place, but many aspects of it hadn't changed. Civilisations were still vying for power, led by rulers who saw themselves as vessels for the gods, and wars were commonplace. Democracy was a flower struggling to take root, occasionally growing in places, only to be washed away by tides of inequality.

A Theory of Everyone

It wasn't until the 1600s when larger changes started to occur. The first glimpses of a global economy were starting to take shape, and economic empires developed, such as the Dutch East India Company. Democracy was finding firmer ground, for example following the English Civil War. Science was also seeing many advances, and the 1600s can count Galileo, Kepler, Descartes, Fermat, Pascal, Hooke and Isaac Newton among its notable alumni.

Up until the 1600s, our understanding of the stars hadn't changed that much, because until then we could only see them with the naked eye. It wasn't until the invention of the telescope that this changed. The first recorded telescope was by Hans Lipperhey, a Dutch spectacle maker, who filed a patent to one in 1608[15]. The invention of the telescope was game changing in understanding our place in the universe.

Galileo took that invention and turned it to the stars[16]. Looking through a telescope gave a much deeper understanding of the bodies above us, whether the craters on the moon, sunspots and solar flares, the rings of Saturn, or the moons of Jupiter.

Using the telescope allowed Galileo to confirm the phases of Venus (i.e. that Venus, like our moon, appears as a crescent, depending on the locations of Venus, the Earth, and the Sun – this can't be seen with the naked eye). This allowed Galileo to deduce that Venus was spherical, and gave some insight into the relative positions of Venus, the Earth, and the Sun. From this, and other observations, Galileo was able to prove Copernicus' theory that the *sun* was at the centre of the galaxy.

Copernicus' theory of heliocentrism, that the *sun* was at the centre of the galaxy, was one of many competing theories at the time. Previous to Galileo (and therefore without the ability to prove any theory one way or another), they had been debated using philosophical arguments, loosely based on logic.

Change and Continuity

The Roman Catholic Church was paying attention to these debates. The idea that the *Earth* was the centre of the galaxy, that had been around for 2000 years (since Ancient Greece), had to some extent worked its way into Christian beliefs. Proposing alternative theories was making the Church nervous. In the early days of Galileo's work, it was merely nerves. For example Galileo was allowed to defend himself at a debate in Rome, and Pope Urban VIII personally urged Galileo to pursue arguments both for *and* against heliocentrism. However, as Galileo pursued heliocentrism further, and proved it more completely, the nervousness of the Church caused them to try him, and he was forced to recant his views. Galileo was placed under house arrest, for most of the remainder of his life, in his villa at Arcetri in Florence.

However, his work on astronomy lived on. The weight of scientific evidence, that advanced our understanding of the stars above, and our place in the galaxy, was too much to ignore.

1859

The 1700s and 1800s saw a wealth of enlightened thinking, with philosophers dreaming of better ways of living, and societies based on monarchism and the elite being dismantled around the globe in favour of power for the people. However, it was also a brutal time, with new weapons of war, and nations vying for power against deep rivalries. The development of the world was also sporadic, which resulted in great conflicts of inequality.

Regardless of the world around us, the individual, average human's perception of it had changed. To be a human in the 1800s was to understand much more about the world. By 1859, the same year Darwin published *On the Origin of Species*, we saw a new breed of knowledgeable human. We had gone from hunter-gatherers wandering the landscape, to bronze age man, who banged drums at eclipses, to the educated few arguing about the philosophical nature of the world around us, to a race of human beings who were comparatively well educated, who understood where they came from as a species, and their position in the galaxy.

When, in 1859, a huge astronomical event occurred, people saw it with wonder, not fear. They saw it with joy, not confusion, and as circumstance, not the will of the gods.

In 1859 a huge solar flare hit the Earth's magnetosphere, and caused the largest geomagnetic storm on record. Auroras could be seen across the globe, even near the equator. The storm caused havoc with the telegraph systems of the time. If a similar storm hit Earth today, as nearly happened in 2012, it would cause widespread malfunctioning and damage of electrical equipment, power grids, and satellites[17].

To have the sky filled with strange moving lights, of different colours, is an awe-inspiring event to perceive. Yet the humans of 1859 were mostly educated enough to understand what was happening.

An Australian gold miner, C.F. Herbert, describes the event[18]:

"I was gold-digging at Rokewood, about four miles from Rokewood township (Victoria). Myself and two mates looking out of the tent saw a great reflection in the southern heavens at about 7 o'clock p.m., and in about half an hour, a scene of almost unspeakable beauty presented itself, lights of every imaginable color were issuing from the southern heavens, one color fading away only to give place to another if possible more beautiful than the last ... It was a sight never to be forgotten, and was considered at the time to be the greatest aurora recorded".

This gold miner's understanding of the event, and their emotional reaction: awe rather than fear, is in stark contrast to their ancestors a few thousand years before. It is an impressive feat for any being of planet Earth, to see such a dramatic and unusual change to the sky above them, caused by an eruption of plasma, from a sun 150 million kilometres away, and to understand it, and enjoy it as a spectacle. Humans had come a long way from their past, and lived in a very different world, in a different social environment, and with new perspectives and understandings.

The change and the continuity

Despite all this change, through farming, civilisations and "enlightenment", some things have never changed.

Compared to early Homo Sapiens, living in caves, roaming the landscape, and living amongst nature, we share many things in common. We are each still driven by friends, families, rivals, contemporaries, love interests, partners, our parents and our children. All of these are universal to any human, regardless of time period. They were important for hunter-gatherers, and they are still important for us, in the present day. And, these are the things that can have some of the greatest influence on our experiences in life.

Similarly, compared to those living in early civilisations, a mere 5000 years ago, we share many things in common. We still have the same social conflicts, and difficulties between parent and child, between neighbours, friends, and lovers, and those from a rival part of society. We have felt the same feelings of power or oppression. We feel about the latest technological development, gadget, trend, fad, our favourite bar or hang-out, and our favourite food, with perhaps little difference to how our ancestors felt about them. The backdrop may have changed, but our daily lives will likely have been consumed by similar thoughts and feelings. These societal experiences have played out countless times since 3000 BC.

Therefore, whilst our backdrop has changed, it is very likely that our lives feel quite similar to our ancestors.

We aren't even that far away from them. The earliest civilisations appeared around 5000 years ago, but this can be spanned by just 60 people living to the age of 84. Just 60 people could have, together, seen every part of civilisation.

Perhaps this helps explain why we are still so guided by our hunter-gatherer roots, that existed for millions of years before we changed lifestyles. We may have become farmers, and then built cities and empires, but we've never shed our hunter-gatherer programming.

Our lurch from our hunter-gatherer lifestyle, to our modern lifestyle, where we find ourselves living in large societies of fixed abodes, closely packed neighbours, complex social lives, and varied professions, has been very recent. We are still that hunter-gatherer, that we were for millions of years, but facing a different environment, and adapting to it in our own lives. It works, and we barely notice it, and we can, at times (or more, if we're lucky), feel 100% fulfilled. But it is a slightly ill-fitting glove, and living in an environment that differs from our programming produces some strange results. Because of this, on balance, it is harder living as modern humans than it should be.

It's unlikely we can ever go back to our old hunter-gatherer ways; the draw of progress is too strong. Or at least, if we don't progress, someone else will. But, we can better understand how the mismatch, between programming and environment, affects our lives.

The next two sections look in more detail at, firstly, the parts of our experiences we share in common with our early hunter-gatherer ancestors, and secondly, the parts of our experiences we share with those living in early civilisations. These two sections provide some basic building blocks of our programming, that will be referred to throughout the book.

Drivers

The parts we share in common with all our ancestors, including ancient hunter-gatherers, broadly fall into 3 categories: Parents, groups, and our desire to maximise our value.

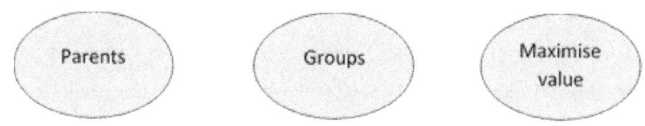

In terms of our programming, these fulfil the drivers to learn, survive, and "survival of the fittest".

On the first category, our **parents** teach us a huge amount during childhood and adolescence. Most of this is subconscious, where the child copies things the parent does. We have very long periods of childhood and adolescence, compared to other animals on planet Earth, partly because there is so much to learn. We are very dependent as youngsters, and this is representative of how we are shaped as human beings, to learn human behaviours that fit in the social environment we grow into (so that we can fulfil our programming of surviving in groups). Our parents act as the primary source of this learning, a type of social anchor, a stake in the sand, from which we can deviate as our circumstances require. Some of our deepest emotions are felt towards our parents, good and bad, and this is because they are that anchor. They can play a major role in driving our behaviours to be human shaped, whether they mean to or not (and in a way that can often be quite frustrating for modern humans).

Our **groups**, and the friends we have, play the role of our main survival mechanism: group security. An ancient tribe provided greater strength, to allow us to survive on the plains of Africa by working together, and so our programming is still looking for our tribes. Not necessarily consciously, but there are many things, good and bad, that push us towards them. For example, our thoughts are often consumed by the goings-on in groups that we come into contact with. Without realising it, we simply gravitate towards them, and this evolutionary group mechanism.

On the third driver, the **desire to maximise our value**, this is the part of us that dreams, that wants to progress, to compete, to get to the top, to adulate celebrities and the rich and famous, and to perhaps even want wealth and power for ourselves. Or, perhaps it is the part of us that wants to move up rather than down, that is hurt when others get ahead, at our expense. It is the part of us, most of all, that seeks attraction with someone that we want, to chase the desirable. It is this driver that is most out of balance in our modern societies. As we shall see, in a tribe, this driver lives side by side with parents, friends and groups. In modern societies, where there are rewards that can appear to transcend those, it can frustrate them, and leave us stretched.

Parents

To illustrate a human's link to their parents, we can look at how the relationship works across the animal kingdom.

Any successful species needs a method of ensuring their behaviours are passed to their offspring. It needs to be robust and difficult to avoid. Again, different species do this in different ways, but it generally revolves around the parents, who created the offspring. In terms of how the parents pass on their learnings, behaviours and emotions, these fall into three categories around the animal kingdom: those that have no contact with their parents; those who only have contact during adolescence; and those that have lifelong bonds with their parents.

An example of the first: those that have no contact with their parents; is the sea turtle. The female turtle lays her eggs on the beach and then leaves. The turtles are born and, even with the mother long gone, the baby turtle immediately knows to make a dash for the sea (quickly, before predators can get them). They then mature and travel the oceans until adulthood. Leatherback turtles have been known to migrate 10,000 miles, crossing the entire Pacific Ocean. In adulthood female turtles know to return to exactly the same beach they were born at, where the lifecycle starts again[19]. And all this is achieved without the turtles learning anything, at least from the previous generation. It's just instinct, which, without contact with their parents, must simply come from their DNA. The turtle likely never even thinks about who their parent is, or was, and even if they did, it's unlikely they'd feel much emotion about it. Emotions are there to direct behaviour, and the turtle doesn't need a behavioural link to the parent, so it is unlikely they'd have those emotions.

The snow leopard is an example of the second. They learn how to hunt and survive from the mother during adolescence, and then around 18-months-old they become independent, and often head out large distances to find their own territory. It is speculated that the reason they travel so far away, from their parents, could be to lessen interbreeding, in a species small in number[20].

There are no visits home, and it's therefore unlikely that the snow leopard spends time thinking about the parent, or feeling that longing to see the parent in adulthood. We may find this strange, but those emotional responses, the thoughts of parents, would be there for encouraging closeness with the parent as an adult. Those thoughts and emotions would encourage the snow leopard to seek the parent out, whereas what we see is that their behaviour is to be independent and separated. If snow leopards did feel that way, they would be less likely to fulfil their evolutionary programming. We find this strange because we empathise by projecting our emotions (how *we'd* feel in another's situation), onto others, including wildlife (and sometimes even inanimate objects like our cars and treasured objects). But often different species will have very different emotional responses, at least in their social relationships.

Finally, some species have lifelong interaction with their parents, and even form social groups with them. Homo Sapiens are in this last category. A large amount of our emotion is tied to our parents, the people that brought us into the world, and who we share the most DNA with. Our ancient tribes would have resulted in us staying in close contact with the parents our whole lives, and we still maintain lifelong links. They are one of the only certainties in life, and therefore provide a large part of the mechanism for learning behaviours that make humans *human.* Our behaviours are tempered and mediated in our social groups, but our parents provide the underlying anchor.

There are two main avenues for a human parent to pass behaviours onto a child. From the child's side, they subconsciously copy things from their parents. Things that their parents do are easier for the child to do. Deviating from that behaviour is harder. On the other side, the parent has a natural desire for the child to copy their behaviour. This plays out as the parent wanting their children to be a reflection of them.

These two forces: whereby the child subconsciously copies the parent's behaviours, emotions and traits; and whereby the parent wants their children to do so, and be a reflection of themselves; is one of the key drivers that result in humans behaving like humans.

Groups

Our parents provide the anchoring point for our behaviours, but we need to apply those behaviours to our evolutionary tactic of participating in groups.

Whether those groups are a small handful of people, one other person, or a large group or nation, our social instincts kick in, and are drawn into the group dynamic.

That group dynamic provides a separate competing influence on us, compared to our parents. In a tribe, where our parents are in our one group, this wouldn't be noticeable. As modern humans, our groups can often pull us in different directions to our parents.

Groups are finely tuned beasts that need to act with common purpose. For hunter-gatherers, this would have been to hunt, travel, and fight off dangerous wildlife, and neighbouring tribes. In order for groups, of individuals, to function with common purpose, they need to have a number of characteristics.

For example, our personal behaviours become interlinked with the groups. This is important, because how we communicate has an impact on other people. We interpret what others say, and it produces reactions in us. In order for a group to communicate in ways understood by those around them, when there are infinite ways we *could* communicate and behave, we need to have common behaviours. This is achieved by copying behaviours from those around us, which when every member does it, results in harmonised behaviours, and a common sub-culture. To the individual, using these behaviours feels good, and makes us feel a part of the group. We learn behaviours that were forged in groups, and then we feel most ourself when using those behaviours.

Groups need to act together. When we face off against a sabre tooth tiger, we need to have an understanding of who is on our side. If there are several strong tribespeople there, we're more likely to act with confidence in the face of a 600-pound beast of teeth and claws. Who is in our group therefore needs to affect how we feel about ourselves, so that our actions are consistent with the group intentions, and it moves as one. We therefore feel similar to those around us, we associate ourselves with them, because when we act, our group is not far behind.

We also naturally absorb information from the people around us. We lack information on ourselves, so we draw it from others. We feel we are a representation of those people. We are their kin, we are similar to them, and we should be treated similarly to how they're treated. We see ourselves consistent with what we see around us. We feel this deeply and clearly, and this is our identity level.

Finally, groups need to have mechanisms for looking out for each other, and accounting for the various group member's competing needs. These don't occur through logical thought, but instead because our programming makes them hard to resist. These mechanisms work effectively in other social groups around nature, who have much more limited communication. There is a level of interlinking in groups, whereby emotions are communicated, transferred and shared, until a balance is reached whereby each person is roughly happy with what they have, compared to the others.

These traits form a key part of who we are, and how we feel about ourselves. We are linked to groups, and interlinked with those around us. Who we are, and how we behave, is often a projection of the group that has our back.

These characteristics still play out in the modern world. If we are friends with someone important, we feel more important ourselves. We copy behaviours from role models, and when we use them successfully, we feel a little more like them. Whatever group we're in, we can get drawn into conflicts, and feel the emotions and dynamics of the group, until they're resolved. We judge ourselves by those around us, no matter whether we're similar or not, because our brain is still trying to perform our hunter-gatherer habits, of linking ourselves to the group in front of us. Then, we can judge how to react, when faced with that sabre-tooth tiger.

Greater value

The third driver, to maximise our value, is probably the easiest to describe, because it is simply that. We just have an urge to seek out better. We enjoy success, and we don't enjoy being treated as less, and generally don't enjoy losing. We dream of being a rock star, or a celebrity. We copy their behaviours, to feel a part of their lives, and we often feel that moving upwards will give us freedom and happiness.

This is really all about survival of the fittest, and wanting to find a desirable mate. It's why those feelings exist, and why they feel good. To be going upwards makes us feel more attractive and desirable. We generally want to have children, and we want to have them with someone we value: the survival of the fittest part of nature. A lot of our actions, emotions and behaviours are driven by that desire. We don't always chase it, and generally finding someone who is a good match for us is better in the long term, but nevertheless the feelings are there.

Maximising our value can strongly influence our emotions, and therefore our actions and direction in life.

Drivers and our modern world

The parts we share in common with those living 5000 years ago, in early civilisations, are the way that large societies influence and distort our drivers.

The drivers, fundamentally, haven't changed. Our programming is still the same as it was for hunter-gatherers. The drivers: parents; groups; and maximising our value; still want to fill the same shapes, and to be absorbed and satisfied in the same way. It is the environment, against which they play out, which has changed (e.g., large societies vs. a tribe).

That environment can make it harder for the drivers to be fulfilled. Living in large societies can pull the drivers in different directions, so that they can become stretched or confused. Or, large social environments can simply add additional (and often unusual) barriers to fulfilling them. This can cause added difficulty for beings who are trying to fulfil their programming. It can cause unusual frustrations and social conflict, as well as affecting our self-belief and perceptions. These difficulties, that we experience in the modern day, are exactly the same as those experienced by people in early civilisations, 5000 years ago. The only fuel these difficulties need are large, co-located, unequal societies.

Three examples of this are: how our more complex social lives and hierarchies make it harder for our *group* driver to be satisfied; how this in turn affects our feeling of self; and how the driver to *maximise our value* can conflict with our *parental* driver.

Complex social lives and hierarchies

On the first example; groups are so important to us as a species. Groups give us laughter, togetherness and belonging. They give us definition, shared joy and purpose.

But, they also contain an element of posturing, positioning and competition. This competition can be stressful, but is necessary for establishing a hierarchy and positions, for allowing the group to co-operate, and have a rough pecking order for mates.

Hunter-gatherers had only one group, and their position in the group was determined in only one way.

That way was likely similar to most group hierarchies across the natural world. The leader of the group is generally the alpha male or female, and generally a natural leader, and perhaps the largest or strongest. This is because nature is harsh and physical, and our early ancestors would have to fight predators, prey and occasionally rival tribes. As a result, within the tribe, challenges happen through an exchange of behaviours, normally involving posturing or physicality. The animal that wins that exchange has the higher social position.

It's likely that as we roamed the landscape as hunter-gatherers, the leader was probably the one that could win a fight, even if most of the time the tribe was harmonious, and relied on the various skills of each member.

As we started to shed our hunter-gatherer lifestyle, and instead live in fixed-location larger communities, we started to get specialisms. We didn't have to know general hunting and survival skills, but instead could now just focus on woodworking or farming. Someone else would deal with defence, tailoring or tool making. Then, in these small societies, humans find that they form social groups with people all of the same specialism. Hierarchies can then form on the basis of how good we were at that particular skill. As societies became more civilised, with laws and punishments, fighting became less acceptable. Even the largest of humans would have to respect and accede to the master crafter in our town, who had plied their trade over a lifetime (even if their brains were still factoring in an element of physical posturing). That master crafter had the knowledge to pass on to them, so they could become a good craftsperson themselves, and contribute to the complex machine of large group living.

As money became more prevalent, groups could be formed on the basis of who had more money, or success. Those with more money can be perceived to be more attractive, and could attain a higher social level within a group, compared to someone bigger and stronger than them. These hierarchies were formed on value, rather than behavioural posturing.

As societies become bigger still, and more structured, we started to have defined roles. Now, hierarchies can be determined simple by who holds that role. For a team of accountants in the pharaoh's treasury department, there is a team leader. The team leader may not be the one who could win a fight, nor be the best at their profession. Instead, they might just have been in the right place at the right time, or been there the longest. Nevertheless, because they hold the position, the others must do what the team leader says, else they won't get the pay rise they need.

All of these forms of establishing hierarchies, whether more behavioural, value or role based, exist to greater or lesser extent in different groups in our present-day environment. They are all necessary for creating stable and peaceful large societies.

However, this creates complexity in our social lives, because as modern humans we have links to more than just one group, and in each group our position is determined

Change and Continuity

according to a different set of criteria. Perhaps among friends it is more down to behaviours. Perhaps at our sports club it could be down to money or prowess at the particular sport. At work it is down to who holds the appropriate roles or positions.

We can therefore find ourselves competing on one criterion one day, and a different criterion the next. At times we can feel that we have instincts that we should be positioned one way, but the prevailing social dynamic in a group positions us differently. We have to keep many plates spinning, which we often do fairly naturally, but which can lead to occasional stress or frustration.

The competition in a group is a bit like playing a board game. Hunter-gatherers would all be competing to the same set of rules, within a well-defined tribe. In contrast, as modern humans, we have greater diversity of competition. In each group, we subtly compete, or argue, that the social rules should be this or that, depending on what gives us the most advantage. We compete over what we're competing on. This can lead to greater stress and frustration, and occasionally the board is knocked into the air, and all the pieces scattered.

Our programming wants our "group driver" to be fulfilled, to find that sense of belonging and security. But, it finds a mix of groups, spread out, and with greater, more unusual conflicts within them. This can add difficulty to our lives, in the same way it did for our ancestors in civilisations, several thousand years ago.

Large societies add greater social complexity, to the groups that we need to fulfil our programming.

Our group driver and our feeling of self

On the second example (of how large societies affect our drivers), our modern social arrangement can also make it more difficult to know who we are. Given how important groups are for making us feel ourselves, giving us support, and giving us belonging and comparisons, when our groups are more spread out, so our self can be too.

If, in each group, we might be positioned differently, and use different behaviours, which becomes our personality? How does our brain aggregate these different experiences, as it tries to find something that ticks the "group driver" box?

We tend to deal with this by focussing more deeply on one group, and forming our identity based on that. For some people it can be their family (though this is rare, in civilisations), for some it is a social group, and for some it can be a role such as a job, or position of responsibility. The person will use the identity from that group to define their behaviours outside of the group. And, they will feel most themselves when they are interacting within their primary group, and less so outside of it.

But this makes interpersonal interactions harder. If we join a new group, each person will be defining themselves according to a group we've never met. Each person has a "self" that has been defined somewhere else. Each person will be trying to mould the present group to allow them to achieve an identity, and use behaviours, that have been forged elsewhere. As we looked at in the previous section, for some people these will be more about behavioural posturing, for some these will be based around their prowess in an activity, or their wealth, and for some it will be based on being a certain position within an organisation, and using the authority of that position. We constantly interact with people who are being influenced by other groups that they are a part of, of which we may know little about.

Further, against our complex social lives, and a need to define ourselves by the group around us, it can result in people being a little "out of position".

Then, our perception of our self can become a little confused. For example, if a non-natural leader is in a leadership role, then, as a human being, they judge themselves by those around them, their contemporaries, and they feel the need the respect of being a leader. Even if they're surrounded by those that could beat them in a fight, or are better at their jobs, they feel the need to command respect. They *are* a leader. It can lead to a split between who they feel they are, or need to be, versus how they come across.

Being a little "out of position" can apply to other social roles too. We can find ourselves in social roles that we aren't all that well equipped for. We can find ourselves with the skills for a particular social role, leader or otherwise, but not the attributes. Or, we can find ourselves with everything needed for a particular role (say as a natural leader), but not the opportunity or circumstances.

All this leads to our spread-out groups making a concrete "self" harder to forge. We are constantly interacting with people who are trying to forge different, incompatible identities, with people who are on different wavelengths (who may not reciprocate our behaviours), or with people who face a split between who they feel they are (or need to be), and how they come across.

Our feelings of self become more fragile. They become more based on an idea that we have to keep returning to, against the competition of other people's.

Our "self" is often based on an idea that is like a life-raft in a choppy sea, rather than being rooted in our nature as a human being.

Our social lives are much less simple than they should be. We can often cope with them admirably, and balance many different influences and situations. However, we perhaps don't feel like we would in a tribe, with one secure group that gave us everything. There, the key fits the lock, and we would feel ourselves the majority of the time.

Despite our modern spread-out social lives being a less good fit, our programming is still striving to fulfil the group driver, and find the belonging, support, and "self" that goes with it. Our brains are often working overtime to try to resolve, and project, that we have done so. This can cause humans to come to some unusual conclusions about themselves or others, or disregard many things that go on around them. We shall explore these aspects later in the book.

Maximising value vs. parental driver in large societies

On the third example, our driver to maximise our value can pull in a different direction to our parental driver. There's just more value to maximise, in large societies and civilisations.

In an isolated tribe, maximising our value is about attaining a small increment. That small increment would be in balance with both the group and our parents (who are likely in the group). A child raised in a tribe of hunter-gatherers wouldn't have dreamt of becoming a rock star, because they didn't exist. The pinnacle of value for them was to be a tribe elder. Therefore, they were more likely to adopt an identity similar to their parents, and follow in their parent's footsteps. The parent must be a good hunter-gatherer, in order to survive, so the child looks up to them. Essentially, the tribal parents are the Homo Sapien rock stars.

The parent recognises the child is following their lead, learning and copying useful skills and traits, and is more able to reward and encourage this, providing the child with approval, love and dependence.

However, as small societies grew, for example around small settlements, this balance was disrupted. Now, there was more apparent value out there than could be attained from our parents. And we want it, it's attractive, and to attain it feels good, at least in the short term.

For example, we can consider a fictional ancient hunter-gatherer tribe who have recently joined a new settlement.

Over time, they had returned to it more and more, taking breaks from hunting, and eventually built a house on the edge of the homestead. During a harsh winter, they relied on the food stores and shelter, and decided put down roots in the town.

The settlement has a leading group that is at the top of the pecking order. They organise the farm, but also still enjoy big-game hunting. The settlement is a hundred people or so, and during the summer months, whilst everyone else is tending the crops, a small group of the leaders heads out, to track and hunt large beasts, using new skills and tools. They bring back impressive trophies, and the big-game-hunters now have the rock star status. They have the adoration of a crowd, and suddenly there is more value available, than can be got from the old tribe elder or parent.

In the recently settled tribe, a parent has a son (or daughter) who is showing great promise at hunting. This pleases the parent. However, the child interacts with the big-game-hunters and is shown acceptance, that their skills would fit in well with the group. They see attraction in one of the daughters of the big-game-hunters, and feel a strong draw towards them, and away from their parents.

Whilst the child has acceptance with the settlement leaders, the parent perhaps doesn't. When the father tries to join the leader's campfire on an evening, where his son is socialising with his friends, the father feels more out of place, and isn't made to feel as comfortable. He feels an urge to go back to his old tribe's campfire, on the edge of town, but frustration that his son won't join him.

When the summer months come around, and the big-game-hunters head out to the hunting grounds, the son decides to go with them (despite the parent's protests), in a slightly impetuous, but entirely human way. The child now identifies with the big-game-hunters, and feels the adoration of the settlement themselves.

The driver to maximise our value is now no longer in balance with the driver from our parents. We no longer want to copy only our parents, and to meet their subconscious desire for us to be a reflection of them. The driver to maximise our value is no longer incremental, but can make large leaps.

How this situation plays out could go a number of ways, good or bad. One common way that it does so is as follows. This way is consistent with the fact that we have long periods of dependency as children, and lifelong bonds with our parents, and these are both representative of the part that the parent-child relationship plays in our programming. This falls into the category of not "that shouldn't happen", but "that happens, *why*".

The parent feels rejected, and sees it as lack of respect. The parent may find it hard to act entirely positively towards the child as a result of this, as the child is copying and looking up to someone else instead. The child now looks down on the parent. The parent is left without a child to look up to them, and being a good parent was important to them. The child responds negatively back, since they aren't getting approval from the parent for their actions, despite appearing to have achieved something good. They want their parent to be proud of them for achieving it, but they find the parent does the opposite. They leave on bitter terms, and whilst the child has elevated themselves, they bear some resentment towards the parent, and vice versa. This is despite positive intentions. There is a difference between how we could behave in an ideal world, and how we are limited and channelled to behave in the world we find ourselves in. However, we should always try to do the best we can in the circumstances.

In large unequal societies, these forces play out. The mechanism for passing behaviours down from one generation to the next is tested, and often produces unwelcome results. The driver to maximise our value is now pulling in a different direction to our parental driver, and instead of being on the same team, they can now be on opposite sides, leaving us with conflicted emotions.

Those conflicted emotions can cause us to behave in ways that are perhaps less beneficial for ourselves or others. For example, particular behaviours, that certain emotions encourage us to do, were finely tuned over millions of years in a small tribe environment. When you place humans in a different social environment, where we experience new (and often unusual) emotions, the behaviours, that those emotions encourage us to perform, may no longer be in tune, and may not be wholly beneficial to ourselves or others.

In our modern societies there can be great wealth out there to be attained, due to the often-great differences between rich and poor.

There are many role models that the child wants to copy instead of the parent. We can find our children can adopt values, identity or behaviours very different from our own, and so it can be much harder for us to encourage and support children as much as we'd like. That support, which can translate as love and value, is easiest passed on when the parental driver is fulfilled.

As hunter-gatherers, growing up in the same tribe as several generations that came before us, we were more likely to have a good relationship with our parents. We were more likely to get approval from our parents, pass rites of passage of the tribe, and grow into a proud, content adult Homo Sapiens.

In the modern world, we may find that, as an adult, we just don't feel it sometimes, and perhaps we just don't quite feel good enough, or completely fulfilled, at least at times in our lives. On average, this will be true of every human being.

The drivers: parents, groups and maximising value, are the basic building blocks of an individual.

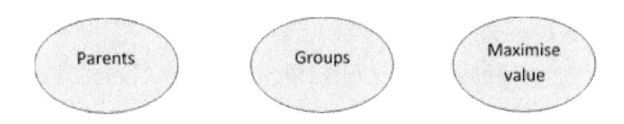

(Parents)   (Groups)   (Maximise value)

Our parental driver provides the anchoring point, and our group driver, and desire to maximise our value, overly that.

For hunter-gatherers, the three drivers were much more aligned. We had one group, that included our parents, and maximising our value simply involved an incremental change within the bounds of parents and group.

In modern societies, our drivers are more spread out, and fulfilled in different places.

In our modern societies, our groups contain competition on new and differing criteria. Having them spread out causes greater difficulty in finding a secure identity, and causes interlinked conflicts, being pulled in different directions, and occasionally feeling out of place. Our large unequal societies provide much greater draw to the possibilities of maximising our value. Our parents still act as the stake in the sand, that we are loosely connected to, but this is now a less comfortable arrangement, against the possibility of greater value outside of

Change and Continuity

the family unit. We can find ourselves a little stretched on occasion, now that the drivers are less in balance.

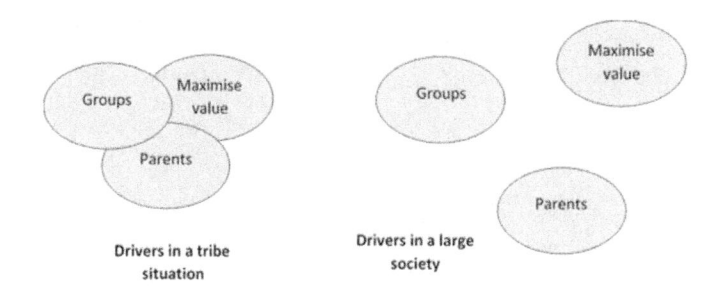

Drivers in a tribe situation

Drivers in a large society

There is one thing that is always certain, we are a human being, facing a modern world that is alien to our evolutionary environment. And, we have a programming that's trying to fit against it, just like everyone else in the world.

The three main drivers: parents; groups; and our desire to maximise our value, are the fundamental building blocks that determine our behaviours. Every human throughout history will have been shaped by these, whether living as a hunter-gatherer, in small farming settlements, or in civilisations.

Our modern world throws some unusual circumstances at them, as described in the last few sections. These circumstances are ones that we, in the present day, share with all humans who lived in times since we gave up our hunter-gatherer past.

We can start to see how our large societies are affecting our hunter-gatherer programming.

Moving forward, we can capture the main aspects of large societies, that affect our experiences of life, in three categories. These are: levels; our web; and our self.

In Parts I and II, we shall explore these aspects in more detail. These three aspects provide a structure for discussing how modern society affects us.

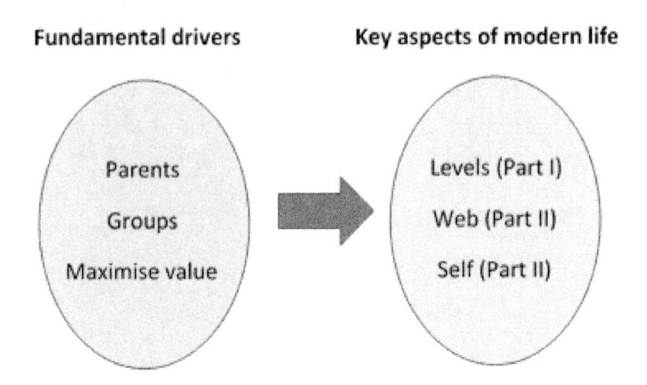

Fundamental drivers

- Parents
- Groups
- Maximise value

→

Key aspects of modern life

- Levels (Part I)
- Web (Part II)
- Self (Part II)

The **fundamental drivers** give us a basis for exploring the **key aspects** of modern life.

Levels (Part I) looks in more detail at our complex hierarchies in our multi-layered social environments, where people are competing on new and different criteria.

Our web (Part II) looks at the nature of our spread-out social lives, and how our brain aggregates our experiences, as it searches for something resembling a tribe.

Our self (also Part II – as our self and web are closely linked) looks at our perceptions of ourself, and how we balance being social creatures with being self-aware.

After Part I & II, Part III looks more at our day-to-day interactions.

Part One

Levels

2

Inherited Hierarchies

The group driver, and the driver to maximise our value, appear to be in conflict.

In a tribe of hunter-gatherers, if each member wants to maximise their value, why aren't they always trying to get to the head of the tribe? Why isn't there constant fighting, with those at the top having to defend themselves against all-comers, all the time? You can envisage a scenario where, after waking up each morning, there is a series of conflicts to arrange the hierarchy for that day. How can the tribe move together, with individuals trying to get the best for themselves?

In reality, to oppose the force of each hunter-gatherer wanting to maximise their own value, there is a stabilising force: their inherited position.

The inherited position is relatively fixed throughout each tribesperson's lifetimes. Whilst rearranging can (and often does) happen, and each tribes-member has an identity that is theirs, they also have a more fixed nature. We are after all, part fixed, part flexible. With regard to hierarchies, part of that fixed nature is represented in our inherited position.

The inherited position creates a bias that makes it harder

to rearrange the tribe. As a result, less energy is spent on infighting. This leaves more energy for the important survival tasks of hunting, defending themselves from predators, foraging, building shelters, and keeping themselves warm.

Whilst these biases make it harder to rearrange the tribe, it can, and often needs to be done. It's just a little harder, and requires overcoming how those biases make the tribespeople feel. The inherited position is merely an anchor, and there is flexibility to allow positions to be arranged according to the specific environment. We are after all, part fixed, part flexible.

We see this ability to rearrange social groups across the animal kingdom. For example, when a leader becomes too aggressive, or less moral and fair, or isn't supported by the group anymore, then the group tends to overthrow them. However, it takes a certain upswell or force for this to happen.

To illustrate this in humans, we can consider a tribe of ancient hunter-gatherers travelling north through Arabia, in search of new animals to hunt. They had passed a different tribe a few months ago, who had told them of better hunting in the north, as they had exchanged news and stories.

The leader of our tribe, who has always been good and fair, is getting older, and is less good at leading long-distance travel. Another, more youthful member, had always dealt with tracking and direction. As they set out on their journey, arguments ensue about whether they should head for the mountains or the plains. The more youthful tribesperson feels strongly about the plains, and feels that the leader is being too cautious. They gain some support amongst the tribe, and eventually decide to usurp the leader. It takes some courage. When they decide to take action, they feel something pressing against them, something in their brain says don't do it. They feel an invisible force that they must overcome. However, the younger tribesperson has strong will, and manages to override

Inherited Hierarchies

those feelings, and, after challenging the old leader, they are successful at establishing themselves as the new one. It feels good, and they feel an immediate elevation in their status.

Yet, they wake up the next morning, and the previous leader is still there. They look at the old leader, who had been in charge of the tribe for their whole life, and something in their brain finds it hard to recognise the new arrangement, with them in command. Those feelings, that they had to overcome to usurp the leader, are still there. They feel number one: they earnt it, and deserve it; but a part of them, frustratingly and confusingly, is still responding as if they're number two. Because of this, they have to be a little harsher to the previous leader, to ensure that they maintain the new arrangement, and be a leader over someone who they had looked up to their whole lives.

The new leader is feeling two things at once. They are feeling some effects of their lifelong position as number two, but also a firm belief, or need, to be number one. The difference between the two is affecting their behaviour.

In the modern world these inherited positions are still there. We all have them, biases that channel and restrain us towards certain positions. They are the part of us that is fixed. They ensure some stability to our groups, whether a small friendship group, or a large society, by ensuring there is some resistance to constant rearranging.

We also have the part of us that is flexible, that can adapt to our circumstances, and it allows us to move around in society, and develop and identity that is ours. Against that identity, the inherited position mostly becomes an unwelcome inconvenience, that often simply makes it harder to be our identity, or to strive for an identity we want. We have an anchor that doesn't move, but we are only loosely connected to it by a stretchy rope, so that we can move around as our circumstances require.

Our inherited position is part of us, and our brain reacts to our environment based on it. We mostly don't notice it, and it is something that happens in the background. It shapes our lives and behaviours, but it only occasionally rears its head in our day to day lives, for example when our behaviours become harder to do. The inherited position is representative of our fixed nature, and is passed down family lines in a cascade.

In the modern world, it's easier to understand when we consider large distances between the positions of people in society. For example, when your average person meets a leader or celebrity, we often feel some of those subconscious effects, that our position creates. Our brain is recognising the difference in position, and we're reacting to that leader or celebrity accordingly. People often find they are nervous, find it harder to speak, or don't know what to say. These are all resisting forces, and are the same forces that our number two had to overcome to become the new tribe leader.

In our social and professional lives, those forces are at play, but on a much smaller scale. We have two things, how we emotionally respond to situations, which is determined by our inherited position, and who we feel we need to be, or are: our identity. The first is more fixed, the second is more flexible. Our behaviours, that we've learnt throughout our lives, will account for any different between the two.

Positions in a tribe are relatively simple. There will be a fairly linear pecking order, which may have small variations depending on what activity the tribe is doing, but nevertheless they will be fairly fixed. When we consider our large societies, where there are effectively thousands or millions of small tribes all interlinked, it can get quite complicated. For example, there

Inherited Hierarchies

will be leaders in groups at the top of society, but also leaders in groups at the bottom.

There are effectively two main ways large societies are arranged. One is our overall position in society, and the other is our social role in the groups we are a part of. We see and react to people in a "societal status" way, as well as an "interpersonal way".

The first is more related to our level or perceived value in that large societal hierarchy, whilst the second is more related to social skills, and perceptions of the type of personalities or attributes that we react to as above and below us.

This leads to two strands of our inherited position: a value one, and a social one.

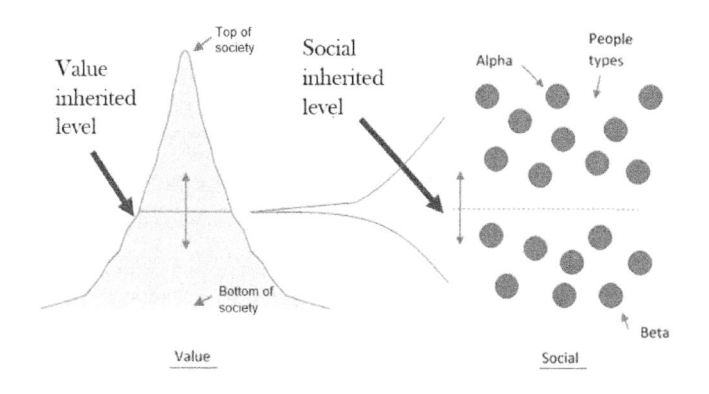

Our *value* inherited position determines who our brain reacts to, without our conscious input, as above and below us in society.

Our *social* inherited position determines who our brain reacts to, without our conscious input, as above and below us in our interpersonal interactions, i.e. the type of people we accede to, and the type of people we don't (in an isolated tribe, we'd only have a "<u>social</u> inherited level", and not a "<u>value</u> inherited level").

The inherited positions are not who the parent thinks they are: that is their identity. As we shall come onto in a scenario (later in this chapter), the inherited positions are merely a slowly changing position, from one generation to the next.

Hierarchies, and the pecking order, play an important part in nature. Because they are important, so they must have an effect on us. We have parts of us that are fixed, and parts of us that are flexible. Considering hierarchies, the part that is fixed is our inherited positions (value and social). These can be difficult to change throughout our lives.

They're relatively fixed because they're a stabilising force. They're the force trying to prevent hierarchies rearranging too quickly, and becoming erratic, with too much energy spent on infighting. They slow down changes in groups (whether a tribe or society), perhaps to a generational pace, so that any changes that do happen can be absorbed and approved of. Therefore, we can change where we are in hierarchies, and our identity can be anything that we can feel supported in, but the further it is from our anchor, perhaps the harder it is to maintain.

Whilst the inherited position exists, and we might notice it in others, we don't really want to believe it in ourselves. To us, there is only one position, our identity. We *are* our identity. That defines us. The fact that we occasionally react, and feel, inconsistent with that identity is more confusion and frustration, rather than recognition of a second level.

If our inherited position is our fixed part, then our identity is our flexible part. After all, in the modern world, people say you can be anything. They say dream big, become a star, emulate your role model. And to some extent this is possible. Whatever our starting point in life, it's at least theoretically possible to move to another, and believe we are that new level.

Inherited Hierarchies

It generally requires one thing – acceptance within the group at the new level. We can't simply decide where we want to go and be there. We may not fully feel it, until we are welcomed, and treated with acceptance, at that level, by the people there.

This acceptance at the higher level, even for a short time, has a powerful effect on us. Our identity can change very quickly from this, and we then believe that's who we are. We judge others in the same way that people of our new level judge others. We associate and believe we're similar to the people around us at the new level. The new level becomes our identity level. Our group driver, to be interlinked and a reflection of the group we associate with, provides us with new self-belief.

We therefore have two levels. We have our inherited position; and our identity, and they can often be different. This forms the basis of the theories proposed in this book.

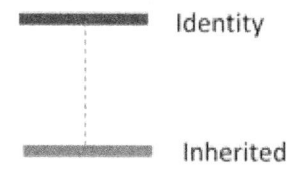

▬▬▬▬ Identity

▬▬▬▬ Inherited

Our identity is **who we believe we are**, who we associate with, perhaps our achievements, our job, and our role in society.

Our inherited position is subconsciously where we fit in, and defines **how we emotionally respond** to the people around us.

There can be a difference between the two. Our identity and our inherited position can be at different levels: they can be *diverged.*

When we are diverged, so that our inherited and identity levels are different, everything is a little harder, and difficult to interpret. At times we may be reacting to things one way (based on our inherited level), but needing to feel about them a different way (in order to fulfil our identity level). We need to be our identity level, because it is the level that defines us, the level that we need to be in order to feel association with the group that we feel closest to: the level we feel most ourselves in.

The main way we bridge the gap between the two, to steamroller over our inherited level, and achieve our identity level more often, is through behaviours. Our behaviours can become a little more obtrusive, in order to ensure people treat us more according to our identity, and not our inherited position.

This is a form of human duality, between our fixed parts, that ensure we follow patterns, and flexible parts, that allow us to adapt to our circumstances.

In terms of where the inherited position comes from, then, as the name suggests, we pick it up from our interactions throughout our adolescence, but, mostly, we pick it up from our parents.

Our inherited level is tied to our parents. They are the source of the parts of us that our fixed, since they are one of the only sureties in life. It also comes from them because they are a force, often unfortunately, that is difficult to deviate from. We have many different forces pulling us towards them, and just as sometimes we have to resist our parents, we also have to resist some of the forces coming from our inherited position. Often we can do both, or reach compromises, without too much difficulty, or even noticing, but sometimes it takes a lot of strength.

Inherited Hierarchies

In order to learn behaviours that are human, we are linked to our parents. We copy behaviours off them, but also emotions. We copy how they respond to people around them, and this replicates itself in us. From this we have an inherited position, as well as behaviours that fit with that position, to allow us to seamlessly fit into social groups we come across, at least theoretically.

The son our daughter of the tribe leader will grow up simply feeling less inhibited taking leadership positions, and feel less of a barrier to taking command of situations. They will learn leadership behaviours from their parent to go with their position as they grow.

The son or daughter of a number two in a tribe, will do similar, with respect to number two. They may feel some barrier to taking the lead, preferring instead to support the number one. Perhaps they test the number one from time to time, as they grow up together, but find that the number one simply has a small advantage, in that the conflict is less of a threat, and easier to dismiss or win.

Our *inherited level* is representative of our anchor to our **parents**. Our inherited position largely comes from our parents. We pick up on how they emotionally respond to different people, and that replicates itself in how we do, without us consciously affecting it.

On the other hand, our *identity level* is representative of our driver to define ourselves in relation to the **group** of people around us, as well as being influenced by our driver to **maximise our value**.

The *inherited level* is more fixed. It is very difficult to change, even throughout our lifetime. It is a stake in the sand after all, and part of the more fundamental tie to our parents to ensure our behaviours don't stray too far from theirs. It gets ingrained in all our relationships, and linked to our starting point in life.

The *identity level* is more flexible. Providing we achieve acceptance; it can basically be at any level. It can jump to the new level very quickly. It tends to only go up. We always hold on to that highest position, even if we are only keeping it in our back pocket.

Because the identity level and inherited level are driven by such fundamental forces, they can have a large impact on how we behave and how we feel, in ourselves, and towards others. They can be a cause of difficulty, especially if they're different, and we're diverged.

There are two main ways we can be diverged: in value; and in social skills:

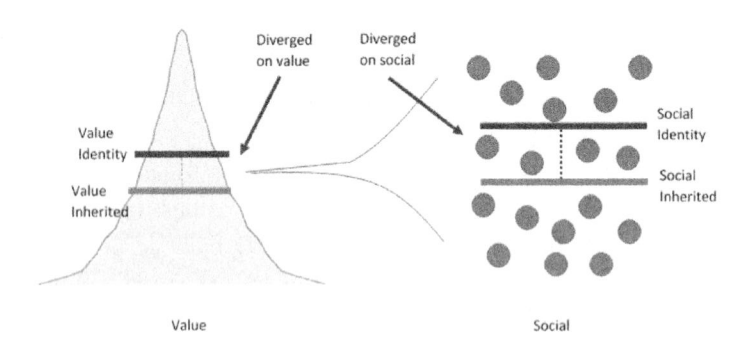

Nevertheless, it gets complicated to consider both at the same time, and often the effect of levels on interpersonal interactions is coming from differences in either value or social skills. In reality, our inherited position is a map that is different in different environments, whereas our identity is normally more singular.

Inherited Hierarchies

We can avoid this complexity however, because in most cases, and most environments, there is only one inherited level that is important, and one identity level. The complexity reduces to those two: how we respond to a situation, and who we feel we need to be in that situation.

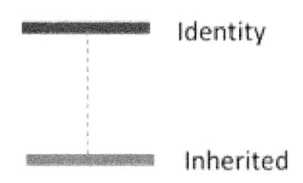

▬▬▬▬▬ Identity

▬▬▬▬▬ Inherited

This simplification is all we need to describe most behaviours that we see in people around us. For most people, we can simply consider that they are diverged or not, in a certain situation, or across key portions of their life, and interpret their experiences and behaviours from that.

In large modern societies, everyone is diverged to some extent. In a tribe, our inherited position and identity are merely about the pecking order, but, in large societies, where we interact with many different groups, different sub-cultures, and have our social lives spread over several groups, we add on a little social resistance. As we will come onto, this "social delta", that causes the vast majority of modern humans to be diverged, means that most people have extra reservations about their social interactions, beyond mere positions, and everyone is behaving as if they were trying to attain positions slightly above their inherited position (including the generations before us).

The "social delta" causes everyone to diverge, as we all face greater headwinds in our life than merely hierarchical positions in a tribe.

However, some people are more diverged than others. Some people diverge in value, and find acceptance at a higher place in society. This often happens through success or wealth accumulation, where we can afford to move to a higher status area, or socially climb. Some people diverge in social skills, and attain positions in groups above their inherited position. This can happen at work, where leaders or managers can attain a leadership role in interactions, which they might not achieve in their purely social interactions outside of that role. Or it can happen when someone has favourable attributes (compared to their ancestors) that allows them to take higher roles in social groups.

However diverged we are, to us, there is only one level, the identity level. The people around us, at that level, are fulfilling an important part of how a human feels about themselves. We are them, and they are us. We move with them, they are the ones we integrate and copy, and who have our back. This is drawn from a key human driver, to fit into a group and integrate with them, which makes us feel a part of them, so it is a strong force. To be treated as less than that identity level can be quite hurtful. But nevertheless, the two levels are there, and have an impact on behaviours and interactions.

This can be one of the greatest difficulties of being a human living in large societies: the conflict between our inherited level, and the need to associate with the group of people in front of us. We can be pulled in two directions at once, and become more stretched, if those two are different.

Our brain is very good at shaping our views to fit. We can disregard large amounts of what's in front of us in order that we are our identity level regardless of our inherited level. We can dismiss certain interactions, people, or facts about ourselves. We are still hunter-gatherers, and our brain is shaping how we feel about ourselves in hunter-gatherer ways.

Inherited Hierarchies

Our brain wants certainty of who we are, and a firm identity, that it would get so easily in a hunter-gatherer tribe.

If people treat us according to our identity level, all is well. If they don't, there can be conflict. Bringing up what you think someone's inherited level is will serve no purpose, the information here is for our own internal understanding. When conflict arises because of levels, for example someone being overly obtrusive, or people not treating others according to their identity level, or people feeling constrained by their inherited level, then, because our levels are such fundamental forces that are difficult to change, we have to make the conflict about something else. We form beliefs, driven by our levels, that allow us to integrate our personal circumstances into society.

Our inherited position and our identity position form a large part of who we are, but unpicking them is often elusive. Plus, there is often little we can realistically do about them. We can learn to live around them, or change our behaviours to better suit them, but changing them fundamentally is very difficult, seeing as how they are derived from our core drivers, and therefore come from quite a deep place. Nevertheless, they play a large role in how we, and others, see the world and behave, and so to understand this, we have to consider them.

As an aside, it's worth noting that interactions caused by levels play-out across any age, but tend to have most impact once the child has reached adulthood, and our personalities become more solidified. In the English language, we don't have a variety of different words that distinguish between adolescent children, adult children, and children of any age. "Offspring" is a little impersonal, so I use the word "child" simply to mean a person of any age, when discussing them in relation to their parent. Therefore where I use the word "child", it can mean a young person or adult person, and hopefully it is clear from the context.

Our max identity

Our inherited level comes from subconsciously picking up on how our parents respond to those around us, and replicating that in ourselves.

Our identity level comes from the highest-level group we've achieved acceptance in.

When we meet new people, we pick up on a lot of information. We may make an initial assessment of them, how they move, and what intentions they might have, and we form a first impression, which is likely to be picking up on their inherited level. Then, often, early on in the conversation, people will drop hints about what their identity level is, and how they want to be treated. It may be a fact about them, an association, such as a group that they are (or were) a part of, or a story of success, present or past. This is their identity level, and is how they see themselves. It is commonly based on their maximum identity achieved.

If we treat them according to their identity level, all is well. Sometimes we can, but sometimes we can't. If we can't, it is normally because their identity is based off a sub-culture that is incompatible with ours, and therefore conflicts with us achieving our own identity level. In this case we have to treat them a little less, which can be a cause of conflict.

The hints that people drop about their identity level are often related to the highest status they've achieved. Our identity only tends to go up. Once we've achieved acceptance at a certain level, it can be very hard to accept ourselves as less than that. This is a representation of our drive to maximise our

Inherited Hierarchies

value. Essentially, if you step back, the human being is attaining a highest level, and then resisting letting go.

If there wasn't a change in ourselves, if we didn't feel more, because of our upwardly jump, then we wouldn't increase in confidence in order to find a mate at this higher level.

The following diagram shows a fictional example of a person's life, with 5 main groups that they've come across. The first friendship group is at school, the second is at college, and then they have three main social groups as an adult. These could be based around work, sport, or social clubs for example.

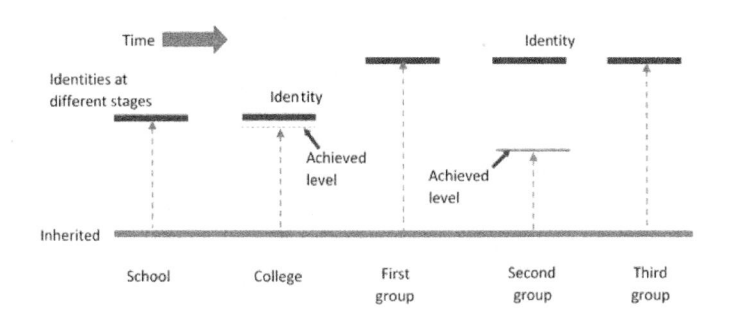

Diagram: Identities at different stages across Time — School, College, First group, Second group, Third group — showing Inherited level (constant baseline), Achieved level, and Identity level varying by group.

This person's inherited level stays fairly constant throughout their life, but their identity level changes.

Their school has a reasonably high standing compared to their inherited level. This can be fairly normal for modern humans, given how an institution that represents hundreds, and has some history, has more status than an individual.

In this example, the person then goes on to college, but the college doesn't have quite the status of the school. The person has no problem fitting in there, and even feels somewhat at ease, because they have their higher identity level from the school to fall back on. They maintain their identity from the school throughout their time at college.

Then, the first social group they come across after college are people of an even higher social status, perhaps met through a job that the person was fortunate to get, and they fit in there. Their identity level is elevated and they now feel like the people around them, in that group. They are quite diverged at this point, but it is probably hardly noticeable in their life. Our brain tries to take our circumstances, and make them feel normal. However strange our circumstances are (and everyone's are to some extent), then providing they're ok, they can feel normal to us.

Next they join a second social group. The behaviours they use in the first social group were copied from those around them, because their natural behaviours are more associated with their inherited level. When they apply these new, copied behaviours to the second social group, they find they aren't quite as accepted. The second group is quite different to the first, despite being at the same level in society, and it is different enough that the person struggles to be treated as if they were of the same level. This feels bad, not being treated according to their identity level, and the person retreats from this group, and is drawn back to the first social group more strongly.

They then find a third social group, at a similar level, with people that they feel more comfortable with. That group is similar to the first, so their behaviours integrate, and they are able to be treated according to their identity, and being diverged isn't a problem.

The person may find it harder to interact with their old school friends, because their identity level has increased since then, and they now judge others from a "higher level". Whilst they may try to interact with old friends at a "lower level" how they once did, it becomes a little harder, and they'll perhaps come across as a little patronising. Also it's also unlikely those old friends will fully recognise that the person they once knew, and felt similar to, now feels at a higher level.

There are many ways a life can turn, but in each case it follows similar rules or patterns. We adopt the identity from the highest group that we've found acceptance in, and our identity can only go up. If we find it hard to maintain that identity, we feel frustrated and it can be hurtful, and we still try to hold onto it.

Our identity level can jump up quite quickly. If we find acceptance, then it doesn't take long for our brain to latch onto that, and absorb it as our new self-definition.

However, even if we don't move up or down in society, or groups, then because each person is diverged in modern societies, due to the difficult social environment we find ourselves in (the "social delta"), the question is not if someone is diverged, but how much they are.

Levels scenario

Our inherited level comes from our parents (because we subconsciously copy their interactions and emotions), and at least a part of our parents wants us to be a reflection of themselves. Therefore how our levels compare to our parents' levels can affect the parent-child dynamic.

We all find ourselves in slightly different places in society, and more so the more multi-layered and unequal our societies are. We then have a contrast between the family dynamic, where the parent is the parent, and the societal dynamic, where the parent and child have (often different) identity levels within society. The parent and child can have very different identity levels, i.e. different status groups they feel accepted in. Each will be drawing definition, and sense of belonging, from those

A Theory of Everyone

different groups (potentially at different levels), and the parent-child relationship has to fit against this somehow.

How our identity level compares to our parents' identity level(s), and how the inherited levels rumble on beneath, can play a big part in the parent-child relationship.

To explore this, below is a diagram showing a fictional example of 5 generations of the same family. Each person is shown with their inherited level, which they've absorbed from their parents (and which is fairly constant throughout their own life), and their identity level, which is the maximum level they achieved in their life.

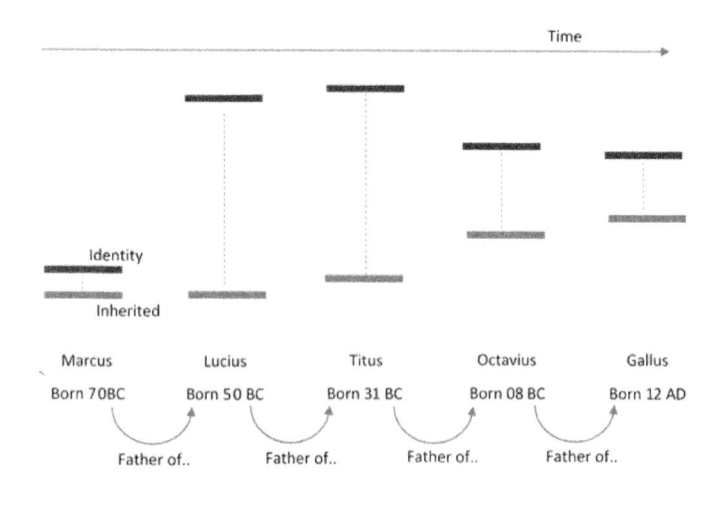

Time

Identity
Inherited

| Marcus | Lucius | Titus | Octavius | Gallus |
| Born 70BC | Born 50 BC | Born 31 BC | Born 08 BC | Born 12 AD |

Father of..   Father of..   Father of..   Father of..

This is just one example of what could happen over five generations. This example, and ones like it, are one of many possible patterns that have played out down generations, for 12,000 years, ever since we gave up our hunter-gatherer lifestyles. It is an example of how our large societies can cause our three main drivers: family; group; and our desire to

Inherited Hierarchies

maximise our value; to head in different directions, whilst our self and emotions are still being dictated by each of them.

This example could therefore be from a family in ancient Maya, the early Shang dynasty in China, Renaissance Italy, Romanov Russia, or, the modern day. In this example, I have chosen this brief story of 5 generations to be set in the Roman empire.

However, before delving into this scenario, to look at how the levels affected their lives, we need to understand a few basic principles of how levels affect the interactions between parent and child, as well as how levels affect each person's experiences of the world.

The effects of levels on our life

Parents

How our levels compare to our parents can have a big impact on the dynamic.

An illustration of this is the hunter-gatherer who decided to head off with the big-game-hunters, for the summer season, at the small settlement.

This hunter-gatherer would then be diverged, because of the elevated identity level achieved through acceptance from the big-game-hunters.

They would also have an identity level higher than their parent's identity level. They would retain this even after they return at the end of the summer. That big-game-hunting acceptance has made an indelible mark on their self, imprinting a belief of being similar to and a reflection of the big-game-hunting group. This is something that our brains never really let go of.

A Theory of Everyone

On returning to their old tribe, this would cause some conflict with their parents. They may still want to behave like the big-game-hunters, or take a higher position in their old tribe because of it. The parents may find this behaviour threatening, and it is going against their evolutionary driver for the child to be a reflection of them, and follow in their footsteps. The parent may act to reduce their child. This is to resist the fact that the child now views the world, including them, and their tribe, from the higher status.

Just like that example, from 10,000 or-so years ago, levels are still playing a role between parents and children. In our huge societies, people are moving around a lot, and it tests the simple parent-child mechanisms. Often a certain amount of restraint is applied from the parent because of this. Parenthood can become a balancing act between encouraging children, and limiting them, so that they are someone we can (theoretically) pass on love and affection to.

We all want to have supportive parents, and to be good parents ourselves. Yet in the modern world this relationship is a difficult one at the best of times. Difficulty gets complicated, and manifests itself down generations, but conflict, between parent and child, is often related (somewhere or another) to levels, and how diverged we all are.

It's difficult as a child to understand that our parents are acting according to levels. Instead we are generally blindsided by quite core emotional needs. Levels are perhaps more apparent to parents, whilst they become irrelevant, or secondary, from the child's perspective.

It is often better not to get too deep into the ins and outs of our parents, it is not necessary for feeling good about the world, nor managing difficulty. Often it is easier and better to focus on a purpose or something that represents our individuality, to find our way in life. However, the parental relationship does

Inherited Hierarchies

tend to underly our world, and occasionally rear its head. And sometimes we have to face it, perhaps when things go awry. Even if we don't, if we can find some better understanding of what's going on there, we can take one step closer to them, and perhaps give us a better understanding of ourselves, and who we are.

Both the relative identity levels, and relative inherited levels, can affect the parent-child dynamic.

The identity and inherited levels are passed to the child through everything the parent does, good and bad. These two levels are deeply ingrained in the parent, as they are in any human being, and so they are passed on to the child in all of their interactions. This is why a relationship between a parent and child is so personal, because how the child feels about the parent comes down to a multitude of tiny interactions across our life, that in some ways represent the inherited level and the identity level.

We feel a need to replicate out parent's identity level.

Even when our parents don't directly put pressure on us, there can be some pressure to attain an identity level that isn't below our parents. Conversely, if we exceed the parent's identity level, then they will reduce us a little in order that we don't judge ourselves as above them. These forces, on both sides, are quite strong, as they come from our core drivers, each of which has a powerful influence on us.

We are also passed our parent's inherited level.

This occurs by subconsciously picking up on how our parents respond to the world around us. We see how our parents react to people and places, and something deep in our brains replicates that in ourselves. This is the part of us that is learning socialisation from the parent, and how the parent is playing the role of the social anchor. It can be frustrating at times. For example, sometimes we find our parent's responses to others annoying, for example when they appear nervous around people we want to associate with. If they were confident with those people, perhaps we'd find it easier to be.

Our inherited level can often also be transferred through more direct action from the parents, which the parent does in order to ensure that their child doesn't have greater social freedom in the world than them. If the child had more freedom, the child would be a much greater threat to the parent in any conflict between them, which would cause the parent to be less kind, open and loving, as they acted to maintain some authority.

In the modern world, the levels we receive can often be a little mismatched. It's not our parents' fault, their levels came from their parents, and theirs from our great grandparents, and so on, but it can mean we are sometimes trying to achieve an identity level against a inherited level that doesn't quite fit.

If our parents are diverged themselves, as most modern humans are, to some extent, it will look something like this:

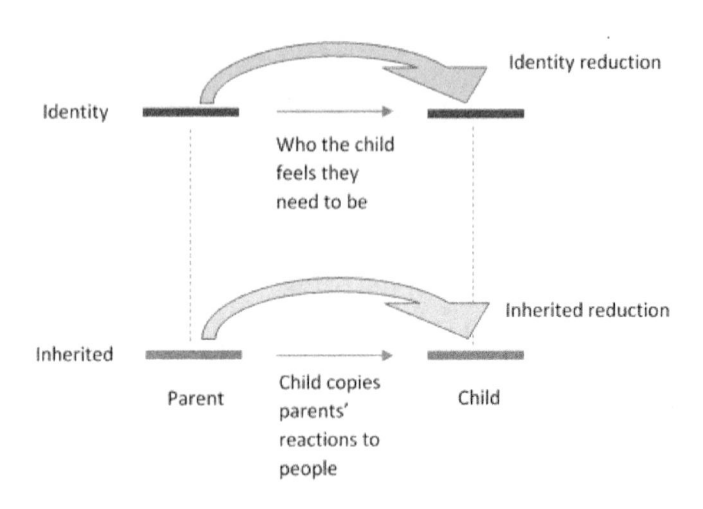

Inherited Hierarchies

The large arrows in the diagram imply some sort of downward, limiting force. In some respects this is true. Some limitation will come from society, from what we can achieve against our inherited position, but a fair amount comes from the parent, inevitably. This is because the parent, instinctively, has to maintain some authority, against a world where the child could "out-value" them. The more unequal society is, the greater chance there is for a child to "out-value" the parent, so the more restrictive the parent has to be. It is frustrating for the child to be limited. In the modern world, these forces, to pass down positions and behaviours from parent to child, are playing out in an unnatural environment.

These downward arrows act on both the inherited level, and the identity level. Some of this will be subconscious, for example the child picking up on the parents' reactions and projections of themselves, and mirroring them somewhat, and others will be more through actions, and the parent-child dynamic, for example the parent verbalising how the child might react, or influencing who the child feels they are.

You can see in the above diagram the parent is diverged, and so the child will be diverged too. The child's levels tend to mirror (or at least be guided by) the parent's.

From this, we can start to see how levels play a part in the dynamic. In reality, in other examples, there can be much greater differences between child and parent, which can cause peculiar and difficult conflicts, as we shall explore in the Roman scenario.

Before looking at how our levels affect our personal life experiences, it's worth noting a point about adulthood.

We have lifelong bonds with our parents. We often, given the nature of difficult parent-child relationships, like to think we are independent, free and distant from our parent's influence as an adult. We can be, and we are to some extent.

But our emotions retain some tie to them. Our programming treats them as the anchor for learning during adolescence, and they remain so in adulthood.

When we reach adulthood, and our own personality and identity firms up, the parent-child relationship can be harder. We both have our fixed points, which are often in different places, and defined in different circumstances and subcultures. Deviating from our identities (the place our personality has settled in) can be hard. This leads to some distance and conflict, which means that when we want support from our parents, which we all do from time to time, as we find our way as an adult (or when we have children ourselves), we can't access it. We can find that that desire for support conflicts with a need to be independent.

This is representative of the difficulty in living in large civilisations, compared to the hunter-gatherer tribe. There, we'd grow into our parents' position in the tribe, passing rites of passage, and gaining their approval as a fully-fledged adult, alongside our parents. We'd have support when we needed it, without feeling less for asking. It is easy to help someone walk a path that we have walked ourself.

Ourself

We've absorbed some levels from our parent, and then we have to face the world by ourselves.

In doing so, in socialising, competing, and finding our way, we have our own two levels: our inherited level and our identity level. Depending on where we find ourself in the world, they can differ greatly from person to person, but one common thing we can look at, which defines a lot about that person's personal experiences, is how far apart those two levels are, i.e. how diverged a person is.

Inherited Hierarchies

Being more diverged as a human can (not always, but can) make our lives a little more difficult.

This is because how we emotionally respond to people and environments, and how we feel we should be responding, are different. We have to work harder on our self-beliefs, change behaviours to compensate, and perhaps find a deeper sense of support in society, in order to maintain our identity level.

Part of the reason for this is that like it or not, we are tied to our inherited level. We may not always feel it, we may develop behaviours that circumvent it, or find situations where we can avoid feeling it, but our evolutionary programming means it can't really change.

It's like we're all on a mountainside. We have a rope tied to us, that is linked to an anchor point (our inherited level). The rope is stretchy and elastic, so we can move up and down the mountain, in between and around other people. At times the rope is slack and we don't notice it. Occasionally however the rope tightens a bit and pulls us towards the anchor. The further we've climbed, the more it might pull. We can resist it, but it takes energy to do so.

It means that when someone challenges us, and adds a little extra weight for us to carry, because we are already fighting a pull from our rope to our anchor, then resisting or responding to that challenge is a little harder.

Below is a less diverged person facing four challenges over a period of time, with time flowing from left to right:

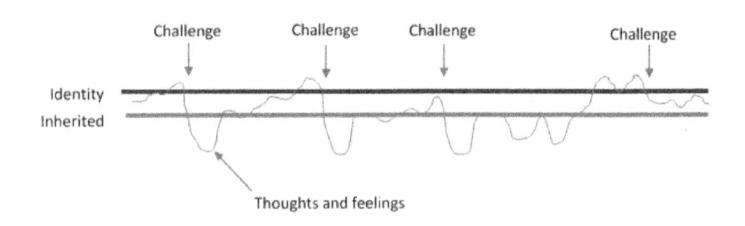

[Figure: Graph showing Identity and Inherited levels with four Challenge arrows; thoughts and feelings dip below identity line and recover.]

The challenges are when someone has said or taken action against us, as part of the difficult social environment we face, perhaps at work, in our families, or amongst our friends.

When our thoughts and feelings are below our identity level, we don't feel ourselves. We feel demeaned, denied a feeling of fulfilment, and feel angry or frustrated.

In the above example, the inherited level is actually helping us recover from the challenge. It isn't too far away from the identity level, so when people knock us down the mountainside, our elastic rope actually pulls us back upwards, and we get on with our lives.

The person will be annoyed, upset or frustrated by the challenge, but they will soon forget about it.

In contrast, here is how a more diverged person responds to the same set of challenges:

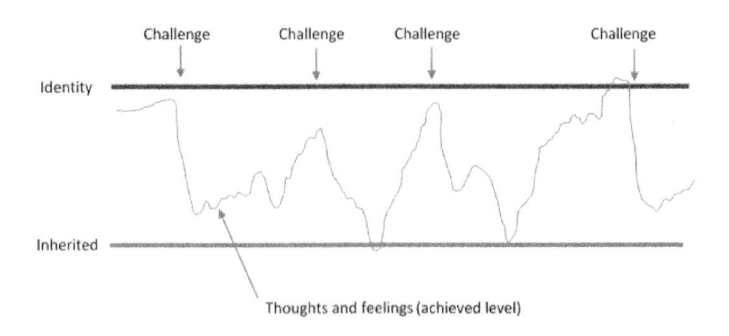

[Figure: Graph with Identity line high and Inherited line low, four Challenges; thoughts and feelings (achieved level) fluctuate widely between them.]

You can see how the challenges have a much greater impact, because of the difference between the inherited and identity levels. That rope, tied below us on the mountainside, makes it much harder to maintain our footing in the jostling world of the level we find ourselves at. We have to expend more energy recovering from the challenge, and maintaining our identity.

As the diverged person is more affected by the same challenges, they need more people to draw on as a source of positive definition, for getting themselves back to their identity, and perhaps greater influence over these people.

There is huge variation in how this plays out from person to person. Some people are largely diverged, but find good environments, where they aren't challenged very often. Others face more competitive environments, where they have more of a daily battle. In both cases the situation is the same though, and when the challenge does come in, the more diverged person will have a harder time recovering from it, in order to be their identity level.

People being diverged is an inevitable side-effect of unequal societies. As people deal with being diverged, they level the playing field. Greater divergence is associated with greater social mobility, which helps bring society towards a common point.

However, what is good for society isn't always good for an individual. In our own lives, being diverged can mean fighting battles on an unequal playing field. Say the two people in the examples above are trying to achieve the same identity level, for example they are colleagues who are working together. For the more diverged person, it is harder. They are facing the same things, but are feeling more of a reaction to it, and a greater headwind. They see themselves as the same identity level, and don't want extra help or sympathy. Nevertheless, the playing field they are both interacting on isn't actually level, and it's bumpy and has ridges and divots. And often those ridges and divots are hidden, invisible, or well-disguised.

Therefore, to be diverged can make our lives more difficult. We can face a greater headwind in achieving similar results to the people around us. In overcoming this, we level the playing field, and the people that follow have an easier time being a human being.

With an idea of how levels affect the parent-child relationship, and how they affect an individual's life experiences, we can then look at how the scenario of five Roman generations plays out.

Levels scenario

Heading back to Rome.

It's 55 BC and Julius Caesar landed on the shores of Britain for the first time. Before then, Britain was a myth, a faraway land. Nobody from Rome had ever been there, and the second-hand stories the Romans heard, about the indigenous people, were exaggerated myths of druids and savage warriors covered in blue warpaint. For Julius to land on the shores of Britain was like landing on the moon at the time, and so it was an impressive feat, that elevated his cult following[21].

Julius was a smart self-promotor, and was ambitious. He sent home stories of his exploits that were told by orators on the streets of Rome, often with a few embellishments in order to further his celebrity. At this time, he was head of the army, and yet to become dictator of Rome, but was amassing popularity and support with every military victory he had across the landscape of Europe.

Marcus, who lived in a small town outside of Rome, was 15 years old when this happened, and Julius was instantly his hero.

Inherited Hierarchies

He played around the local cobbled streets outside his parent's modest home, brandishing a wooden sword and shield. As his father was a blacksmith, he was the envy of his friends with a replica legionnaires belt.

Marcus grew up to be a blacksmith himself, following in his father's footsteps. His life, and the lives of four generations that came after him, can serve as an example of how inherited position and identity can change from one generation to the next.

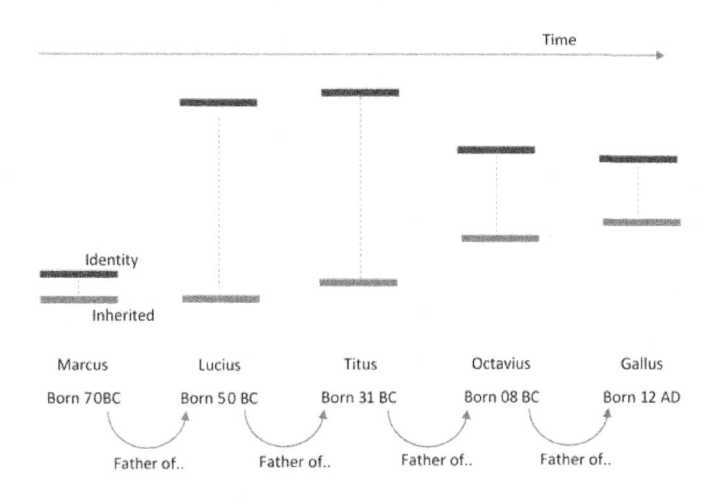

Time

Identity
Inherited

Marcus	Lucius	Titus	Octavius	Gallus
Born 70BC	Born 50 BC	Born 31 BC	Born 08 BC	Born 12 AD

Father of..   Father of..   Father of..   Father of..

This example follows the male half of the family, but it could equally be applied to the female half of the family too, or with some intermixing. We tend to be more influenced by family members of the same sex, since on average there are more similarities, but every situation is different.

Applying the theory from the previous section, we can now assess how the changing levels, of the five generations of his fictional family, played out in the relationships, and to the people themselves.

A Theory of Everyone

Marcus learnt his trade from his father, in the family business. Life is fairly straightforward for Marcus, he is popular among the townsfolk, and after work he often went to the town forum to have a few drinks with his friends, who he'd grown up with. He felt content, and himself.

His inherited level was similar to his identity level. He was playing a part similar to his father, as well as a few generations before that. How he reacted to people was similar to who he felt he was. He was happy in his life, but gave little thought to the world around him, they didn't bother him and he didn't bother them. Despite the changing world (Julius Caesar had become dictator in 45BC, and was assassinated in 44BC), Marcus was relatively unaffected. Blacksmithing was a trade in demand, and his life wasn't strongly impacted by the social and political landscape.

Marcus fell in love with a local girl who he'd always had a crush on, and they had two surviving children, a boy Lucius and a girl Aurelia. At the time infant mortality was high, and Marcus had lost three children. He often thought about them, and wondered what type of people they'd grow up to be.

His children Lucius and Aurelia were quite different. Lucius was academic whilst his sister was artistic. Marcus wanted Lucius to follow him into the family business of blacksmithing, but whilst Lucius showed an interest, he was also finding success in school. He was good with numbers, and enjoyed maths.

Marcus tried to praise Lucius for his maths work, but it didn't seem to work. He didn't feel his praise for maths really felt genuine, and this seemed to push Lucius away more. One day a recruiter from the Roman Imperial treasury came to the school, to give a talk on accounts, and explained how a *rationarium* was being prepared, listing all of Rome's finances for the first time. In it would be public revenues, cash in the treasury, cash with tax officials and cash in public contractors[22]. The recruiter explained how this was revolutionary, and the next step in the development of their great civilisation. He wore fine clothes and jewellery, and carried an authority that made an impression on Lucius. Being good at maths, the recruiter talked to Lucius personally, and encouraged him to put in an application when he finished school at the end of the year. Lucius excitedly told his parents that evening. They tried to be supportive, but didn't seem to completely share his optimism, which annoyed Lucius.

Lucius did put in that application, and was successful. He moved to the city of Rome, and became an accountant. When he was leaving, his father was distant and didn't seem supportive, and Lucius got annoyed and they didn't part on the best terms. Marcus was pleased for his son's achievements, he wanted Lucius to follow his dreams, after all he remembered having dreams of his own, but it was going against his programming. It felt like Lucius thought blacksmithing wasn't good enough for him, or that he didn't look up to Marcus enough to follow in his footsteps. The path Lucius was following slightly intimidated Marcus. He wanted Lucius to find his own individuality, but that individuality was having ramifications.

After a while, Lucius was starting to challenge him in ways he wasn't used to, and he found himself more opposed. It wasn't that Marcus was easily intimidated, but Rome had always been a distant thought. He'd been there a few times, and didn't like the noise and bustle. He found Romans superior, and they had odd and different behaviours, and he always longed to go back to his home town.

But Lucius fitted in there. Accountants had good social standing in Rome. He was good at his job, and it felt rewarding, it felt as if he was making a difference to the world.

A Theory of Everyone

In 27 BC Augustus became the first Emperor, and the Roman Empire began in full force. It was an exciting and optimistic time to be a 23-year-old in the capital city. Lucius earned a good salary, more money than he'd ever seen, and bought nice clothes, pottery, and eventually a house in one of Rome's suburbs. Because of this, Lucius's identity level was that of a wealthy Roman accountant, who he felt was changing the world. He couldn't help but feel far above the small town he came from.

However, Lucius's inherited level was still similar to, and linked to, his fathers. Throughout his life, his brain had followed cues from how his parents reacted to other people, including those from the city of Rome. When his parents came to visit, they seemed nervous and out of place, and often made derogatory comments about the locals, and this frustrated Lucius. Lucius needed to associate with those around him as an equal, since that is his identity, and found it uncomfortable seeing his parents feel uncomfortable there.

Through this process the inherited level is transferred from parent to child, even in adulthood. Lucius' mind is picking up on, and replicating, his parent's reactions.

Lucius started to reject that he was similar to Marcus, and instead felt similar to the role models around him. Nevertheless, he found working with wealthy Romans, who'd grown up in the city, with their private tutors and large houses, a little intimidating. He was just as good at the job than them, but his inherited position was responding to them as if they were above him, whilst his identity was that they were equal. He found himself competing with them as if he was an equal, but found it was as if he was facing a greater headwind.

He made friends with someone similar to him at the business, who also came from a small town. He focussed deeply on his work, aiming for targets, and trying to get good

Inherited Hierarchies

appraisals. He became a team leader, not least due to his focus and attention to detail, and adopted the new position, and the behaviours that went with it, with some gusto. He enjoyed this, and those behaviours that he used at work, as a team leader, filtered into his personality. He met a wife at a chariot race he attended, with his friends, and they fell in love.

He fell out with his father Marcus. When Lucius walked into his old town wearing fine clothes, and acting like a manager, Marcus felt compelled to disapprove and reduce Lucius. He was still the father, and wanted the respect from that, and some authority, but instead found Lucius judging him from a superior position. Marcus wanted respect as a father and a blacksmith, whilst Lucius wanted support from Marcus, as well as to be treated as an elevated Roman accountant. Neither got what they wanted.

It might seem like this dynamic, and these reactions, are arbitrary, and perhaps that they could be overcome with a strong will, or a different approach. However, it goes deeper than that. If society is seated around a stadium, in some sort of social pecking order, then the different places in society, that Marcus and Lucius find themselves in, are like Lucius going and sitting in a different section of the stadium to his father. The dynamic, and social forces they experience, are representative of the thousands of people now seated between them. They are trying to have a parent-child relationship, whilst at different places in a society of millions.

Both were bitter and sad at this. Marcus felt that his son wasn't respecting him, and was frustrated that he couldn't show love and affection. It was also frustrating for Marcus, because he couldn't fathom Lucius' point of view. After all, Marcus was an upstanding member of his town, and had many friends, but that wasn't enough for Lucius. Every now and again he would try to praise Lucius for being an accountant, but it just didn't come off right, and seemed to annoy Lucius more.

Lucius felt frustrated because his father wasn't approving of him, nothing he did was good enough for Marcus. Lucius couldn't understand Marcus' behaviour, he felt Marcus should be pleased and proud of him for his achievements, but it wasn't felt.

This is what levels can do, and what happens when the parental driver, the group driver, and the drive to maximise our value, become out of balance. Both want what they feel they should get from a father or son, but that now conflicts with the situation in front of them.

Lucius found work occasionally stressful, and often conflicts at work caused him to spend a whole evening frustrated. He sought dependence more deeply in his wife, who helped him reaffirm that he deserved to be there, which he did, his work was very good. Occasionally he showed his frustration at work, and found himself blaming others in his business for sometimes minor mistakes, and sometimes, in private, blaming his father for making his life difficult.

The dynamic between Lucius and Marcus is very difficult to resolve. It is down to levels, which always complicate situations. The social dynamic, driven by groups, and the desire to maximise our value, are in direct conflict with the parental driver.

Marcus can't admit to Lucius that he is at a higher level. Lucius can't let Marcus treat him as below him, with authority, as a son.

Even if Marcus could somehow be entirely supportive, Lucius is actually battling his own inherited level, which neither Marcus nor Lucius can have a say over. Lucius' levels, including his inherited level, (which is derived from Marcus, whether either of them likes it or not), are what Lucius has to face the world against. Lucius finds increased frustration at having to maintain an identity level distant from his inherited level, and because the inherited level is drawn from the parent, the frustration often manifests itself in that direction.

There are many ways this can resolve, and many compromises that can be reached. Occasionally, when things are going well, he and Marcus get along. Lucius feels he has a good life, and feels fortunate. He has broken the mould, and played a part in the intermixing of Roman society, but neither of those are easy, and the reason for that comes down to levels.

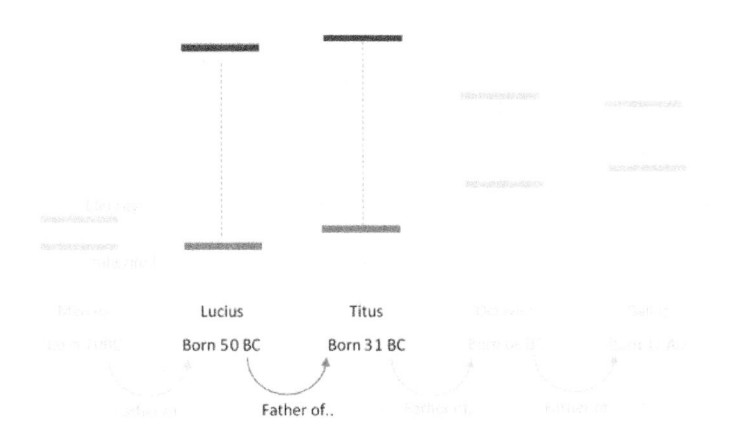

Lucius — Born 50 BC
Titus — Born 31 BC
Father of..

Lucius had three surviving children, a boy, Titus, and two girls, Cecilia and Livia. His children grew up in the suburb of Rome, very different to Lucius' upbringing as a small-town blacksmith's son. Titus grew up with all the privilege and wealth of the son of a Roman accountant. His father Lucius had grown up as the son of a blacksmith.

As such, Titus' inherited level was higher than Lucius'. But it was only a little above Lucius'. Even though Lucius' identity was as a fully-fledged, moderately wealthy citizen of Rome, having spent his adult life there as an accountant, his son Titus' human brain picked up on the fact that Lucius was reacting to people as if they were above him. This would happen both consciously and subconsciously, for example by watching the difficulty that Lucius experience in his life and work.

Not only this, but Lucius didn't want Titus to feel completely at ease in the environment, because he didn't. If Titus was at ease, he would have a distinct advantage in any conflict between them. This conflict can come from, for example, when Titus was a teenager. As teenagers we try out new behaviours, and test our parents a little, which is part of our mechanism for ensuring interaction, and forcing levels to be passed down. In modern societies, where we have to reduce our children a little more than we needed to as hunter-gatherers, this can lead to more conflict. So Lucius, even though he didn't want to, felt compelled to make his son Titus a little less secure. This is how the inherited level is passed from Lucius to Titus.

This was confusing for Titus. His father Lucius projected himself at one level, but didn't quite give Titus the support to achieve it himself. As a result they were not emotionally close. When Titus faced difficulty, his father didn't seem to really understand, and instead encouraged him to focus on achieving success in his career in order to solve his problems. Titus found that he saw his father one way, but his father spoke as if he was something else. When, occasionally, Titus opened up to Lucius, he found Lucius talk to him from a level that he didn't feel he justified, which felt uncomfortable. As a father, Lucius often was distant with Titus, as if he was protecting something.

They were amicable, but Titus moved to the other side of Rome, blocked out some of Lucius' behaviour in his mind, and instead had a very close-knit group of friends, who enjoyed Roman theatre and comedy.

Inherited Hierarchies

Lucius was even a little derogatory towards his son's friendship group. Lucius wasn't a part of such a group himself, as he had always felt a little of an outsider, and felt a little threatened by Titus' acceptance there.

It was tolerable. Titus was finding success, as an architect specialising in aqueduct building. The Roman Empire was entering the Pax Romana, a period of 200 years of relative peace and stability, and there were plenty of aqueducts to be built. Titus travelled across Italy and even into Europe with his job, and thus obtained a similar identity level to his father Lucius. Lucius was proud of Titus. He told his accountant friends of children's successes, and they became competitive over them. But he found it very difficult to praise or show this to Titus, and instead kept him at arm's length.

When we're diverged, it can be difficult being emotionally close to people. This is because we want two things: we want them to see us at our *identity level*, which is who we feel we are; but we also want them to support us and understand our *inherited level*, which is how we're responding to the world (and often the cause of our difficulty). These two things are often incompatible. The closer people are to us, the more they see and experience our emotional reactions, and how we see the world, which is our inherited level. If our inherited level is a long way from our identity level, we often are quite guarded of it, since if it is exposed, it can be harder to maintain our identity level.

Children, who want to be emotionally close to their parents, and who are noticing and copying their parent's emotional responses, are exposed to their parent's inherited positions much more than the average person on the street. As a parent we sense this, and can sometimes keep our children at arm's-length, to keep our inherited level defended, and our identity level maintained.

All these mechanisms are part of a cascade, that, one way or another, causes traits and behaviours to be passed from parent to child. Titus felt that he was quite different to his father, yet because Lucius was diverged, Titus was also diverged. Due to levels, Lucius had never received comfortable praise from his father Marcus, and so he found it hard to give to Titus. Because Lucius focussed on his job and career, Titus also found himself focussed on his job and career.

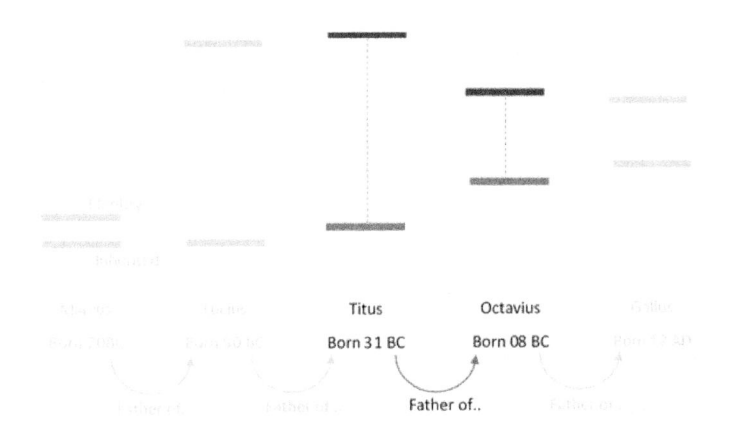

Titus — Born 31 BC
Octavius — Born 08 BC
Father of..

Titus married, and had a son Octavius. Titus wanted to be a better father to Octavius than Lucius had been to him, but as Octavius grew up, he found himself doing some of the things Lucius had done.

Octavius' inherited level was a little higher than Titus', because they'd been living in the suburbs of Rome for two generations now, so it just seemed more comfortable to Octavius. Nevertheless, Titus still found that occasionally he had to make life a little more uncomfortable for Octavius, to match his own subconscious feelings.

Titus' primary focus in life was his close group of friends, who's main interest was the latest plays and comedies that travelling actors would perform. As a group they were a good collection of respectable individuals, and it formed quite a large part of how Titus felt about himself. He felt sure Octavius would look up to him when Octavius made his own friendship group. However, when it came to it, Octavius' became friends with a different kind of group. They were more outgoing, and enjoyed fighting like gladiators, and going to the local games. The Coliseum of Rome wasn't to be built for another 70 years, but still there were many games going on, and it was a part of Roman society. Octavius didn't look up to Titus how he thought he would, and they fell out as a result.

Octavius didn't have the aptitude for maths or design, that his father Titus did (or his grandfather accountant Lucius did), and so took a less well-paid job as a games designer. He enjoyed this greatly, as he got to work with designing sets and challenges for gladiators to face. But he just didn't feel Titus really appreciated him. Titus wanted to show it, but couldn't. When he tried to say how good he thought Octavius' games were, it just didn't sound right, and Octavius found it patronising. How Octavius' *identity level* compares to Titus' can have an influence on the dynamic, regardless of intent or goodwill (although efforts to show approval are always welcomed in the long run).

Octavius and Titus weren't emotionally close. Titus tried to project it, but it was clear his focus and behaviours were strongly tied to his friends. As his son, Octavius could sense that Titus was diverged, and that his reactions didn't quite match his identity. Whenever he was open with his father Titus, it always felt like Titus ignored those reactions and instead talked down to him, as if those insecurities didn't exist. If Octavius pointed this out, Titus became distant and defensive. To an individual, there is only one level: the identity level. To Titus, he was one and the same as his group of

A Theory of Everyone

friends, and the idea that he felt unease at that level was inconceivable, at least to admit. Octavius felt he had to face a headwind in life (which he saw markedly in his dad Titus, due to the large divergence), whilst pretending those headwinds didn't exist (like his dad Titus).

Octavius enjoyed his work, and despite the conflict with Titus, had a good life. He lived to a relatively old age for the time, just long enough to see the building of the great Coliseum, which filled Octavius with excitement and marvel.

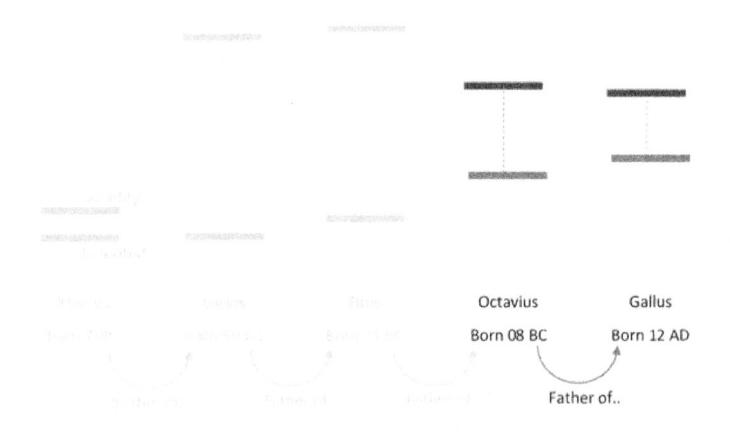

Octavius   Gallus

Born 08 BC   Born 12 AD

Father of..

Octavius had married, and had a son Gallus. Octavius and Gallus were closer than any of the previous generations. Gallus' inherited level was consistent with a citizen of Rome living in the suburbs, as his family had been living there for four generations. He had friends and a job similar to his father Octavius, and so was more comfortable in life. He found his father Octavius difficult at times: Octavius never quite felt good enough, and so treated Gallus in a similar way. However, Octavius was more open with Gallus, and able to explain his

Inherited Hierarchies

situation, and so Gallus was able to live with the relationship more easily than some of the generations before.

Of all the generations, Octavius and Gallus had the most similar levels. It meant that Gallus, like his great, great, grandfather Marcus, had a place in life that matched his father, and likely behaviours and traits to go along with it. Perhaps Gallus had the most comfortable life. Perhaps Gallus was the "best" son, and perhaps Octavius is the "best" father, but neither are fair statements. There is so much out of our control when levels become involved, and much of it comes down to chance and circumstance.

It took four generations for the strong divergence, that Lucius experienced, to be lessened, and for the inherited level to slowly rise, one generation to the next, so that Gallus actually felt comfortable as a citizen of Rome's suburbs. This was just a small jump too, there are much bigger jumps out there.

It is easy to describe five generations in a short passage, and see the contrast and developments, but for each of those generations, one of those unique circumstances was their whole life. We may be one of those generations, unaware that our circumstances may have been dictated by events several generations ago, and that our relationship with our parents perhaps bears the hallmarks of the relationship between our great grandparent and their parents.

This is just one example of what *can* happen and why. It is representative of the forces felt by modern humans, and how they play out on our lives. Any difficulty felt can be greater or less from person to person due to a large range of factors. Sometimes issues arise that are a cause of great difficulty, and sometimes there is some fortune involved and the difficulty is never exposed. Even with difficulty, which everyone feels to some extent, we can find happiness in our lives, levels are certainly not a barrier to that.

Should Marcus have prevented Lucius from taking that job, and following his dreams?

Would Lucius have thanked Marcus for preventing him becoming an accountant, even if Lucius could have had a comfortable life as a blacksmith?

Even if he knew how it eventually panned out, would Lucius have chosen to be a blacksmith, and missed out on the chance to know what it's like to live as a citizen of Rome, own expensive clothes, and know what it feels like to be at the forefront of the developing world?

In each case, probably not. There's perhaps little that could have stopped Lucius resisting the draw to maximise his value. It would be quite hard for a person to deny themselves the opportunity to feel success and elevation, even if they knew it would come with difficulty.

The impact on the lives of these five generations are a result of each generation's inherited level and identity level, and how those levels compare to their parents. The circumstances of Lucius' divergence caused impacts down the generations. We see this all around society. We can't help being diverged as modern humans, and it is more a case of *how* diverged we are. And, as we have seen, and perhaps you believe (or not), it can have a big influence on our relationship with our parents, and our experiences of the world.

The social delta

The social delta is the reason why the vast majority of human beings, who live in large societies, are diverged.

The social delta lowers the inherited level of each person, so that they face an additional headwind in maintaining their identity. Every person's inherited position then becomes more of an unwelcome inconvenience.

Inherited Hierarchies

The larger the society, and the greater the inequality in it, the larger the social delta.

In a tribe, levels are merely about position. If we adopt the same position in the tribe as a few generations of our family beforehand, we will not be diverged at all. We will feel entirely comfortable in that position, and have a set of natural behaviours that fit it. Our identity level, who we feel we are, and our inherited level, how we emotionally react to those around us, are the same.

In large societies, our levels are about positions **plus** the social delta. Even if we adopt exactly the same status in society, and the same social position in our friendship groups, compared to several generations of our family before us, we will still be diverged a little. Each person faces additional headwinds to simply feeling fulfilled in a comfortable social position (assuming we even have a comfortable position).

Large societies cause a social delta for two main reasons. One is the spread of our social lives across several groups, and the other is inequality, which gives rise to the possibility that the child can "out-value" the parent.

In terms of having social lives spread over several groups, this causes additional headwind because each group has a slightly different sub-culture. They may have their own cliquey language, their own jokes, things they value, enjoy doing, and things they don't, and disapprove of. There will be groups we feel better represent us, but it's unlikely we'll have a group that completely matches our values and interests. Given our social lives are spread over several groups, we will often come across groups that have different sub-cultures to the ones we are most comfortable in. Therefore, at least parts of our social lives will contain greater hesitancy and reservations about truly expressing ourselves. Or, if we express ourselves without reservations, then we may face resistance and conflict from time to time.

Even in the groups that best represent us, with our closest friends, we may have to bend and adapt our views, values and interests to fit in. Perhaps some of ourselves fits better in one group, and a different part of our individuality fits in another, but it's rare for all of ourself to be truly represented in one group.

Compare this to a tribe, it is more likely that our views, values and interests grow in unison with all the people that we integrate with, since we stay with that one group our whole lives. Who we grow into, fits what we grow into.

However, perhaps more importantly, our spread-out social lives (and the difference in sub-culture from one group to the next) affect the parent-child relationship.

In large societies, when children grow, and find groups that represent them, it is likely that these groups don't include their parents. The child absorbs the sub-culture and behaviours of those groups, and, it's likely that those sub-cultures and behaviours differ from the ones their parents feel most comfortable in. In any parent-child relationship, there will be some conflict, and the child will challenge the parent, whether in finding boundaries, finding individuality as a teenager, or establishing themselves as an adult. If they challenge the parent from the viewpoint of a sub-culture the parent doesn't recognise, or behaviours the parent isn't comfortable with, then the parent will reduce the child more than they would otherwise.

The parent has to reduce the child in this way, in order to maintain authority, despite the differing sub-cultures and behaviours of their respective identities. The parent reduces the child to ensure the child isn't too comfortable in sub-cultures very different from the parent's. If the child was, then the parent would have a harder time maintaining their position of authority, which their core drivers, and deep instincts, encourage them not to yield.

On the second reason for the social delta: inequality, this also affects the parent-child relationship, because there now exists the possibility that our children can "out-value" us.

If they attain acceptance in a higher group, then their group driver causes them to feel a part of that group, and feel similar to, and a reflection of, the people in it. They judge others from the viewpoint of that group. They expect to be treated consistent with how someone else of that group is treated. When they apply these to the parent-child relationship, they can then look down on the parent. They are being pulled towards a position higher than the parent, whilst the parent is trying to maintain the upper hand themselves.

The parent naturally tries to maintain authority. This results in a situation where, against the mere possibility that the child can "out-value" the parent, the parent has to apply extra restraint, in order to balance their authority as a parent, with the social position that their child may attain.

The greater the inequality in society, the more restraint the parent may have to apply.

They have to apply greater constraint and caution (alongside encouragement), in order to prevent their children being drawn towards the top, and becoming someone that they can't interact with: someone that looks down on them.

Greater inequality also affects the first reason for the social delta (our spread-out social lives).

The more unequal a society is, the more people have to gain and lose. This causes people to seek greater security in groups. Groups become more cliquey and insular. If the mountainside is steeper, and those below (or above) us are driven by a greater desire to usurp us (or resist us), then we seek greater security in closer friendships. The sub-cultures of individual groups become more different and distinct, in order to provide that security.

The result of each group being more distinct is that it is less likely that they fully represent us, and we have to bend further to fit into a narrower set of views. Also, it raises the chances that a child's sub-culture, that they feel most comfortable in, and that represents them, is different from their parent's. This increases the constraint and reduction that the parent has to apply in order to maintain authority. This in turn leads to a lower inherited level, and therefore a greater headwind to achieving an identity level.

Therefore the greater inequality in society, the greater the social delta.

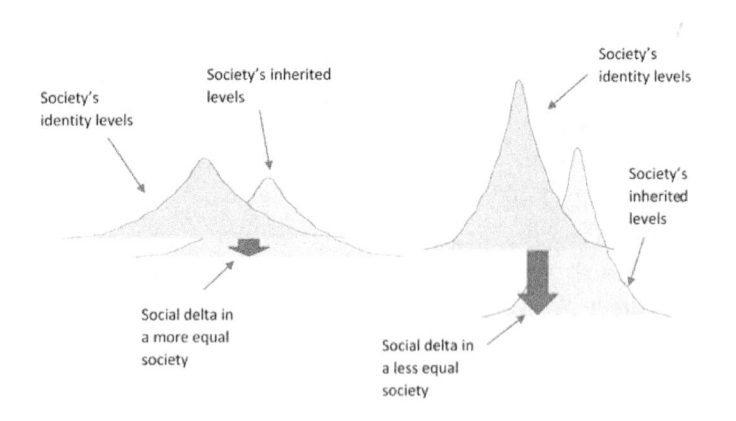

Society's identity levels / Society's inherited levels / Social delta in a more equal society

Society's identity levels / Society's inherited levels / Social delta in a less equal society

The cause of the social delta (that is causing everyone to be diverged), is our spread-out social lives, and the possibility of a child "out-valuing" the parent. Both reasons are exacerbated by greater inequality in society.

The social delta has its source in the parent-child relationship. As parents try to be parents, against an unequal

Inherited Hierarchies

society of spread-out groups, they apply additional constraint, which causes additional divergence. Humans then find they are trying to be "complete", and feel fulfilled, against a difficult social backdrop, and without the full support of the parent.

To each individual, we then find an additional headwind in being our identity. For example, we may only feel ourselves, and be treated according to our identity level, in pockets. In certain groups, we do, in others, it can be a fight to be treated how we want. Often, even in our closest groups, it can be a fight to be treated according to what we feel is our identity.

This is the "social delta". Positions aside, each person will feel an additional headwind to being their identity level. On average, the social delta is lowering the inherited levels of each person. The larger and more unequal a society is, the more this is the case.

This is why, as modern humans living in large societies, the question is not whether someone is diverged, but how much.

3

Levelling

Levels also play a part in group dynamics.

In towns and cities throughout history, people have been forming groups with people from different backgrounds, walks of life, and who've had very different experiences.

When a group forms, our social instincts kick in. Our hunter-gatherer brain assesses the goings on in the group with some importance. The dynamic of the group, what it represents, and how we are positioned in the group, can have a big impact on us. Our focus tends to be drawn into the group, and any conflict there, in isolation from the society around us.

Those hunter-gatherer instincts are there to move the group towards a common point, where there is order, harmony, and each person's needs are accounted for. However, when the group is made up of people from different parts of a large, unequal society, this process can be harder than it should be.

Each person in the group, because they are from different backgrounds and experiences, will have different preconceptions about how and where they fit into the group. Their backgrounds and experiences will affect how they subconsciously react to the group in front of them, as well as where they feel they need to be positioned.

Each person in the group will likely be diverged to a greater or lesser extent. For example, one person may identify as a leader, but find they have to do so against a strong headwind of a low inherited position. Another may feel out of place in a group of higher social status.

When a group of modern humans comes together, they tend to be a slightly mismatched melting pot of different respective levels. Below is an example of 8 people who have just been thrown together in a new group.

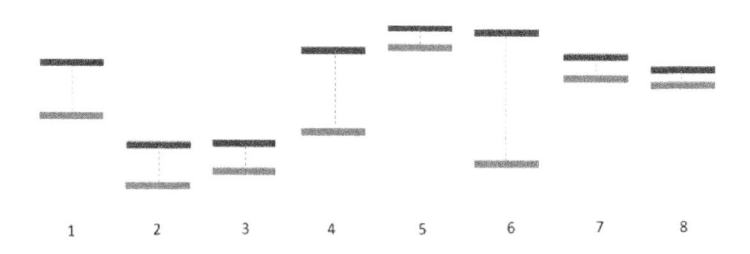

They could be a group of frontiers men and women, banding together to head across the Rocky Mountains, in the early 1800s, in search of wealth, and a better life on the West coast of America. They could be a group heading across the silk road from Chang'an in 700 AD, when Tang dynasty China brought about a golden age of arts and culture. It could have been a group in the aristocracy of Hapsburg Austria, or a group of slaves in the Mesopotamian empire. The levels are relative to each other, so apply to any human beings, in any part of society.

This coming together of different levels is a melting pot of a situation, but our social instincts deal with it fairly well. We tend to pick up on the other people's inherited and identity levels. People signal who they feel they are, how they want to be treated, compromises are made, and a rough structure starts to form.

The group resolves around a single new sub-culture, which will be an amalgamation of the different sub-cultures of the new members. The group finds a level of commonality, and, as the group establishes itself, each member feels acceptance at the group level. Our brains starts drawing definition from those around us, copying and interlinking behaviours, so that we become a reflection of those around us, to allow the group to move as one. A group structure forms, with rough positions and alliances, until the group dynamic looks like this:

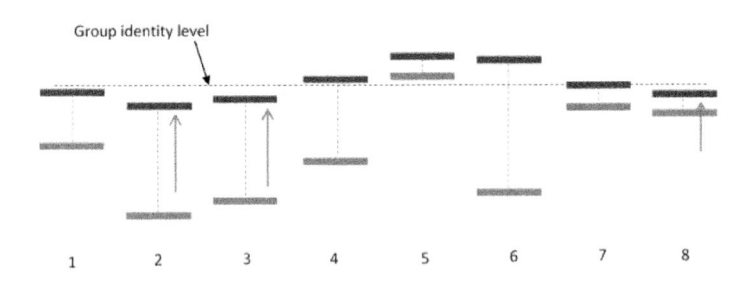

The inherited levels won't have changed, but the identity levels have been affected by the formation of, and acceptance within, the new group.

Particularly for persons 2 and 3, and lesser so for person 8, the acceptance in the new group has raised their identity level. This is the jump in max level described before. It can happen very quickly, and this group then becomes those person's highest acceptance group, and therefore their new maximum status.

Levelling

Their identity will quickly form as a reflection of those around them in the new group. They will judge themselves by those around them, seeking comparison, feeling elevated by their acceptance, but also finding new competitions, and perhaps new social pressures too. Looking outwardly from the group, they will now judge others from the viewpoint of the new group, including old friends, and even family.

However, despite the commonality and coalescing of the new group into a single structure, each person is linked to other groups that also influence them, and the group will appear, and mean, different things to each member. The members in the group are also anchored to different points, some far away from the group's identity level.

The external forces are manifested in different levels of divergence on individuals, which result in the members of the group being obtrusive towards each other, and competing and posturing in order to achieve identity levels, in the group, against the totality of their social lives.

As each member is diverged, to a greater or lesser extent, each has to be obtrusive to maintain their identity level against the pull from the elastic to their anchor: their inherited level. Those who are more diverged will be more obtrusive, and so the inherited levels (the anchor points of each person), are feeding into the group dynamic.

The playing field isn't level beforehand, different members of the group are trying to achieve their positions, with differing distances to their anchor point. Some are facing a greater pull towards that anchor point than others.

This isn't always a problem, far from it, it is the norm in the modern world. In fact this obtrusiveness is the levelling mechanism. It is sharing the difficulty of being diverged. It is evening out the difficulty felt by some more than others, and, within a group, and across society, it is resulting in a more even playing field.

The obtrusiveness is also making it harder for those with identities *above* the group identity level to maintain them. They face some of the obtrusiveness of others overcoming their inherited levels, and feel less able to fully project a personality representative of a higher status level. That personality will have come from a different group. If they fully expressed it in the current group, it would be trying to move the group away from the common group identity level; and make it harder for those who are diverged to maintain their own identities in the group.

As a result, in the group, those with the highest identity levels will have them reduced a little. They will still maintain their identity levels, but elsewhere, and find they have to let go of it a little when in this group. Overall, each person in the group has had their identity moved towards a common level.

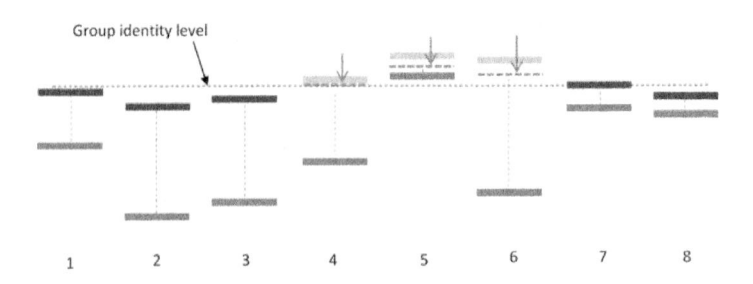

For those that the new group has given a boost to, the group will be quite important to them, as it is the source of their max status, and therefore their identity.

They are also now more diverged, which means greater distance to their subcon, and greater pull towards it, from time to time.

Levelling

On the other hand, for those reduced a little, the group will mean much less, and they will instead rely more on other groups they are a part of, where they can achieve their identity level more uninhibited.

Our inherited level, and need to be our identity level, are strong forces. They are also relatively fixed by circumstances, so this process of levelling is almost impossible to circumvent. It happens one way or the other, even if people are trying to avoid it, trying not to be obtrusive, or trying not to integrate.

We tend not to think of groups in this way, it is a process that simply happens, based off our social instincts, and the emotions they produce. Nevertheless, it can explain much of the interpersonal behaviour we see.

The impact of levels on the group dynamics, and the interpersonal relationships within the group, can now be briefly looked at. Most conflict comes down to the relative levels of the people involved.

Group interpersonal relationships

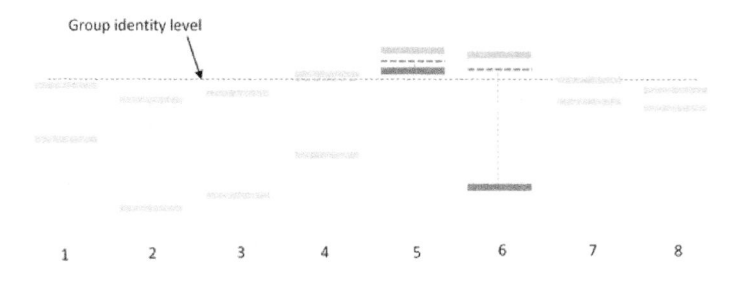

Person 5 has the highest identity and subcon, so they are likely the leader of the group. However, person 6 has an identity close to 5, but a much lower subcon. It's likely that at times person 6 thinks they are the leader of the group, until they are gently overruled by person 5.

Person 5 occasionally has to keep person 6 in check, because, if person 6 gets too confident, they tend to be a little disruptive of the group, or treat people in ways they aren't happy with. For example, person 6 may try to lead and support people from the viewpoint of their identity level, but to others, it feels like it is coming from their inherited level. That can feel uncomfortable to the others. The members of the group sense the difference in inherited positions between person 5 and person 6. As humans we pick up on a huge amount of information, and read body language and expressions quite accurately, even on brief first impressions. To be led by someone we don't feel justifies the position can be frustrating.

In order to try to maintain their identity therefore, person 6 will have to be more obtrusive towards the others. They are unlikely to blend into the group seamlessly.

Perhaps person 6 could form an alliance with person 5. However, this would be unlikely to be a two-way, close friendship, and instead be more of an alliance of convenience.

Person 6 may find it difficult to interact with the group when person 5 isn't there, partly due to their obtrusiveness, and partly due to needing the group to treat them according to their diverged identity. Without person 5, the rest of the group may not support person 6's identity as a leader.

Levelling

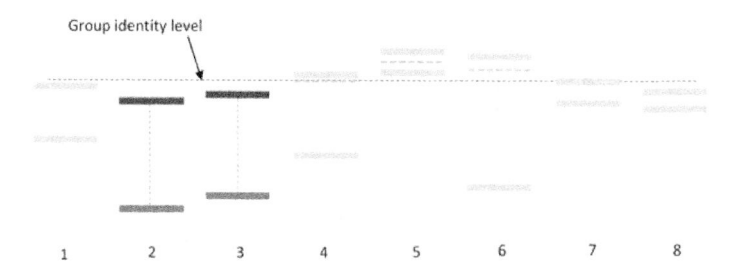

Persons 2 and 3 have the lowest inherited levels. To them, the group represents something that elevates them. They are able to meet the group level and find acceptance, and this is likely through an alliance with each other. As they both have similar inherited levels, they will see the world, and react, in the same way, so they have greater potential for being closer. They will perhaps be a little cliquey, and be less close to those around them, or, alternatively, they may take on a more supportive role to the other group members. In group situations, it's likely that persons 2 and 3's focus will be more on each other, as friends or competition, and they will pay more attention to what each other is doing than other members of the group.

Persons 2 and 3 can also be peacemakers and leaders in some way. They have quite a secure position in the group, albeit in the lowest position, which allows them to be a stabilising factor. However, perhaps they aren't wholly happy with being in the position they find themselves in, and should unusual circumstances allow, they may wish to raise themselves up a little. We all have that desire, to maximise our value.

A Theory of Everyone

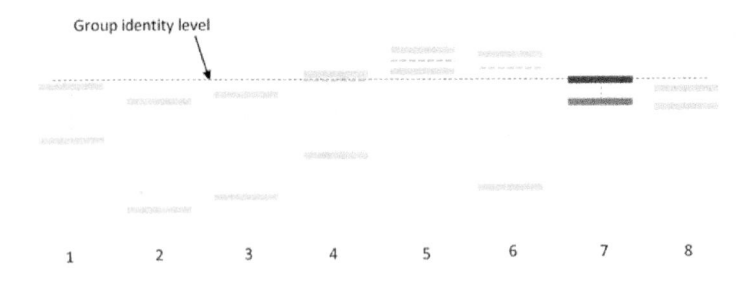

Person 7 is in the middle of the group hierarchy through their identity, but the least diverged. They're happy in their position, for example perhaps their parents took similar positions comfortably in similar types of groups, and therefore they don't play too active a role in the group, preferring to stay by the side-lines. Occasionally, someone else in the group tries to challenge them, but because they aren't diverged, they're not too bothered, they can brush it aside more easily, and people leave them to it.

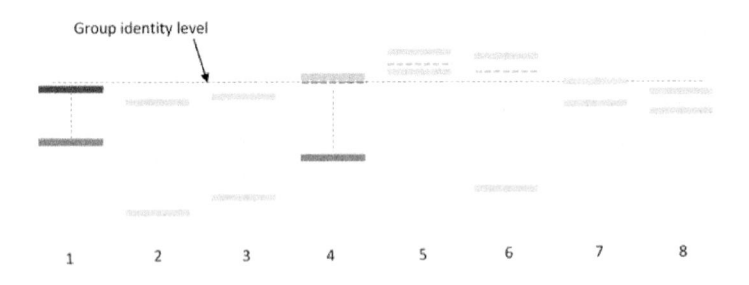

Persons 1 and 4 are the middle of the group, and are somewhat diverged. They sense that they are similar types of people, and, like 2 and 3, perhaps form an alliance, and become quite competitive towards each other. This competitiveness is because both sense the other's inherited levels, but, as is natural for a human being, believe themselves

100

Levelling

to only have one level, their identity. We tend to see others according to their inherited level, but see ourself according to our identity level. Each will therefore feel themselves above the other. This can cause a "cross-conflict":

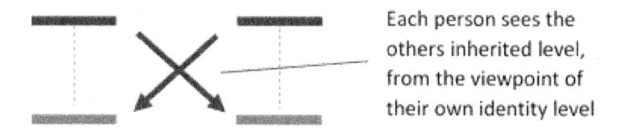

Each person sees the others inherited level, from the viewpoint of their own identity level

This arrangement can escalate relationships somewhat, because it is something that cannot be resolved fundamentally. Both want to establish themselves a little above the other, but neither can (due to their own inherited level), and they can be drawn into conflict or competitiveness as a result. Perhaps this is tolerable or enjoyable at times, in a friendly banter type way. In some ways competing with the other person is a method of maintaining their identity level. Or, perhaps it pushes them apart.

Often, these two people, in such a cross-conflict, will have different values, for example different reasons why they should be positioned above the other. Perhaps these are drawn from other core groups that each of the pair are a part of. Neither can recognise the others values, because it would allow the other person to establish themselves above them. Through this type of competition, our own values are reinforced, and harder to stray from.

Therefore, we tend to observe others according to their inherited level, and only treat people according to their identity level when we can, i.e. when it doesn't conflict with us achieving our own identity level. And, whilst we see others according to their inherited level, we see ourself according to our identity

A Theory of Everyone

level, and struggle to believe that we have an inherited level, that may be apparent to others.

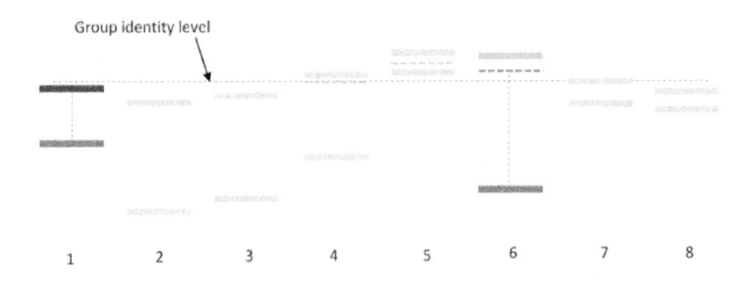

Looking at the friendship that persons 1 and 6 might have, person 6 has both a higher identity and a lower subcon. This arrangement can often produce strange results, and it is unlikely the two are close. Person 6 feels they have a higher identity that person 1, and this has been established in the group sub-culture, but, due to their lower inherited level, they actually feel more out of place in the group from time to time.

Person 6 will be more affected by goings on in the group, and be more emotionally invested in it. Person 6 will be more affected by person 1, than person 1 is by person 6. In conflict between them, person 6 has a higher position, but further to fall.

This can often set up a feedback loop.

This "leveraged-conflict" can result in person 6 being quite controlling. In order to maintain their identity, against a less secure position, they have to be more obtrusive. They have to more greatly rely on the group structure, that enables their higher position, and impress that on person 1. Person 1 senses the lower inherited level of person 6, and so to be talked down on by person 6 is uncomfortable.

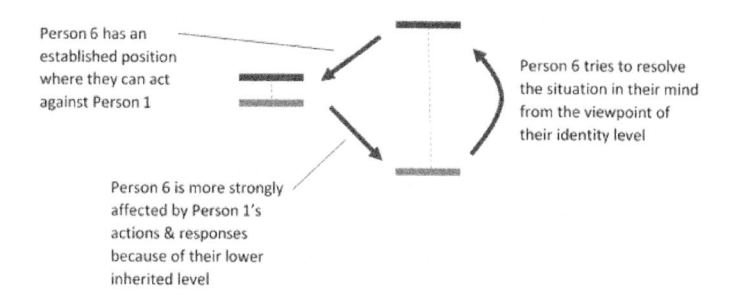

Levelling

Person 6 has an established position where they can act against Person 1

Person 6 tries to resolve the situation in their mind from the viewpoint of their identity level

Person 6 is more strongly affected by Person 1's actions & responses because of their lower inherited level

In a friendship group, it's likely some distance will be put between persons 1 and 6, in order to minimise tension and conflict. However, there are many examples in life where this type of leveraged social relationship can occur.

One example is when the group has specific roles of responsibility, for example in our profession. If person 6 is a manager (hence the higher identity level), but one of their employees has higher inherited level, the manager may feel insecure in their higher position, and rely on the role, as well as impress the organisational structure on others.

There will be huge variation in how it could play out, depending on the personalities and situation involved, and it may not be a problem at all. If persons 1 and 6 have strong support elsewhere, that maintains their positions, they may not even notice this arrangement.

This group is an example of how our modern social environment, where people are diverged, and with identities forged in different places, can cause conflicts. The differing levels, that are caused by the melting pot of different people coming together to form a group, can collide. Our brains cope with the complexity of the situation, and our social instincts often find compromises and solutions naturally, but levels are hard to cover up completely, and generally greater stress and conflict ensues at times.

For hunter-gatherers, who only had one group, and the group structure and sub-culture was well established, these types of interpersonal conflicts simply didn't happen.

Levelling across society

With each group being pulled together towards a common point, this effect occurs across society. In every group, there are social instincts trying to find commonality, and so there is a general trend in society pulling it all together, slowly and methodically over generations, like a tailor stitching a garment together.

We see this when we look throughout history, where power, wealth, rights and freedoms are generally moving in the right direction, towards greater equality.

There are many forces causing this to be so. However, there are also many forces opposing a move to greater equality (otherwise we'd get there in the next few weeks). For example these include: greed; the difficulty in moving around large amounts of wealth and power; the need to hold onto wealth (and be unyielding) vs. the desire to usurp it; the need to compete with contemporaries (with whom we are interlinked with, wherever we are in society); and, not least, the way that an adult human being's perceptions of the world become quite fixed in adulthood (so that they can be a reference point for their growing children, but, as a side effect, they become more resistant to change). Nevertheless, it appears that the forces propelling us towards equality are more powerful than the forces that oppose it.

Levelling

When the world is a more equal place, where a similar quality of life can be lived wherever we are born, the world will no doubt be a better place to live in. We'd be able to enjoy life as fully as anyone else, and live with a similar quality of life anywhere in the world. We'd be able to enjoy our cultures, respecting similarities and differences to neighbouring ones. We'd be able to compete amongst our social circles with some enjoyment of it, rather than it being stressful, with too much on the line. When/if there is conflict in the world, each person would have less to gain, and less to lose, so can be more amenable, and compromise more easily. We would feel less stretched, and be able to prioritise, and feel, the fulness of family and friendship, which, like our hunter-gatherer ancestors, are some of the most important parts of our life experiences.

With greater monetary equality, our three fundamental drivers become less stretched, and can take the arrangement that occurred naturally in our ancestors for millions of years. Our lives will then feel more balanced:

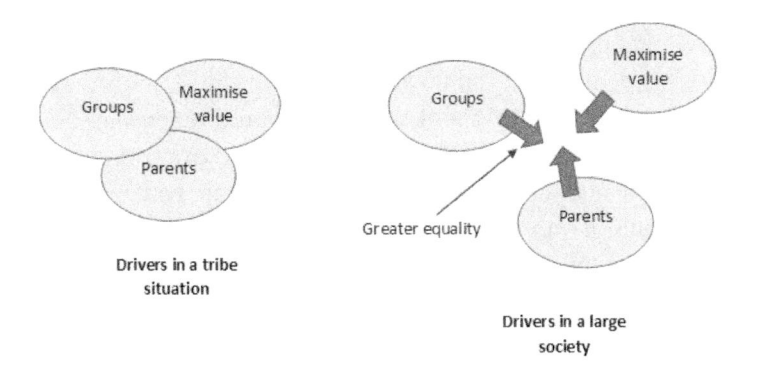

Drivers in a tribe situation

Groups, Maximise value, Parents

Drivers in a large society

Groups, Maximise value, Parents — Greater equality

We'd give up that feeling of glory and power, but those are short lived, fragile rewards that last only until the next person takes them from us. They are an out of balance driver, that rarely leads to long term fulfilment. And, with a shrinking world, it will become harder and harder to enjoy excess, when we never live too far from those with less. Currently, the top 26 wealthiest people in the world have the same wealth as the bottom 50%: the bottom 3.6 billion people. Perhaps they should all meet up for a conference to debate whether this is a good thing or not.

It's unlikely we'll ever be completely equal, some hierarchy needs to exist for large groups of humans to live side by side, but we can certainly get closer to a more equal, and fairer world. And, whether we want to or not, it appears to be the natural progression.

Levels summary

Levels are very important to us, whether considered against an individual, a group, a parent-child relationship, or across society. They represent something tangible, a pecking order, that is something that is key throughout nature. As these pecking orders exist, so they must have an effect on us, and drive our behaviours and emotions.

Levels represent our desire to maximise our value, and survival of the fittest. They represent our driver to draw definition and identity from a group, to become part of it, and act in unison with it. They represent our driver to draw learning from, and follow, the generations before us. They represent our need to be anchored. They represent the part of us is fixed, and part of us is flexible. They represent the fact that we can adapt to the world around us, but fundamentally remain human, and display the same characteristics that caused our species to become so widespread, and arguably successful, in the past.

Levelling

However, whilst levels are tangible, the way we experience them isn't. Whilst they drive much of the behaviour around us, we generally don't see it that way. We experience levels in an obscure, indirect way, and often our focus, attention, and understanding are diverted onto conflicts in front of us, that appear unique and unrelated. Our brains are very good at assessing and acting according to levels, but our conscious thought tends to be diverted and caught up on conflicts and experiences in the foreground instead (we shall come onto this in the third part of this book, where we look more at the interactions that we experience on a daily basis).

Finally, we have our own levels.

We have our inherited level, that defines how we react to the world around us. We generally ignore this in ourselves, and believe we only have our identity level. Nevertheless, we draw this inherited level mainly from our parents, by copying their reactions to people around us, but it also in a small part tempered by the world we grow into.

Then we have our identity level, that generally revolves around the maximum status group we are a part of. It is normally found in a pocket of our life, and we generally try to bend our social situations, that we have on a daily basis, to be more favourable to it.

In the modern world, our inherited level and identity level can be far apart, and we can be diverged. As we saw, most people are diverged, hence why we can only achieve our identity level in pockets. The more difficult the social environment, for example caused by greater inequality or complexity in society, the more diverged each person will be. The more difficult the social environment, the more each person (including our parents) faces a greater headwind between their inherited and identity level, and a has a harder time finding places where they truly feel themselves.

Levels are often inconvenient and frustrating. They are largely down to chance and circumstance, and we have to live the life in front of us no matter how they turn out. We are more a shepherd of our circumstances, trying to do the best we can, than in the driving seat, most of the time.

To understand ourselves, others, and what is going on in the world, we have to at least consider levels, and how strong a driver they can be to human behaviour. It's perhaps not a good idea to think about them too much, or discuss them in the open, but they are there nonetheless. They form a part of the modern human experience, often playing out in unusual and complex ways.

Part Two

Web & Self

4

Our "Web"

Moving on from levels, we shall look at the two other key aspects of modern life: our "self", and our "web".

These two aspects are interlinked, because much of our self is drawn from people around us. To understand "self" we have to consider our spread-out social lives (our "web"), and to understand the impact of our "web", we have to consider our "self".

In this chapter, we shall consider our "web".

In the modern world, instead of having a close tribe, we have a "web" of spread-out social contacts.

Instead of being connected to just that tribe, we're connected to a number of people across society, in different groups.

The people we're connected to, our "web" of social contacts, form part of a larger web across society, and the world. The people we have links to, in our personal social web, have their own webs, to other people, many of whom we don't know.

It is said that we are only 6 degrees of separation away from anyone in the world, which shows how interlinked our social connections are across society.

This forms our modern social environment. Our societies are arranged in these large webs of social links between individuals.

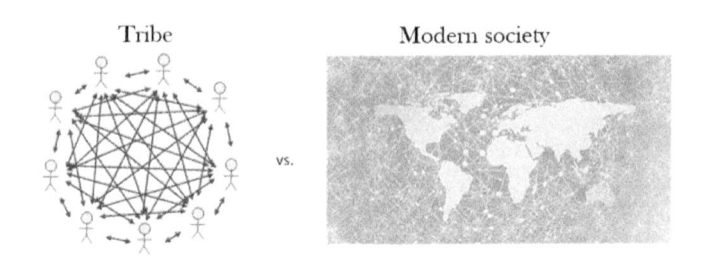

Tribe vs. Modern society

Having our social lives spread over several groups, interlinked with many others, is such a stark contrast to our evolutionary social lives. Given how much social beings rely on others for definition, belonging, bonds, giving us a sense of who we are, and allowing us to feel ourselves, this contrast is important to understand. Sometimes it works well, sometimes it doesn't. In any situation, it can help to understand how it works.

From a distance, our interlinked societies resemble a giant herd, or bee hive. However, whilst we share some characteristics of them, we don't socialise like them. Instead, when human groups reach a certain size, they tend to compartmentalise into a collection of smaller sub-groups. Each of these sub-groups is then suited to our programming, which evolved within smallish groups. Therefore, whilst our societies resemble, and are the size of, hives or colonies, each person seeks out small groups within society, as if we were still hunter-gatherers looking for a tribe.

These small sub-groups are all connected. They are connected for many different reasons. For example, because each group interacts with neighbouring groups, or because

Our "Web"

each group aligns themselves to a common idea or culture (for greater protection and security of value), and, not least, because each person is a member of multiple groups. Being a member of multiple groups means each person is influenced by, and influences, one group one day, and a different group the next. This causes cross pollination of ideas and values between groups, and a general cohesiveness of the many subgroups that make up society.

For human beings, like every social creature that lives in groups, our programming is reliant on others. This is for defining who we are through comparison, for bonds of friendship, belonging and support, and reciprocated behaviours (which can make us feel most "us").

For our ancestors, they got all of this from their one tribe. These self-contained groups, that included their parents, and had little external influence (or greater potential external value), are well suited to providing all of what each human being needs.

Their tribe provided them with a sense of definition, comparison and feedback. It provided them with people to bond with, parents to guide them, a group to be able to work and hunt with, to socialise with, to use common behaviours with, and it provided them with a sense of self.

We still need all these things, but now we don't have that one tribe to provide it. Instead, we have multiple groups. What we need therefore gets spread out.

Our parents are in one group. Perhaps our closest rival (friend or otherwise), or who we consider our closest comparison, is in another group. The person we turn to for support is in a further group, and the people we work with are in another group still.

What we used to get from one tribe is now fragmented across our web of social contacts. And, the people that we draw these things from, have their own links to others. We can end up with links across a spread-out landscape (and end up pulling and manipulating our personal social life to get what we need, in competition with others).

Within the giant interlinked web of society, we can consider our own personal links. These are to all the people and groups that we form a part of:

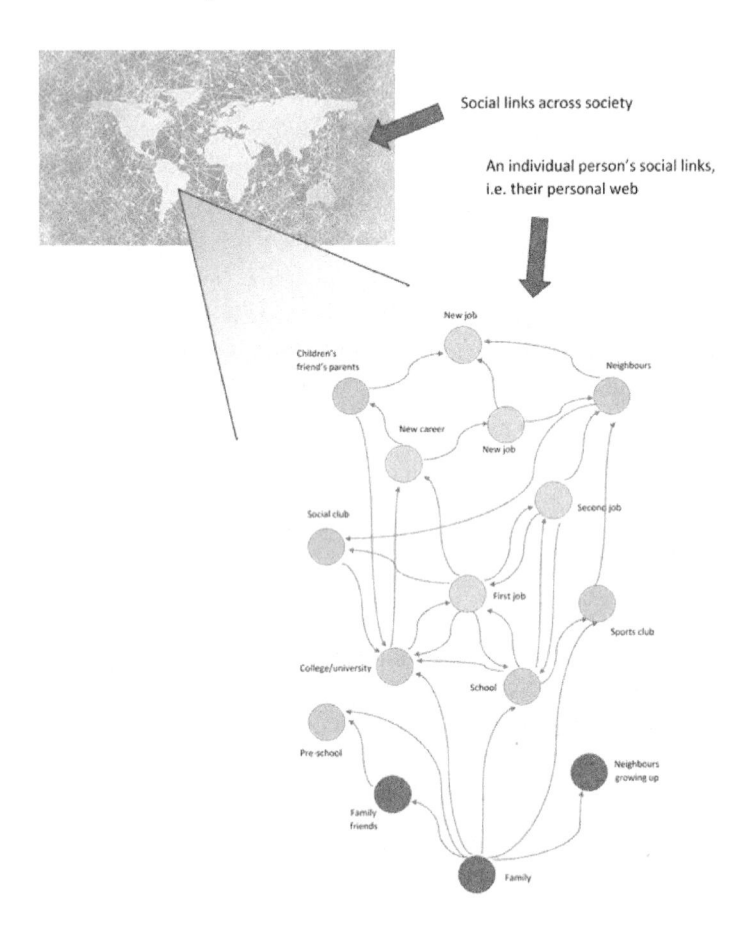

Social links across society

An individual person's social links, i.e. their personal web

New job
Children's friend's parents
Neighbours
New career
New job
Social club
Second job
First job
Sports club
College/university
School
Pre-school
Neighbours growing up
Family friends
Family

Our "Web"

This fragmented social environment could be a cause of difficulty for our poor brains.

But our brains can cope with this admirably. Our brains keep track of all our social links at a very deep core level, and this works effectively in everyone, including very young children, who are seeing the world for the first time.

For example, we can share bonds with several groups, each feeling different and unique, and this can feel entirely comfortable. We can use different behaviours in each group, whether they be family, friends or colleagues, and in each case, we can feel like the behaviours are somewhat ours, and "us". It doesn't always work like this, but it can, if the circumstances are right.

However, living in webs can, on balance, be more difficult, stressful and frustrating than living in a close tribe. Not because our brains fundamentally struggle with the arrangement, but for three main reasons.

One we have mentioned already, which is that we are trying to get all the feelings we would get from a tribe, from a spread-out arrangement. We can compete with others for our basic group needs.

The second is that the web around us, that we rely on, and which affects our feelings of self, fulfilment and security, keeps changing.

The third is that we feel influences from our web even when not physically located with the people in it. When separated from people in our web, we still feel their influence through "tied thoughts". Our tied thoughts are when our mind wanders onto various people we know, and we imagine or remember interactions with them. These "tied thoughts" play the role of maintain links to our different groups, even when we're geographically separated from them. This arrangement causes difficulty because our interlinked webs often don't fit against each other perfectly. Conflict can arise that our tied thoughts get stuck on, which can cause frustration with people not currently present.

This arrangement also causes difficulty because, overall, this creates an unusual social environment, where everyone is behaving according to invisible influences, from people not present, that we may not even know.

Rearranging webs

On the second point, that everyone's webs keep changing, this can affect how we feel about ourselves.

In a tribe, the social dynamic will be more static. We are with the same people all our lives, living in a close group with a strong sub-culture. We would be using the same behaviours most of the time, with a defined, secure position that we are comfortable with. We know that the positions of those around us, that form a large part of who we are, are unlikely to change dramatically, because of the close interlinking within the group. This is like a small puzzle, where each puzzle-piece fits with those around them, and together they form a picture that doesn't change over time.

In comparison, our modern webs are much more prone to change. We are now a giant puzzle, that keeps on going, and many (or most) of the puzzle-pieces don't quite fit against each other. The puzzle keeps rearranging, as different pieces try to fit against a new set of pieces. We want to be a piece in a well-fitting puzzle, but it is difficult to achieve. We find we want to see the overall picture, but it is more blurred and changes.

The people that make up our personal web have their own set of influences. They make new friends; we make new friends. They find successes; we find successes. Sometimes people come towards us, and we find new companionship, and

Our "Web"

sometimes people drift away from each other, or pull in different directions. Perhaps old friends, that we once shared good times with, don't want to anymore. Perhaps we find that old friends, who's behaviour we once enjoyed, *we* don't enjoy anymore. People that we once felt close to, can drift away, and develop new behaviours, or a new identity, and this can affect how we feel about ourself, better or worse.

If the people around us influence who we are, and how we feel about ourself, then if their positions and behaviours change, it affects how we feel, and it can be frustrating, annoying, and sometimes hurtful. Our personal web of links, to people and groups that play some importance in our lives, is playing the role of a tribe. Our brain is looking for that tribe, but now finds it spread out.

In a tribe, we almost have a pact with the other tribe members, or at least it's mutually beneficial to work together, and head in the same direction. This works because we will always be with those people, and there aren't any external influences.

In our webs, we're being influenced by an environment that is prone to change. No such pact exists, because everyone is being influenced by a different set of groups. We may want to make such a pact with a friend, and it may work for a while, but no two people are being drawn in exactly the same direction. There is always some pulling in different directions, as we are influenced by our own, different webs.

Our influences are like pieces of string connecting everyone. The strings represent where our thoughts go, who is significant to us, and who is close to us. As people move around and rearrange, change their life circumstances, and grow towards and away from people, they feel tugs and connections to those close to them. If people find success, and feel elevated, they might find people pull downwardly on their strings a little more. If people feel low, they might feel support and uplifted from those linked to them. If we move too far, up, down, or sideways, we pull on the strings of those around us, which causes them to pull on their own strings. People moving around causes ripple effects through society's web, and there is a general humdrum and tension in the strings, as people jostle and move. Our societies are like a choppy sea that's agitated by everyone pulling on their strings, rather than a sea of calm where each person has secure positions and feels comfortable in them.

This arrangement of strings can include all sorts of peculiarities. One example of that is the standoff created by someone level-jumping. If one person finds success, and is elevated compared to someone they were close to before, then their link can become a bit of a tug of war.

The person who is elevated feels their new identity. They now judge people from that new higher viewpoint, and want to be treated according to it. However, the person they were close to previously doesn't see it that way.

The person who has jumped up forms a part of their old friends' web. That old acquaintance will struggle to see their friend as higher, and "better" than them. They still see the person they first met. Our views of other people tend not to change too much, even if our view of ourselves is more flexible. As a result, in their interactions, the old friend pulls down, whilst the person who was elevated pulls upwards. Neither can move that easily, so a standoff occurs.

The strings connecting everyone are therefore full of people pulling us one way or another. Some we want, some we resist. Some are resolvable, as people move closer together, but others aren't, and the feeling of being pulled in a direction, up, down, or sideways, is something we have to live with.

Our "Web"

When all is going well, we can feel at ease, and that we navigate this environment successfully. Some people simply have fortunate circumstances around them, so that their web isn't too difficult to navigate, whilst others face difficult social circumstances.

On average, living in a modern web, with spread-out links across society (that is constantly rearranging), is less suited to our programming, which is reliant on others, than living in a tribe.

Tied thoughts

On the third point, as to why webs are more difficult to live in than tribes: our "tied thoughts" (having influences from people not present); adds complication, and can cause strange results in a few ways.

Before that though, why do we even have tied thoughts? Why can't our mind just be free when alone?

If our "self" is to a large extent a reflection of feedback and comparisons to those close to us, and of our positions versus others, then we need to have a mechanism to keep track of these when geographically separated. Social beings such as ourselves evolved such a mechanism in our tied thoughts.

In a tribe, we're with those we draw this "self" (definition, position and comparison) off all the time. We'd be fairly constantly in a "socialisation mode", where interactions are sent back and forth, and positions are maintained through challenges, and the group structure.

However, situations arise where the group can become separated. If this happens, their interlinked definitions need to be maintained, as well as some urge to come back together.

In one example, say a tribes-member decides they want to be a solo hunter, and try a different way of life. They head out into the wilderness tundra and start their new life, by themselves. However, they will still have links to the people they knew, and this tribes-member will find their thoughts wander onto their past tribe.

These "tied thoughts" urge them back to the human behaviours of survival in a group. They would miss the bonds of friendship and family, and they would think about what people close to them used to say. Or, they would miss the feeling of hunting in a tribe, and feel an urge to seek that out, at least after a while, or when things got difficult.

In another example, we can consider the hunter-gatherer that left to join the summer big-game hunt, from the example described earlier. Their tied thoughts, and the tied thoughts that members of their old tribe would have, would cause their old positions to be maintained, to some extent.

As the hunter-gatherer tried to fit in with the big-game-hunters, and learn the new improved hunting behaviours, they may find their tied thoughts drift onto how members of their old tribe would respond to them doing this. Perhaps their closest friend in their old tribe would be most upset about this arrangement, because that close friend drew much of their position and definition from that previous alliance and companionship. The closest friend isn't too happy about their friend leaving and "improving", and they might scoff and disapprove of their friend's change.

The hunter-gatherer that left, would feel this, even if nothing was said. Their thoughts might wander onto what *might be said*, and imagine how a new dynamic might play out. While in the hunting grounds, distant from their old tribe, then, through their tied thoughts, they actually feel the effects of old dynamics, *as if that person were present*. This in turn affects their emotions, and makes it a little harder to integrate into the new tribe, even whilst geographically separated from the old. They might feel scoffed at, even if no-one is there doing the scoffing.

Therefore whilst that person is with the elite hunters, their tied thoughts are projecting, representing and maintaining the links and positions to the people they have some bond and connections to, in their old tribe.

Definitions remain somewhat interlinked even when humans are geographically separated. Our mind wanders onto, seeks out, and imagines possible interactions, that represent the dynamic between us and that person, even when they're not around.

This happens a lot for us modern humans, good and bad. We think of others, our friends and family, a lot when we're not with them. We imagine socialising with them, get "thinking of you" moments, and we feel an urge to get together and relive past good times. However, our thoughts also get caught up in conflict, we struggle to get someone out of our minds, and we feel pressure and insecurities of others, even when they're not around. This is why this arrangement can be difficult compared to a tribe.

Our definitions are all interlinked, but not in a well-fitting small puzzle. We are interlinked in a giant puzzle where all the puzzle-pieces don't quite fit with those around them.

Our definitions are all interlinked, but not in a simple, well ordered arrangement of strings between a group of people. The pieces of string that link everyone across society are a jumble, a bit of a mess, and occasionally get caught up and knotted.

As a result, our tied thoughts can sometimes be uncomfortable and frustrating. They are there to draw us towards people and maintain positions and links, but often we simply can't (or don't want to) move towards people that we have these thoughts and links to. Our tied thoughts can be negative, and persist, where we can't resolve a conflict with someone some distance away.

As a result, we feel the difficulty of our spread-out social lives through our tied thoughts. The complication of our respective webs is felt, regardless of geographical distance.

This environment, where our social lives are spread over several groups, and our social links are maintained by tied thoughts, just as much as they are behaviours, requires a certain amount of separation. No person can avoid being pulled in more than one direction, so if people are pulling on strings less, then each person has an easier, less stressful time maintaining their social links. However, this is difficult to achieve, pulling on strings less requires greater "self", but this is hard to come by.

Despite all this, on average, this arrangement just about works. Even though our social lives are spread over several groups, our mind moves around them, keeping a check of how we fit into each, and imagining how different people might react to us if they were present in our current situation. As this happens in each person, then a rough (though not entirely satisfactory) social structure is maintained across society.

Invisible influences

Our tied thoughts create a confusing social environment where each person is reacting to influences from people that aren't present at any one time.

When we're interacting with people, they may be responding and behaving according to influences from people we don't know, or have never met. We may never know who pops into the heads of people we interact with, and how it makes them feel. Everyone's personal web is quite unique.

Our "Web"

People find things easier to do that people in their web would approve of. When they do those things, they feel approved of, even if the people around them at that particular moment aren't approving. Their tied thoughts may even be imagining how someone in their web might approve, what they might say or do, or how they might join in, and it gives them a feeling of if that person was *actually there* and approving in person. Similarly, people find it harder to do things that people in their web would disapprove of.

This can sometimes leave us thinking "I don't understand why someone would behave like that". However, it's likely they are behaving like that because someone, who we may not know, who isn't there, is influencing it, or might approve of it.

When people challenge or provoke us, it can often feel quite personal. It can be upsetting to have someone take out a frustration on us. But often they are driven by the influences of people not present. For example, perhaps they have difficulty with someone in their web, or a conflict from the previous day, that was still in their mind.

In the same way, sometimes *our* thoughts may get tied up in a particular person, and it may frustrate us or lower our mood. It may make us a little more irritable. We may take that out a little on the people around us, who are unaware of our thought processes.

With our webs interlinked with those around us, so are our emotions. As social beings, emotions are shared and mediated in groups. When faced with our spread-out social lives, this sharing and mediating of emotions happens in a more confusing way.

The transference of emotions and circumstances happens through invisible tied thoughts. People are being influenced by links that we can't see. Difficulty elsewhere can develop into difficulty in front of us. We can even get transference in our own thoughts, as they move from person to person faster than our emotions change.

All this gets very confusing, and we still need to resolve conflicts in front of us. The point is that this is happening all around, and creates a confusing, more difficult social environment. It's not that human beings struggle with the arrangement, it's just that the arrangement causes a bit more struggle for human beings, given our programming is suited to a different environment.

A side effect of this is that our intuition becomes compromised. Behaviours can appear more irrational and harder to understand, and we don't have all the facts to be able to draw accurate conclusions from our interactions. People often respond to this by blocking out others behaviours, and more blindly focussing on their own.

In contrast, in a tribe, we've grown up with the same people, seen all their experiences, seen the large majority of their interactions (with their parents and others), and we know all the people they're tied to. We therefore have all the facts. We see the root causes of issues, rather than transference, i.e. second-hand issues. We can better understand others, and know more how to help or support them.

Then, in that tribe, our social skills, understanding of social dynamics, and our intuition, and knowledge, of what human beings really want or need, is likely improved.

In contrast, in large social webs, humans can lack a huge amount of information, that contains other people's motivations. People are being driven by influences that we aren't aware of, and we often have to deal with second-hand issues, when the root cause is some distance away. Then, human beings can often become unaware, unsure, or self-absorbed, from time to time.

Our "Web"

A person's web

Looking at a practical example of a person's web, we can consider the following.

As a person grows through life, their own personal web develops. New groups, and people, add new links. Some improve our web, and make other (perhaps difficult) links easier to bear, whilst others perhaps don't. Some links we wish we could cut out, but, perhaps unfortunately, it is hard to do so.

For modern humans, the first group we come across in life is our family, who raise us through the early stages of development. As we grow older, we likely have social groups at school, and clubs that we attend. We do courses, and perhaps go to college or university. We then take jobs, fit into work hierarchies, take orders, give orders. Then we come across more social groups as an adult, for example partners, neighbours, our children's friends' parents, and more. This personal web is ticking the box of our personal tribe, that our brain is expecting on entering the world.

A typical web therefore looks something like the following:

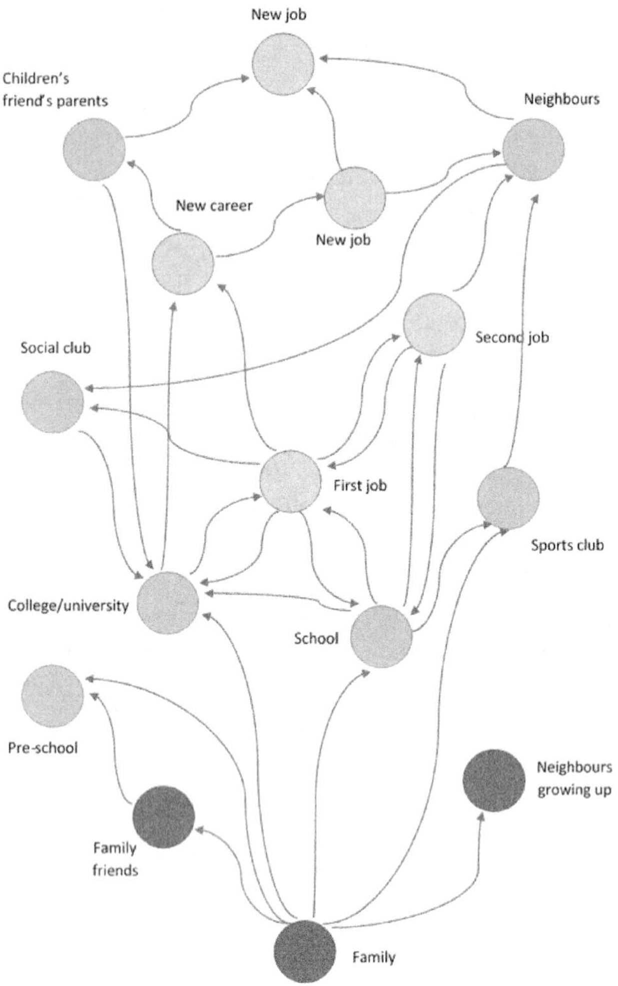
New job
Children's friend's parents
Neighbours
New career
New job
Social club
Second job
First job
Sports club
College/university
School
Pre-school
Neighbours growing up
Family friends
Family

There are arrows from one group to the other because we tend to use the definition from one group as a way to present ourself in a different group. We may interact with people from, say, our first job, depending on our school experience. Perhaps we even talk about our school experiences, or people

Our "Web"

we knew there, so that we signal to others the kind of people we associate with, and who approves of us. That is our identity level, and how we want to be treated.

Then, if we're lucky, our job goes well, perhaps we are successful at it. This success then feeds back into our school friends, who, in this example, we're still in contact with. The success in our job changes how we socialise with those school friends. Perhaps we have a little more confidence, and we tell them about our work, signalling to them that our identity has changed a little, and we wish to be treated slightly differently. Perhaps we've learnt new behaviours in our job, and we've absorbed them into our personality.

Now, we have a successful job, and, if we're fortunate, this still fits with our old friends. Perhaps this gives us confidence in finding a partner, and we go after someone we really want. We feel confident and attractive, and in part they are attracted to us because of those associations and successes. Then, because we have an attractive partner, we feel more confidence still, and use this in our work and friends.

Sometimes it can seem like a house of cards, with each group and link propping up another. It's quite rare for it all to fall over, but it does mean that if we find conflict or difficulty in one group, it can impact how we fit in, or feel about, another group, that it was propping up. Essentially, the different parts of our life are all interlinked, and changes in one part can affect our whole web.

It doesn't always feel like a house of cards. At times it can feel comfortable, and each group is how we want it, and some semblance of balance is achieved.

However, it is often difficult and rare for this balance to be achieved, because it's not entirely within our control. Each of those groups and associations that we have, that define us, and form a part of us and who we are, are full of people who might want different things. They may feel very differently about the groups that we share, and it may be propping up their web in a very different way to how it fits with us. This can cause some conflict, in how each person wants a group to feel, and what they want that group to be about.

With spread-out social lives, our ties and bonds to people, that are important to us, can be more fragile.

Pulling on strings

What is it that holds all the connections together? Well, we're social beings, so we need a certain amount of togetherness. Other people are important to us, and we are important to other people.

Human beings need a certain amount of tension in the strings that are our links to other people. People want other people to care about them, to matter to others, and be important to them. If a human being doesn't get these, however much they want freedom to be themselves, they feel compelled to pull on other's strings.

In a tribe, we have a ready-made belonging, and bond of togetherness, but in a large society it is sometimes elusive.

Instead of our needs being laid out in front of us, they are more spread-out. Instead of feeling comfortable in a tribe, and our focus being fulfilled evenly in that tribe, our focus is now more fragmented, and some of our social needs are fulfilled in one place, and other social needs are fulfilled in a different one.

On average, people manage with this, and find a social structure that works for them. However it does have a side effect or two. It can cause us to zone in on a few people more than others, in a good or bad way, at least at times. Our focus is now deeper in some people, and less in others. Sometimes they will be someone similar to us, a close rival perhaps, friend or otherwise, or sometimes they will be someone opposite. Sometimes they will be someone we look up to, and sometimes they will be someone who looks up to us. When people zone in on us, we are drawn in to reciprocate, to some extent, although every situation is different. If someone will react strongly to us, if we met in person, at some time in the future, we might find our focus drift more onto them in our lives, however wanted or unwanted.

We need a certain amount of pulling on strings, but now we are all pulling in different directions, and pulling in some places more than others. Some people get more than they need, some don't even realise this is happening, and others don't get enough.

In terms of fundamentally where this need comes from, perhaps it is an uncomfortable truth, but a lot of this need comes from the foundation of our webs: our family and parents. Our parents are one of the only certainties in life, so it makes sense for them to be the source of the more fixed parts of our programming. It doesn't have to be fulfilled here, it can be fulfilled in partners, friends and others, but it tends to be where the need comes from.

As we've discussed, in large multi-layered societies, the relationship with our parents can often be unsatisfactory, or at least not entirely satisfactory. There can be a huge number of different circumstances that cause this dissatisfaction, given how large society is, and how complex relationships can be. For example, we could diverge from our parents, or they could be strongly diverged. They can lack self, and their attention is always elsewhere, or they are distant and defensive. They can get trapped in tight webs and have uncomfortably strong views, or pressure and reduce us in order to maintain their identity as a parent, in an unyielding way. They may be preoccupied with maintaining their own house of cards, and not have spare thought to give to others.

As a result, often our parents are a no-go area, or at least difficult and painful to tackle head on, and we spend much of our life with our focus somewhere else in our web. This will also be true of our children as they grow up, however comfortable we feel in our identity and our social life.

This comes down to the crux of modern human beings, which is drawn from the nature of our spread-out social lives. Our parents provide the anchor for our programming, and sit at the foundation of our web. But our focus and attention are in the social groups we have links to. Difficulty from our parents can get transferred and projected into those social groups.

For contrast, a tribe that includes our parents will have much less transference, and our anchor, and what makes us feel ourselves, is aligned.

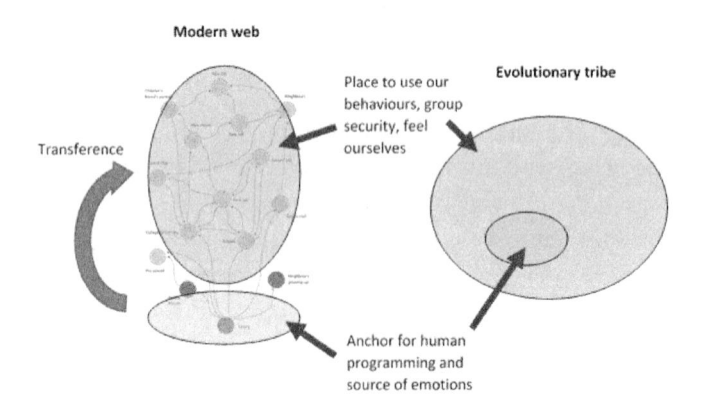

Our spread-out social lives cause transference. The source of emotions tends to be our parents, but it's possible and easier to manage these difficulties in our social webs. It's not our

Our "Web"

parent's fault per se, our modern social environment creates many pitfalls and difficult circumstances, and our parents had their own parents to deal with.

We are born into the world with the pre-condition and need for groups and anchors, and we find them, but they aren't quite in the ideal configuration for our programming's expectations. We adapt, but there are some side effects.

It doesn't have to be a problem for a person day to day, or even for achieving happiness, but the less we get positive definition from our parents, the more we deepen the interactions in a different group in order to compensate, so that our focus is more consumed in that group, and less by our parents or family. This is why we pull on other's strings, and why they pull on ours, and why some people pull on strings more than others.

When we create a house of cards, it's in order to defend against the raw difficulty of facing our parents without our web. However good people want to be as parents, and however good people's intentions, in modern societies the parent-child relationship can simply be difficult (although we should always try to do our best as parents).

As a result, our whole web can become tighter. The tighter our web is, the more we draw others into our web, and the more our focus is on those in our web. We may not want to do this, but often we are quite limited in having freedom to act how we'd like to. It's human nature to try to be the best person we can with what we have, it's just that, sometimes, what we have, is less than what we'd like.

The giant web of society is a jumble, a bit of a mess, and the strings can occasionally get caught up and knotted. Our societies are like a choppy sea that's agitated by everyone pulling on their strings. Difficult parent-child relationships cause the level of disorder in the social web, as well as the complexity that results from our spread-out social lives. We pull on other's strings, where we need a certain level of closeness, and others pull on ours. Sometimes it works, sometimes it doesn't.

Our web often doesn't give us the social freedom we want. Sometimes we can feel that more success would give us greater freedom from our web, that it would elevate ourselves above it, and we'd be stronger and less affected by others. Sometimes we want to move to another country to get away from our web, and feel that distance would put people out of our minds, or give us a fresh start. Sometimes these things work, sometimes they don't. Sometimes we just have to find what works for us.

It's a subtle point, but perhaps it's not freedom we really want, but instead to be comfortably constrained, in a group of people behaving how we like.

Each person's web is likely very unique, so it comes down to each person to decide how best to manage their own web (and there's always help out there if at times it gets difficult).

Our personal web can be good, our web can be bad. We don't have a huge amount of control as to the people in it. We are more a caretaker of our circumstances, trying to do the best we can, rather than in the driving seat.

The point is, according to this theory anyway, this is how it is. This is how it is for us, for others, for everyone. It can be fundamentally harder for a human being living in this arrangement, with a spread-out web, compared to a balanced interlinked tribe, where everything is in one place.

Our "Web"

Tied and act for

Having our focus strongly on one group, and having strong tied thoughts, doesn't always have to be bad.

If that one group is close, and we have a secure position within it, then having the feeling that those people are with us all the time, having our back, can make life a little easier. They can be with us in spirit, be on our side in conflict, and make us feel ourselves, even when those around us aren't. They can even laugh at our jokes, and approve of our behaviours, even if those around us don't.

To illustrate this, we can consider the case where someone becomes very deeply tied to a particular group. They may find that they can disregard many of the challenges and small-scale conflict in the world around them, because they feel supported through their tied thoughts.

This often occurs when a group becomes very close, and often develops from a group that has known each other during adolescence. The closeness comes because at least some of the members of the group do not have close ties with their parents, and need strong social bonds to focus on instead. The tied group could be any group however, such as a group from college or university, or colleagues from a job.

A tied person's web looks something like the following diagram.

A Theory of Everyone

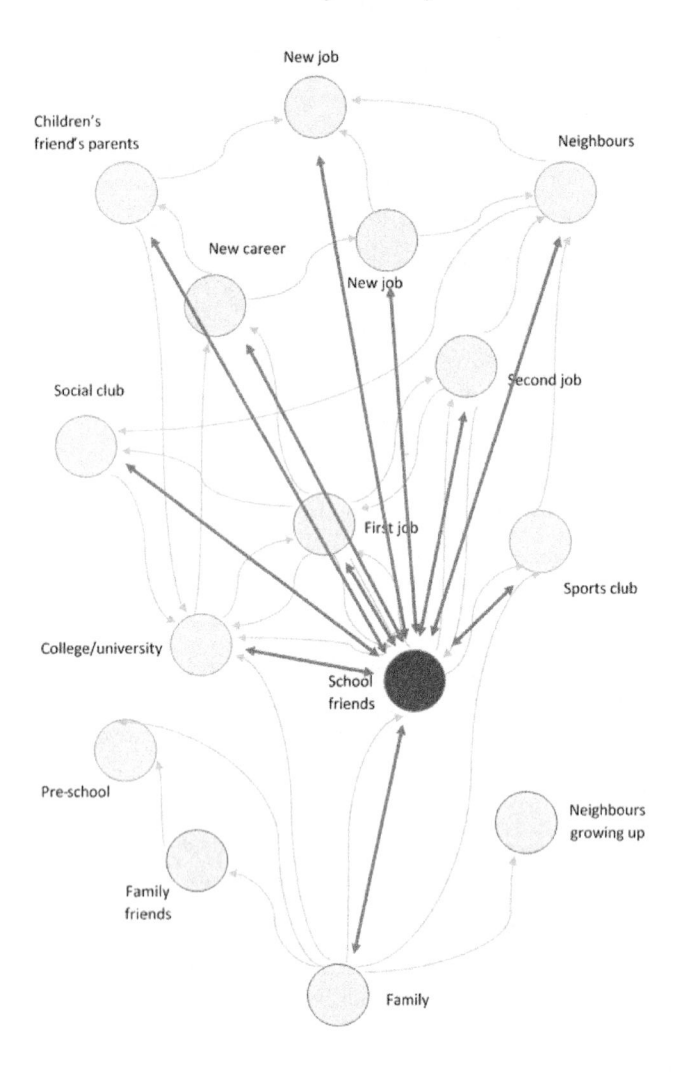

Figure shows a network diagram with "School friends" (dark circle) at the center, connected to: New job, Children's friend's parents, Neighbours, New career, New job, Second job, Social club, First job, Sports club, College/university, Pre-school, Neighbours growing up, Family friends, Family.

The tied group becomes the focal point of their entire social web. Each new interaction is not so much linked to a previous, but instead linked back to the tied group.

Their emotions, beliefs and values are all strongly linked to that one group. They view the world vividly from the viewpoint of that group as a whole, and they feel they represent that group (even if others may not see it on first impressions).

However, because their emotions are dictated by the group, they lose some ability to empathise with those outside of the group. They can become a little disconnected from the emotions of those around them (that aren't from the group), and find it easier to disregard or not even notice emotional difficulty in others. Their emotions are not so much influenced by those around them, but instead influenced by how someone in the group might respond if they were present. Thoughts of the tied group can cause them to become giddy, with a rush of good feeling, and when human beings feel these types of emotions, they tend to block out, or override, the emotions of other people around them.

A person that is strongly tied to one group can of course still be kind, supportive and good, but not in a way where their emotions are necessarily connected to those they're interacting with.

Whether someone becomes tied to a particular group comes down to a range of factors. Some do, some don't. Many people have looser connections to the groups in their web, or medium strength connections to two or three groups. People generally become more tied to a single group out of necessity. The more difficult our circumstances, and the more unequal a society, the more we need greater group security. We need this group security to defend against the values of neighbouring groups, who, when things are unequal, may have very different values. We need this because the more unequal society is, the more people are diverged, and the more people need islands of positive feedback where we're treated according to our identity, rather than a choppy sea where we're not. We need this because the more unequal society is, the more constraint is applied by the parent.

Someone who is tied may have that greater security, and even a more peaceful and stress-free life at times, but there are compromises. Being strongly tied to a particular group can have its downsides. For example, the person is more limited in how they can behave, and therefore more likely to come into deeper conflict with those of incompatible values. Secondly, their focus can be strongly elsewhere at any one moment, and this can be frustrating for those close to them. Thirdly, the person can have a negative impact on others without realising it, or meaning to, which can come back to bite.

On the first point, the tied person finds they have to act in ways the group would approve of, or else someone from the group would pop into their mind and disapprove of them. Their views on what is right and wrong can often become quite narrow. This can affect how they judge or assess other people when they meet them. For example, they will judge them according to how that person would fit in, and be treated, if they joined the group that the person is tied to. This can sometimes create a deep conflict with someone who has incompatible values.

It can also have an impact on what type of parent that person becomes, because how they go about parenting will be strongly dictated by their tied group, rather than being based on nurturing their children.

On the second point, being so tied to one group can affect our close interpersonal relationships with people outside of the group. Those other people may find it occasionally frustrating, because it appears as if the tied person's focus and emotions aren't reacting to them, but instead to people not there. Humans feel valued by focus and attention, and being important to others, so this can leave them feeling a little less valued. This may be true of a partner or our children for example. It doesn't affect the intention of the tied person, they

Our "Web"

may still want to come across as loving and caring, it just affects what is actually transmitted, and how it makes the other person feel (although again, effort goes a long way). With children, this can often cause them to replicate their parent's behaviour. They don't feel value coming from the parent directly, so in order to feel valued, they seek out their own deep, tied group.

If the parent is successfully integrated into a strong tied group, often the child will copy similar behaviours and values, and find it easier to replicate this situation. The parent and child may not be close, but there may be little conflict between them, due to the fact that both the parent and child simply focus on their respective tied groups, rather than each other. There may be frustration and difficulty there, but it never has a large effect on their lives. This can even carry on down generations. It is one example of where quite large divergence is passed from parent to child, without difficulty being exposed.

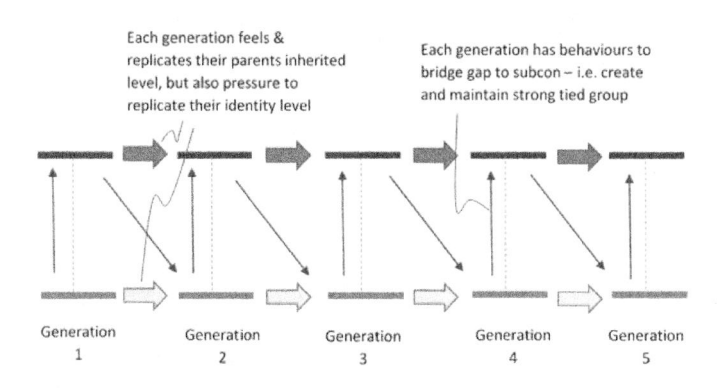

Each generation feels & replicates their parents inherited level, but also pressure to replicate their identity level

Each generation has behaviours to bridge gap to subcon – i.e. create and maintain strong tied group

Generation 1   Generation 2   Generation 3   Generation 4   Generation 5

On the third point, having our focus and influences coming strongly from one group, can mean that sometimes we act more blindly, without realising the consequences on those around us. We are simply unaware, can't relate, or just deeply believe we are coming across one way, when the reality is that we are pressuring someone, or conflicting with them, without noticing. We can live more in a bubble, and do actions that others can't understand, or that are dangerous and reckless even. We do so because of that strong tie to a single group, and less of an emotional link and understanding to the people around us.

We can also act more blindly within the tied group. People in the group may see it as a pseudo-family group. A person may become more consumed in the tied group, and transfer external issues into it. The difficulties felt by each person with their actual, respective families can transfer in, and cause large conflict. Other people in the tied group can become manifestations of difficult relationships outside of the group, but now those conflicts are playing out in a second-hand way. This can often occur when the tied members have children. This can be, for example, because they may realise that their social reputation is inconsistent with how they want their children to see them. Or, because they become more aware of their own life circumstances, and the consequences of their own parental relationships.

Being strongly tied to a particular group can be an effective coping strategy for our spread-out social lives, but it comes with caveats.

It's likely that the strength of ties we have are based on our needs, and if we need to form a deep group, and pull others towards us, then that is what we'll do. Our personal web tends to develop organically, with each connection formed in a nuanced way, based on the ones before.

Our "Web"

Relationships

Relationships with partners obviously form part of our web, and often a key aspect of it.

Relationships can be an important part of our lives. We are shaped by our key drivers to maximise our value and have children. Desire, love, trust, sex, bonds, support and value are all intertwined in them. We can feel the power of comfort, support, family, security and purpose through them.

However, whilst they can be very important, this section on relationships is quite short. The reason for that is partly because you can apply anything about an individual, or a group, discussed elsewhere in this book, to them, and partly because most of an individual's self, web and primary friendships (and obviously siblings and parents) are formed before the relationship. As a result, whilst relationships can have its own nuances, difficult, and conflict (and there is much to say about how to resolve issues and trade compromises in a relationship), much of a person's self, web and positions are formed outside of the relationship. Whilst a lot of our focus can be on finding a desirable partner, once we do so, a lot of the difficulty we still have, as modern humans, is still present in our circumstances outside of the relationship. The relationship is then quite high level in the structure of our web. Often, the relationship is then about supporting each other in managing issues outside of it.

In the context of this book, which focusses on the individual, and a first principles, basic building block approach to human programming, relationships then form a smaller part on how a person forms and behaves (and experiences life based on that). Our lives are often forged outside of relationships, and then applied to them.

Any type of relationship can work. Opposites attract, or similarities attract. Often we are attracted to people with similar levels to us, since they experience and react to the world in similar ways to us, but a difference in levels can also be a basis for a strong relationship.

Between very diverged people, there may be less closeness, and instead more support in individual endeavours, for example at work. Between medium diverged people (which are the most common), there may be some closeness, but a fair amount of each person's focus is consumed in their respective core friendship groups. However, each situation is different.

Our relationships as modern humans are likely quite different to how they would be as hunter-gatherers. Often modern relationships are about status and security, against a difficult modern social environment, and about fulfilling social norms and influences, rather than simply a union between two people. With people around us jostling and rearranging, the relationship becomes a source of continuity, and people often refer to their partner as their rock.

However they are, and however they were, relationships are often the goal and focus of our lives as modern humans. Much of what happens in life is about finding someone we desire and value, and the competition that goes before that. It's just that, as modern humans, the competition, and modern society, often continues somewhat after that someone is found.

The reality of being a modern human

To summarise this chapter, having social lives spread over several groups is a significant change compared to our hunter-gatherer lifestyle. As a result, this modern social arrangement

Our "Web"

can have a significant impact on the way we experience and feel about the lives we lead.

In a hunter-gatherer tribe, we'd stay in the same tribe our whole lives, and it'd be the tribe our parents were in. Whilst being a hunter-gatherer would have been tough, and there would have been dangers and difficulty in the natural environment, it would have felt right. Everything that our programming wants to achieve, in order to make us feel good and fulfilled, would have been possible to achieve in that environment. It's unlikely we'd ever question who we were. That environment is our natural environment, that our ancestors lived in for millions of years, before we decided to start living in small settlements (around 12,000 years ago) and large societies (around 5000 years ago).

In the modern world of big societies, everyone has webs and links, and unfortunately there is inequality.

Our focus is on one, two, or a few social groups. These likely don't involve our parents. We feel most ourselves in one of those social groups, rather than when interacting with our parents, and the result of this is that conflict is often about second-hand issues, having transferred from the source onto the world in front of us.

With our main source of identity in a group, away from our parents, our parents reduce us a little more than they would naturally, in order that we don't challenge them with behaviours, and values, which may be very different to theirs.

We have complicated, interlinked webs. These are like pieces of string connecting us, but they are often not well ordered, and instead get caught up in each other, and occasionally knotted. We rely on our web for all the things that a tribe would give us, but it doesn't stay still. People move towards others, but then move apart, and perhaps change their personality and identity. People we once used behaviours with, that made us feel ourselves, now don't want to, or vice versa.

We can struggle to know who we are, and feel pressure or stress from competing with others for successes that, if we were honest with ourselves, we don't really care about. Security and calm are hard to come by, and we can get unhelpful tied thoughts from friends and rivals alike. Those tied thoughts, whose noble purpose it is to keep is linked to our tribe, instead now pull us in different directions, and leave us feeling a bit weakened, and make it harder to behave exactly how we want to.

Relationships can be a source of continuity and support in the choppy seas. For modern humans they are often based on that, whilst our focus is more directed towards people outside of the relationship.

It's therefore almost impossible in this modern world to replicate the feelings that we'd get in a tribe, our natural environment. But we still want them, and we feel compelled to try and seek them out, as if we could. We long for the warmth, belonging and security, even if we're side-tracked by the accumulation of success and wealth.

Often, we try to go upwards, higher jobs and more money, with the impression that this will give us more freedom from our web. Sometimes it does, sometimes it doesn't. We may try to avoid negative emotions, or clear an area around us where we feel content, perhaps at other's expense. We find it hard to explain or understand our lives, or it's confusing how others behave. People are being influenced by people we've never met, or project one thing whilst hiding another. Then we find that we take actions for one reason, but tell everyone it is for a different, more socially acceptable reason. Difficulty is hidden behind closed doors.

Our "Web"

Modern humans therefore often try to interact as if they were content hunter-gatherers, because that is what our programming is urging us towards, but the reality is that we live in an environment where it can't be wholly achieved. Our spread-out social lives make our lives harder, whether due to rearranging webs, uncomfortable tied thoughts, people pulling strongly on strings, or transference.

It can be very hard, and there are no easy solutions, but it is getting easier as the world moves towards a more equal place to live in.

5

Our "Self"

Looking at the third key aspect of modern experiences: our "self"; we shall now consider our self-perception, and how we balance being social creatures with being self-aware. It is a key aspect of *modern* life because it is part of our programming that works well in a tribe situation, so that it is fairly inconsequential (and just happens in the background), whereas in our modern social circumstances it can work less well, and occasionally become a source of difficulty.

People sometimes say to us: "just be yourself".

It sounds good, and it's normally said with good intentions. But this often leaves us thinking: "great, but what do you mean by that!".

"Just being ourselves" is often an elusive trait. We can spend a large amount of time, in life, working out who we are, and finding a place in the world where we feel ourselves. To other people, they may look at us, feel our behaviours, and hear our voice, and it seems complete to them. But to us, it can be less so.

To us, our self is less concrete, and more flexible. For example, when we meet new people, what impression do we

Our "Self"

want to make, and how should we act? Do we try to be exactly who we are, or behave how we want to be? Do we act according to who we might become in the future, or copy the behaviours of people that we look up to? All of these are possibilities to us, and we can be unsure as to which is the right one to go with. When someone else says "just be yourself", they generally mean that they like our behaviours and we shouldn't have to change, but against the complexity of modern life, where there are a myriad of pressures and influences, it perhaps isn't received in quite the way it was meant.

Some people seem to be able to "just be themselves" more than others. We get a sense of this when we meet people, and have an intuition that picks up on when people are "just being themselves". It's difficult to pinpoint exactly what it is about them. It's not necessarily related to confidence, but perhaps more a surety of who they are, a lack of doubt in their behaviours, and an ability to express themselves more naturally and comfortably.

We might say these people have a "greater sense of self".

But then it gets complicated. Each of the following people might fit that description. Each may feel uninhibited socialising, and feel they know exactly who they are:

Some people seem self-sure, grounded and comfortable in their own skin.

Some people seem confident, brash, focussed, and strongly directed.

Some people seem like they're acting and playing a role. They seem very confident, but we get a sense that they are using behaviours that aren't theirs.

The idea of "self" is therefore difficult to pin down. Different people will have a different idea of what type of person has greater "self".

There are many ways to define what "self" actually is, and then many avenues by which to explore it. In these chapters, we will consider "self" as the idea that our internal view of ourself can be different from the external view. The internal view is who we feel we are, and what makes us feel ourself. The external view is how others see us, and how we come across. Then, people with a "greater sense of self" are ones where the internal view and external view are more consistent.

The person that says "just be yourself" is looking at the external view. The external view is more concrete and defined. They see how we look, how we sound, how we come across and how we make them feel.

However, we see the world from our internal view, and all those things are often elusive to us. Our internal view is more of an idea or impression. It is formed of comparisons, feedback and associations. It can also be formed on missing information, disregarded truths, and inconsistencies. It is the deeply lodged perception of ourselves that our brain interprets our interactions against.

As human beings, there can be a difference between how we think we come across, and how we actually come across. There can a difference between how we think we look, and what others see. There can be a difference between how we think our behaviours make others feel, and how they actually felt.

All of these are related to an internal view and an external view. In the modern world, the internal view and external view can be very different for an individual.

This doesn't really matter. Providing there are places in our lives where our internal view is accepted and integrated, it doesn't really matter whether it's similar to our external view, at least for ourself. Providing that, in places, we can act consistent with our internal view, and use behaviours that feel ourself, then we can *be* ourself.

How we actually come across, what others see, is blocked from us, so, instead, feeling ourself generally only relies on using behaviours that feel "us", and being treated how we like.

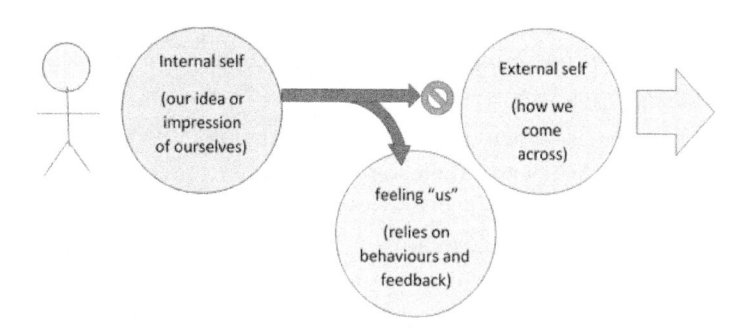

[Diagram: A stick figure next to three circles. "Internal self (our idea or impression of ourselves)" with an arrow blocked from reaching "External self (how we come across)", and instead flowing down to "feeling 'us' (relies on behaviours and feedback)".]

And this is enough for a human being, how we come across is irrelevant to us, providing that, in places, we can be ourself.

This way that our "self" works, will have evolved in the tribe environment. As a result, it works very well there. It's unlikely that hunter-gatherers would have questioned who they were. That conundrum is more of a modern challenge, that results from our modern environments and social backdrop.

Firstly, in expanding on this theory, we will look at a more theoretical approach to the various aspects of self that we derive from the world around us, and secondly, we will compare it to an existing theory of our "locus of evaluation".

The internal vs. external self

With a human being, there can be a difference between how it feels to be our "self", and how we look and come across to others. In fact, the two can be quite separated. Our internal view of the world can be very different to the external view, that someone sees of us. We can have very little appreciation of how we come across, compared to how we feel about ourselves.

The "how we come across to others" part is largely unattainable to us. Even with photos, mirrors and videos, we will have an incomplete picture of what others see and feel, when they interact with us.

Conversely, when we think of other people, we get quite a vivid mental image of their personality, their looks, and how they make us feel relative to everyone else. When we think of a close friend or family member, we likely think of a face, how they sound, how they make us feel or how they come across. But when it comes to ourselves, the characteristics that make other people so clear, are characteristics that we don't have access to, or are hidden from us. We can't see or hear ourselves, at least in the same way that we perceive other people. We don't know what emotions we conjure up in other people. If we meet someone new, it's quite possible the impression we thought we gave, was quite different to the impression we actually made.

Where our internal self comes from

The internal "self" (the impression we have of ourself), develops as we grow through adolescence. We draw definition, comparisons, and take feedback from those around us. A human-being enters the world with little idea of who they are, or where they fit in, yet by the end of adolescence they will (theoretically) have a much firmer internal idea about their self-definition.

There is nothing inherently guiding our internal self to be consistent with our external self. They are two separate things.

Our "Self"

How we come across (our external self) is more fixed, but how we feel about ourselves (our internal self) is far more flexible, and subject to change.

We draw our internal view from those around us. We draw it from our family, our close friends, and our job. It is driven by the groups we are a part of, and we feel similar to, and a reflection of those groups. Our internal self is an idea, a rough picture made up of fragments of information. In our mind we have a collection of our mannerisms, gestures, memories, features, and previous social interactions, that together form an overall impression.

The internal view is an idea or impression we have of ourselves, and it is what our brain uses as a foundation for our interactions.

Because our internal self is drawn from those around us, then the environment we grow up in can affect how it forms. A tribe is likely to produce the most consistent self, a small settlement less so, and a giant interlinked society less so still. Large societies result in much greater variation in the internal self, and therefore less consistency between the internal and external self. This can be due to our spread-out social lives, or the chance for fame and glory. For example, the internal self is flexible, and therefore gets diverted and drawn away from us by our many different groups. It is also strongly affected by our drive to maximise our value, and we dream about who we might become (even if on the outside we are still just a human being).

Our modern world can create many situations where the internal view, that develops during adolescence, becomes separated from the external view. Being diverged is one of them, where our identity level is different to our inherited level. There are many others though too, for example if we receive unusual feedback, or if the people around us have lower self, or if we have attributes, opportunity, or the possibility to fit in with people who come across very differently to how we do. This can be a cause of duality, where we feel there are two aspects of ourself, both with some realism, but both different. None of these are a problem, providing there are places where we can act according to our internal view, and feel ourselves.

When the internal view and the external view become more separated, it can sometimes lead to the situations where people think "who do they think they are". With the internal view, humans can think all sorts of things about ourselves, very different from how we actually come across. A person can be oblivious to a great many things, and seem nonplussed by it, or, alternatively, frustrated with other people, for not treating them according to their internal view.

However, people that have "greater self" may have an easier time forming close relationships, for example with their partner or their children. The closer we are to someone, the more we experience their core emotions and reactions, and their internal self. It is easier to project behaviours, play a role, and provide a front, when there is some distance.

In our modern social environment of interlinked spread-out social lives, we all lack self to a greater or lesser degree. It's quite unlikely that who we feel we are in the modern world is consistent with how we come across. In order for our internal self and external self to be consistent, well, we'd need a tribe environment. As we will see, the mechanism for feeling ourselves described here is well suited to tribe environments. It both fits with the structure of tribe environments, and contributes to harmonious, interlinked tribes with strong sub-cultures. In contrast, the modern world creates many more situations where it is harder to know what "ourself" is. Perhaps sometimes we feel it, but at other times we don't feel ourself, or we don't know where we fit in.

Feeling most ourselves

Whilst our internal self sits in our subconscious, and can affect how we feel about interactions, we mostly don't think about it or focus on it. Instead, in our conscious thoughts, "self" becomes more about our behaviours and the feedback we receive. When we are able to use behaviours that feel "us", and people treat us in a way that is consistent with how we see ourselves, and want to be treated, then we *feel* most ourselves.

Feeling most ourself is a good thing, it feels right and pleasant, compared to feeling lost and unsure of ourselves. When we feel most ourself, we tend not to care about how we come across, we just be. We tend to feel most "us" when interacting in a core group. We tend to focus on, or be concerned with, how we come across, when away from a group situation, by ourselves, or when we're about to meet new people.

Self is a difficult concept for a living being. With an outward view on the world, and not being able to see ourselves how others do, it will always be a partial picture. Then, it can work well in the environment that the beings programming developed in, but in other environments, it can work less well.

"self" within a tribe

For millions of years our ancestors each lived in one tribe their whole lives, spending the vast majority of their time, day and night, with the same people, that likely included their parents. The groups would tend to arrange themselves into a rough hierarchical order, with reasonable stability and harmony.

Being collocated, and in constant contact with our tribe, would mean much fewer situations where we're distant from a group, or meeting new people. Who we are, or how we come across, would be much less important, because we'd be more constantly in a "socialisation mode" within a group. Then, our "self" becomes more about our behaviours and the feedback we receive, and our internal self is a painting that's stored at the back of the attic, out of sight, out of mind (the best place for it).

With each tribes-member having a secure position in the group, and regularly using the behaviours that make them feel "them", not feeling themselves never really comes into the picture. With "self" becoming more about just behaviours, then, because each tribes-member has behaviours that were developed in that tribe, and were integrated, reciprocated and interlinked with the other tribes-members, then the feelings of being lost, or lacking "self" would have been much rarer.

This would result in each tribes-member having a strong sense of who they are, and feeling themselves the majority of the time, both in adolescence and adulthood.

These tribes-members would still have had little idea of how they came across. They would never even have seen pictures or videos of themselves. Their **external self** was still unobtainable to them.

For example the earliest recorded mirror was dated to about 6000 BC, when in Anatolia (modern day Turkey) they would polish obsidian, a volcanic glass, to create a flat reflective surface[23]. Before that, the only way our ancestors would ever have seen themselves would have been very occasionally in a flat pool of water. Homo Sapiens emerged 200,000 years ago, and Homo Erectus (our predecessor), 2 million years ago. Therefore the majority of our evolution was without mirrors even.

When mirrors have been given to modern day remote tribespeople, they have remarked that it's the first time they've seen themselves, and take a while to recognise the movement in the mirror as being the same as the movements they make.

But those tribespeople, who have never seen themselves, are often friendly and content. They can be welcoming of outsiders, have good social skills, and an understanding of behaviour, and what is right and wrong.

Developing in a tribe, whether as a remote modern-day tribe, or an ancient hunter-gatherer one, would result in greater "self". A tribe-member would come across as if they had a greater sense of self, but not because they were fully aware of their external self. They would come across as self-assured and grounded, but more because of the environment they developed in, rather than knowledge of how they came across. Their internal self would more closely match their external self, simply because of the circumstances, rather than an excess of information.

A tribe produces a realistic and consistent **internal self** for a few reasons.

Firstly, they would have grown up in an environment close to their parents and siblings. These are the people that we are most like in the world (not always, but in the majority of cases), and the people we share most DNA with. We'll look similar to them, have similar features. We'll pick up on and copy gestures and mannerisms from them, and we may sound like them, move like them, or talk like they do. Our internal self absorbs information from people around us, in forming the idea or impression of who we are, so if we spend a large amount of time with close family members, as we would in a tribe, our self is likely to be more realistic.

Secondly, tribes are also very interlinked. We form a part of the tribe, and the tribe forms a part of us, in a symbiotic relationship. This will be true of each tribe member. If there are 9 people in a tribe, then each person sees 8 others. They treat each person as a comparison to the others, and fit each person into the tribe structure according to what they see.

There will be fairly constant and consistent socialisation, and therefore verbal definitions nudging each other this way and that. The tribe will be fairly independent and isolated, so there are no external groups or influences, and each member's identity is consistent with this interconnected social structure. The tribe then becomes a very effective mirror, and through the countless interactions, each person builds up an impression of themselves that is realistic and consistent with their external self.

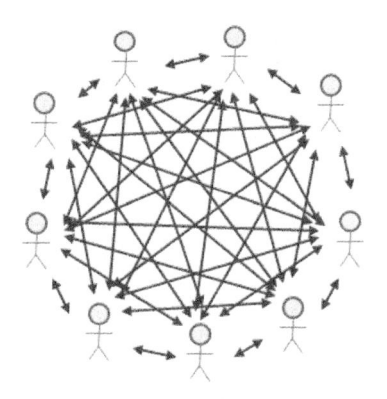

Thirdly, the tribe will have a very defined sub-culture. It will likely be based around behaviours, rather than value or roles. Having a narrower set of criteria to judge oneself by, and compete over, provides more security of self. With only one, well defined set of criteria, for positioning ourselves relative to others, we have an easier time forming a picture of ourselves. It leads to less variability in the challenges we receive, and the feedback we get will likely be consistent over our whole lifetimes. It's unlikely that one day we'll be competing with others on one set of criteria, then the next day that criteria changes, leaving us less sure of how we are positioned. We'll be less likely to have to adapt our behaviours from one

Our "Self"

interaction to the next, and therefore we'll be able to freely use the behaviours that feel most ourself most of the time. Our internal self will have developed in this strong sub-culture, that we form a part of, and be positioned within it, and received consistent feedback based on it, and so naturally be quite consistent with how we came across.

These three reasons, and potentially others, lead to a strong sense of self, and a consistent self, in a tribe.

Of course it won't be perfect match between the internal and external self, but it is unlikely to be too far off. Inconsistencies in the internal and external self, that we may see in the world around us, tend to be a by-product of our modern societies. They tend to originate from the unusual social circumstances we find ourselves in: having social lives spread over several groups; the intermixing of society; and the draw of being more than just a human being. For example, when a large group of humans form, for example as happened when hunter-gatherers started farming in a settlement, or as civilisations grew, different status levels were created. This makes the flexibility of our internal self dream of what we could be, driven by our desire to maximise our value, and soon we are no longer content with just being a human being, and we need to be more.

If that kind of dreaming somehow occurred in an isolated tribe, it would have a knock-on effect to the other members of the tribe, due to the interlinked nature, and that person would quickly be brought back down to earth, fitting in based on what others saw. The feedback and verbal definition, that plays a strong part in the interconnected nature of the tribe, would prevent a tribes-member having an inconsistent self. Because of this, and the close interlinked socialisation, it is unlikely in this environment that any member can feel grandiose, unrealistic, self-inflated or exaggerated self-beliefs.

Similarly, with the tribe being a mirror for our self, other types of mismatched selfs are less likely too. It is less likely that someone who has positive and desirable attributes won't feel like they do. It is less likely that people feel a little lost, or not quite themselves. A tribe provides an environment whereby an internal self grows that is consistent with our external self.

"self" outside the tribe

If a person in a tribe has a better sense of self, what are the consequences of this? From their point of view, the difference between having greater self, or not, isn't particularly perceivable. Our brain tends to take our circumstances and make them feel normal (partly because our circumstances are the only ones we've ever known). Therefore what is the point, or what are the benefits, if we are lucky enough to have greater self?

Let's say an adult tribes-member becomes separated from the tribe, and joins another. The new tribe isn't too dissimilar, but has its own quirks and sub-culture.

With a greater sense of self, the newcomer's internal self (who they feel they are and how they feel they come across), is similar to the impression they actually make. The new tribe interact with what they see of the newcomer, and find little surprises. The vibe that the new tribe get, from the first impression of the newcomer, is similar to how the newcomer appears to want to integrate. What the newcomer appears to believe about themselves, is consistent with how they come across, and fitting them into the new tribe is a smoother process. It requires less communication, less trial and error, and less of a back and forth, before a harmonious tribe structure is found. The newcomer's actions and intentions appear more predictable, and therefore conflict is kept to a minimum.

With a greater sense of self, our tribes-member's feelings of themselves are more rooted. They feel they know who they are, and, whilst their new tribe is different to their old, they still feel grounding and surety within it. When members of the new tribe challenge them, they feel less affected. They are less likely to feel the need to influence those around them, to bend the new tribe structure towards their own. They can join in with the new culture's traits and traditions, without feeling that it is taking too much from their core.

A greater sense of self causes us to get less tied up in conflict. With an impression of ourselves similar to how we come across, we are more likely to get consistent, realistic feedback, and less likely to ruffle other's feathers. With our internal self grounded in realism, it is less affected and influenced by those around us. Someone with a less consistent self is more prone to having it change, be influenced by others, or feel the draw towards making their internal self bigger and more powerful.

The newcomer in the tribe has displayed that greater sense of self, and finds an easier time integrating with, and feeling less influenced by, their new tribe.

The flexibility of our internal self

Before looking at self in a modern environment, we can briefly look at how flexible our internal self can be.

A fairly extreme (but nevertheless widespread) example of the flexibility of self is one seen throughout nature, which is when one animal is raised by another from a different species.

It is not unheard of to find an animal that thinks it's a different animal. We even see this in our pets occasionally. Perhaps we have a dog that thinks it's a cat, or a goose that thinks it's a dog, and so on. Sometimes our pets will even copy human characteristics, and act as if they aren't aware they are a different species to their owners.

These animals will adopt behaviours appropriate for the species they "think" they are. Of course we have no idea what they are actually thinking, but we have some intuition. When we see a dog behaving like a cat, we say "they think they're a cat" quite instinctually, rather than merely "they are behaving like a cat".

This normally requires the animal to have grown up with a different species. As their internal self draws their self-definition as they grow, and they slowly absorb behaviours (that later make them feel themselves), they do so by absorbing these from animals very different to them. Their internal self would then be wildly different to their external self.

Perhaps we meet a shark, and we treat it like a shark, but then we find that it appears to think it's a dolphin. Or, we meet a dolphin, and treat it like a dolphin, but then we find that it appears to think it's a shark.

This happens in humans too.

There are cases of humans raised by wolves who, before they came across humans, thought they were a wolf. Their programming takes what they see around them, and they believe that they are similar to, and a representation of, that group.

For example there is the case of Dina Sanichar, who is said to have inspired Rudyard Kipling to write the Jungle Book in 1895. Raised by wolves in India, he was kidnapped by hunters, and spent his 20-year adult life in an orphanage[24]. He walked on all fours, found clothes uncomfortable, and felt most at ease socialising with a fellow person in the orphanage who was also raised by animals.

Dina thought he was a wolf. He had behaviours that were wolf-like. He ate like a wolf, and sharpened his teeth on bones.

Our "Self"

His internal self had fully formed around the idea that he was a wolf.

Or, perhaps it's not that he believed he was a wolf, but perhaps it's just that his brain approached all his thoughts, interactions and social bonds from the point of view of a wolf, since that is what it has absorbed in his life. When he has time to think of himself, it becomes uncomfortable to contradict those aspects, and think of himself as otherwise. To contemplate that he was in fact human would be to go against, and change, his social links and bonds. It would be uncomfortable, and he would dismiss and avoid those thoughts, and instead return to thoughts of his kindred wolves. He would be aware that his hands were not paws. He would be aware that he didn't look like a wolf. But then these would have been overridden and disregarded in favour of the idea that he was one. When he interacted with others, his brain defaulted to the impression, in his internal self, that was wolf-shaped. There is a self-image deeper than our consciousness, or what we see of ourselves, that determines our emotions and interactions.

Our internal self appears to be so flexible, that the idea and impression we have of ourselves moulds itself to the groups we come across as we grow, whoever they may be.

The more our internal self has to flex, to shape itself onto those very different to us, the more side-effects occur. For example Dina was quite uncomfortable in the orphanage. He shunned most socialisation, and didn't appear to overly enjoy it. Like any social being, whether wolf or human, he would have felt compelled to socialise. With an internal self very different to an external self, any socialising would be confusing and frustrating. Either amongst wolves or humans, he would be searching for a strong sense of self, but never getting rewarding feedback, and never finding comfortable interactions, that allowed his self to be fulfilled.

Of course this is a highly unusual case. Dina would have grown up very isolated from humans, and unaware of their existence, with no-one to explain his situation to him.

Nevertheless, this is how flexible our internal self *can* be. The same thing is happening, in a much less strange, and more realistic way, between us and our friends, in terms of the behaviours we copy, who we feel we are, and how we feel we come across. Our impressions of ourself are often a reflection of the groups we form a part of. We behave, feel we come across, and expect to be treated, in ways consistent with those associations.

"self" in the modern environment

In our modern environment, we don't have that close interlinked tribe, where a realistic and consistent self stands the best chance of forming. Instead, our social lives are spread over several groups, and we grow amongst friends and family alike. Each group may have very different people and behaviours. We regularly meet new people, who perhaps behave, and see the world, very differently to us. We can find ourselves in unusual social positions or roles. And there are riches to potentially enjoy, so that our flexible internal self wonders who we might become.

We are bombarded with influences telling us how we should look, and unrealistic standards of beauty. We are surrounded by gaps, mismatches and incomplete pictures in our social environment. We try to act like personalities that appear to transgress modern difficulty. We get irregular and odd feedback, good one day, bad the next.

Selfs get distorted, and less consistent. Some move one way, some another. Some become inflated, some diminished.

Our "Self"

Pockets of "greater self" and "lesser self" get worked into groups, families, and down generations, as the world around us changes over time. We have to work quite hard to ground ourselves, and focus on a realistic self, or hold on to an idea that works.

In this modern environment, how we feel about ourselves is still being dictated the same way it was for millions of years, before we gave up our hunter-gatherer lifestyle, about 12,000 years ago.

Our "self" is interlinked by comparisons. Who we feel we are is in a large part drawn from comparing ourself to those around us. The fragments of information that form our internal self are drawn from the interactions we've had, but now those memories, gestures, mannerisms and snapshots are all from very different places.

Our "self" is still interlinked with those around us, like it was in the tribe. It still follows the pattern of being shaped by how others see us, similar to how the other members of a tribe would act as a mirror to each other, and our feeling of self gets drawn from feedback. When other people try to define us, it can have a strong impact on us. Often how other people define us has a more powerful effect on our self, compared to us trying to control how we feel about ourselves, by ourself.

Through feedback and comparisons, the idea or impression of our internal self forms. However, whilst our self forms in a way that is suitable for a small tribe environment, our modern social environment is very different. We have spread out social lives, and multi-layered societies. This often results in less grounding, and instead, highs and lows, gaps and crevices, ladders and pitfalls, and our internal self is often less consistent with our external self.

Having social lives that are spread across several groups (for example a family group, friendship groups and work colleagues), causes a large change is how our "self" forms.

For example, we feel an influence from each of them, and each of them imparts some "self" on us. We might feel ourselves when interacting in each of those groups, but behave slightly differently in each. Often our closest friend or friendship group is separate from our family group, and has a different sub-culture to our family's. We then have our work colleagues, and our job often requires a different set of behaviours to our social lives. In our modern communities, we simply can't find a completely self-contained group, which is the environment that the part of our programming that defines our "self" is appropriate for. In reality, we have to occasionally use behaviours that don't quite feel ourself in some groups, and find pockets of our lives where we can feel ourselves.

Also, with large unequal societies, we can often find ourselves copying behaviours and mannerisms from role models, rather than those around us (for example, our parents). We try to act like whoever is the star of the moment. We replicate their gestures, movements, or ways of speaking, sometimes without even realising it. We try them out ourself, and, if we pull it off, we feel a little more like that role model. We feel good, and we feel an association with the person we've copied it off, and perhaps imagine we come across like they do. However, it may look very different, when we use that mannerism, compared to when the person we're copying it off uses it. But our internal self is unaware of this. Using it makes us feel a little more like the role model, and it's imparted something onto our identity. The fragments of information, that make up our internal self, are now being drawn from sources potentially very different to us.

Our "Self"

We all end up with less self, i.e. our internal self is less consistent with our external self. This is entirely a modern problem, and a side effect of leaving the tribe environment we evolved in.

To some, having less self isn't a problem at all. People may have little self, but have a place or group where they feel themselves, and they block out and disregard all the inconsistencies. Providing we have a place where we feel ourself, and can use the behaviours that make us feel "us", it doesn't matter too much whether our self is consistent.

For others, having less self can be a big problem. We can be frustrated that others don't see us similar to how we see ourselves. We can feel lost, or like an imposter, or we can look in the mirror and find we just don't feel similar to the person looking back at us.

Having greater self is an asset for dealing with our spread-out social lives, where we are being pulled in different directions. With greater self, our thoughts are less influenceable, and we can be less drawn into conflicts, or have our thoughts wander to others.

The amount of self that we have, and that people have in general, is difficult to change, and more a reflection of our circumstances in life, and the social backdrop around society. It develops and absorbs information from our social environment as we grow, and can become quite deep rooted. Our internal self is like a leaf in the breeze, and whether it lands near our external self is down to chance and circumstance.

We perhaps can't change our fundamental amount of self, but we can better understand it and tackle some of the side effects. For example, with our self residing more in others, our focus gets drawn more onto others. We can tackle that part of our self by learning to draw that focus back towards us. We can also gain greater self-definition by finding a purpose, idea, hobby or activity that really makes us feel "us", and therefore feel ourself more.

Self and levels

Our internal self: the fragments of information that form an idea or impression of ourselves; that our brain uses as a foundation for our interactions; can be full of inconsistencies.

Some of those fragments can be high, some low, and perhaps neither are representative of how we come across.

For example we have some impressions of ourself as imposing, but other impressions where we are shy. Perhaps we have some fragments where we are tall, but others where we are short. We may have some where we are old and wise, and others where we are still a teenager, or still looking upwards to our primary authority figures. We may have some fragments where we are attractive, but others where we aren't.

It could be that none of these really have much accuracy, compared to our external self: what others see.

The source of these inconsistencies can be as varied as the inconsistencies themselves, but most can be linked to our spread-out social lives and societal inequality, that produces such a range of social circumstances, some good, some bad. All of us will have had varied feedback throughout our lives, and some places where we fit, and others where we don't. Sometimes our actions are accepted and reciprocated, and at others times they are rebuffed.

One source of inconsistency is if we change significantly during adolescence, or if we change after adolescence. Our internal self forms as we grow, so if we change after that, then we may have fragments from who we were during adolescence, and fragments from who we are after adolescence. This can increase the chance that we find it hard to have certainty over who we are, and increases the chance that we have a certain amount of conflicted emotion in our feelings towards our self.

Another source of inconsistency is being diverged. Then, our reactions to the world around us, and the associations and identity level we have, may be very different. We are likely further away from our parents in society, and instead feel more similar to those around us socially. We are likely to get more inconsistent feedback, and perhaps have a smaller area where we feel ourselves. Our behaviours, gestures and mannerisms are more likely to be copied from role models and authority figures, and the source of our fragments of internal self more diverse. Our internal self becomes less grounded and more influenceable.

The highs and lows of our fragments will in some way reflect our two levels: our inherited level and our identity level.

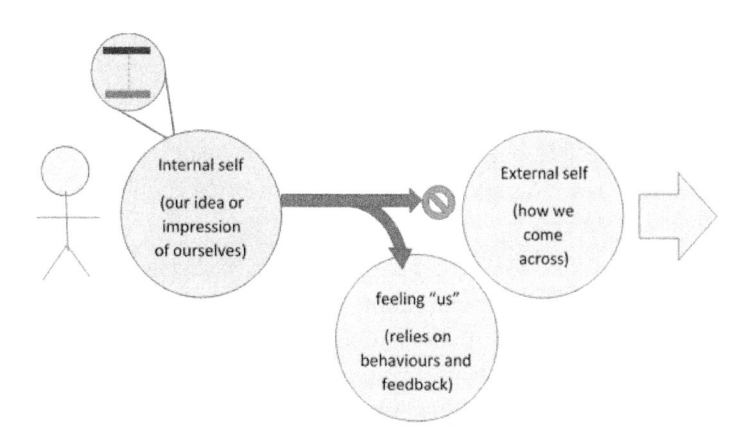

Our identity level is generally when we're at our best, and so may produce some of the highs of our internal self. Our inherited level is what we're all fighting, and is generally a representation of the difficulty of modern societies, and so contains some of the lows.

It therefore adds another layer of complexity to the idea of an internal self. The previous parts of this section discuss the internal self as a single concept (in order to illustrate how it can be different to the external self), however the internal self perhaps has two parts.

The fragments of internal self, that we have, can either represent **fixed** aspects, associated with our inherited level and our parents, and drawn from adolescence, forming a deeply lodged perception of ourselves, that our brain tends to revert to at times. Or, they can represent **flexible** aspects, associated with our identity level, and drawn from the groups we most associate with. The flexible aspects will be more associated with how we want to come across, and include fragments of gestures, mannerisms and snapshots that allow us to feel similar to our role models and contemporaries.

Despite the highs and lows in the fragments of internal self we have, it's quite possible that none of them really capture how we come across.

To briefly consider a further aspect of complexity, then it is not only our internal self that has two aspects, our external self does too. For example, the impression we make will depend on who's viewing it.

There will be some aspects of external self that are **specific.** Perhaps in certain environments, or with certain people, that either strongly align to our sub-culture, or oppose it, other people are more likely to see an impression that is influenced by sub-culture. This often happens at work, where we need to be a little characteristic and stereotypical, and the impressions we give, and view of others, will be more based around abilities related to the job.

However there are some aspects of external self that are **universal.** For example when we see ourselves in videos or mirrors, and just can't feel similar to what we see. Or in certain close relationships, or with our children, they are more likely to see an impression without the influence of sub-culture. In some ways the universal aspects of external self are about the way that, on the outside, we are only ever just a human being.

Nevertheless, despite the possibility that our *internal self* can have fixed parts and flexible parts, and the *external self* has specific parts and universal parts, then we can ignore these and treat them as singular aspects, in order to make the points made in this section.

Someone with greater self, and therefore more consistency between their internal and external self, is more likely to come across as expected, and have a greater fundamental awareness of their rough impression, and their traits and behaviours. They will find it easier to fit into different sub-cultures, and bend and shape themselves, when necessary, without feeling it takes too much from their core. They are more like a dolphin that thinks it's a dolphin (but that can occasionally act like a shark), rather than a dolphin that thinks it's a shark.

People from all walks of life can have better or worse self. Our modern society produces many ways that the idea we have of ourselves can form in a way that is different to how we come across. As the world slowly becomes more equal and easier to live in, a good self will be easier to find.

Mirrors, photos and videos

In theory, the more information we have on how we come across, the more accurate and consistent our self should be.

However, this is not necessarily the case. Firstly, the information we get is often incomplete, and only gives a snapshot, or partial impression, of how we come across. Secondly, we evolved for millions of years in an environment whereby our self was dictated without any of this information, and so it tends to favour that method. Our brains are very good at disregarding information we feel is inconsistent.

In the modern world, we have lots of photos, videos, recordings and mirrors that give us information on what we look like, and how we come across.

We can spend a long time looking at ourself in the mirror, trying to decide if we're attractive, trying to decide if one of our features is good or bad, or spend a long time shaping that one part of our hair, none of which really gives us an accurate impression of the impression we make on others. We can see something in the mirror, and simply not feel similar to what we see, good and bad.

When we watch videos of ourselves, it can often be uncomfortable. People often don't like to view recordings of themselves, there is something about it, that makes us not want to see ourselves in that way. We say "I don't look like that do I?", or "I don't sound like that do I?".

Photos are just a snapshot, and don't necessarily represent what others see, even if we want the good ones to (and delete all the photos of ourself that we don't like). We can look different in photos depending on the angle or lighting. A photo can capture a momentary emotion, good or bad, that isn't representative of our lives, but nevertheless can create an impression on those that view it (including on ourselves).

Our self, how we think we look and come across, still develops in the age-old way, based on those around us as we grow. When faced with modern additional information, our brain tends to take what we see in photos and videos, and moulds and distorts it *onto* our self, rather than using that information to *help define* our self. We tend to take information on ourself, such as videos and pictures, and view it from the perspective of our social reputation, or focus on how it might change our social reputation, rather than absorbing it into our programming's deeply lodged perception of ourselves.

Mirrors, photos and videos of course affect our self-image, good and bad. However, when we aren't looking at them, our brain actually may not store that much of the information we just saw. When we are in a socialisation mode, mid conversation, or with a group, it's likely that our focus becomes more outward. In that socialisation mode, our emotions and reactions are being determined by our internal self (the rough idea or impression we have of ourself), rather than an accurate impression of how we come across.

The internal self, the impression we have of ourself, can actually be quite dissimilar to things we see of ourself in mirrors, photos and videos. We genuinely dismiss lots of things about us, good or bad, that don't fit with our social reputation or feedback. Our brain favours the internal self approach used by our ancient ancestors, rather than being driven by an abundance of information we have in the modern day.

For example perhaps we have a gesture, movement or feature, that we know is there, but that just never forms part of our self-image. Perhaps we don't like it, and disregard it. It simply doesn't form part of the self-impression we have. We can become, in a small part, like the boy raised by wolves, who knows he doesn't have paws, but still believes he is a wolf. We know we have a certain gesture, movement or feature, but to consider it is uncomfortable, and it simply doesn't fit with our social links and identity.

Given that modern humans have a poor sense of self, where our internal self often differs from our external self, extra information can sometimes confuse the picture. If mirrors, pictures and videos didn't exist, we could simply *be* our definition, feeling ourselves in blissful ignorance. We'd never worry if something about us was good or bad, or find confusion in the idea that we can't feel similar to what we see of ourselves. All we'd have would be a rough idea of who we are, and providing people treated us like that, and we could use behaviours that felt us, that'd be enough.

Photos and videos are of course an important part of modern life. However, perhaps due to social media, people can focus on them too much, and use them excessively to craft images of themselves, for social reputation purposes only.

They can play a stabilising role however. For example, despite that fact that our external self is only ever just a human being, our internal self can feel powerful and exalted, or small and worthless. Perhaps, when we try not to look at them through rose tinted glasses, or with despair, photos and videos serve as a restoring force, and a reminder that we are just a human being after all, like everyone else in the world.

Self summary

We can consider all this with respect to ourselves, but, if you believe it, it will therefore be true of everyone else as well. It raises the idea that all the people we interact with, who appear so distinct, individual and memorable, may actually have little idea of what others see. How they believe they come across may be very different to the impression they're making.

When we see a person interacting, their brain may be approaching that interaction as if they are a very different person to the one we see in front of us (better or worse). Their internal self may be different to their external self.

Self can be difficult for modern humans. It's probably not worth worrying about too much. We can try to put ourselves in other's shoes, or consider how we feel about other people who behave like we do, and use that to build a better understanding of how we come across. However, whilst we should always be looking out for, and considering others, perhaps the more important thing to do is to try and find a place in the world where we can *feel* most ourself. Perhaps this is a place, perhaps it is a person, or perhaps this is a purpose.

After all that, all we can really do is "just be yourself". We try to find things that make us feel ourselves, and find people that treat us how we like, and everything else is largely irrelevant. We try to find environments where we can use some sort of variation of the behaviours that we picked up in late adolescence (which are often the ones that will make us feel most fulfilled in our adult lives). Perhaps the narrower the people, places or behaviours that make us feel most ourselves, the more we compete and come into conflict with others, but nevertheless, as modern humans, a large part of us is driven to find it nonetheless. Therefore, whilst it's sometimes confusing, the advice: "just be yourself", is good advice to give.

On a final note, in our search to find our "self", there are some things that are more likely to make a human feel themselves more than others. One is the natural world, the environment we live in. People often associate being in nature with "being at one with yourself". Places and activities in nature stand a greater chance of making us feel ourselves. The behaviours we use there are more similar to ones we evolved with. The feedback we get from our natural environment, the sights and sounds, are more realistic of us *being a human being*, and a part of the natural world. We are less likely to be consumed by fame, wealth and status, and less likely to feel unsure of ourselves, whilst in the wilderness, compared to in a big city.

Our focus

Comparing the "internal self"/"external self" consistency theory, proposed in this chapter, to a more established one, we can consider our focus (i.e. from the concept of a "locus of evaluation", a term first used by Carl Rogers - who had a big influence on modern psychology and counselling, from his work in the mid-20th century[25]).

The idea of our "focus" (or locus of evaluation) is another way of looking at "self". Self then becomes a concept that can reside close to us, or more distant to us. If it is close to us, we have more ownership of it, whereas if it is distant from us, then our self more resides in other people, and how they judge and define us.

To bridge the gap between the two theories, we can consider why having inconsistency between our internal and external self (i.e. having less "self") may cause our focus to be more on those around us, and why we'd then judge ourselves more through comparison and feedback.

The more self we have, the more our thoughts, and who we are, resides with us. Our self is centred on us, not in a self-absorbed way, where we focus on our comparisons to others, but instead in a grounded way, where it is less influenced by others.

The reason for this, with regard to the internal/external self consistency theory proposed in this chapter, is because the more self we have, the more we come across as expected. What people see of us, is similar to how we feel we come across. The impression we make, matches our expectations and behaviours. A person with a more consistent self is more predictable, and as a result slots more easily into different places, gets into less social conflict with their peers, ruffles less feathers, and integrates into new groups with less trial and error. For a person with a more consistent self, their interactions are more comfortable. With a more consistent self, our internal self contains more realism, and is therefore drawn less to new groups, possible futures, and the heights we could achieve.

The result of this is that a person with a more consistent self has less conflicts for their thoughts to wander onto. They also aren't reliant on a narrower pocket of their life, where they do feel themselves, and so their thoughts feel less of a draw towards close friends, or groups not present. Their behaviours are more comfortable, and more easily reciprocated by anyone. More comfortable interaction means our mind wanders less onto fantasies, or imagined interactions (where difficulty is removed).

As a result, a person with a more consistent self has more ownership of their thoughts. Those thoughts spend less time on other people, good and bad.

Therefore a person with a more consistent self will have a locus of evaluation, and a focus, that resides closer to them.

Our focus is therefore perhaps a by-product of how consistent our internal and external self are. An inconsistent self can be the cause of a focus (or locus of evaluation) that is more distant to us.

We all lack self to some degree. In our modern world of complex spread-out social lives, it is unlikely that anyone has a truly consistent self, and everyone has their thoughts tied up in other people one way or the other. However, there is variation from person to person as to how much self someone has. For those lucky few who have better self, it can give a certain freedom in their thoughts and awareness, and allow them to see the wood for the trees.

With two ways to consider "self": the consistency model; and the focus (or locus of evaluation) model, we can consider two more topics. One is how we can improve the amount of self we have, and the other is how much self we can pass to others. These are quite complex topics, so it is helpful to have more than one viewpoint.

On the first, if we wish to **improve our "self"**, then considering our *"focus"* is a good way to do it. Our locus of evaluation was developed as part of therapeutic practice, and through that practice we can find understanding, focus on ourselves in a non-comparative way, and find a certain amount of self-affirmation. Then we can bring our thoughts a little closer to ourselves, and feel more ownership of our place and direction in life.

From the perspective of the *consistency model*, if we wish to improve our self, then we can consider how we come across, who we are, and what impression we make. We can try to change our approach to situations based on those. We can find acceptance in traits and attributes that we have, that we previously tried to dismiss, and to bring them into our self-definition.

However, with this, perhaps we are simply changing our behaviours, defences and reputation, in order to better integrate our circumstances into the environment we find ourselves in, rather than fundamentally changing our internal self. We may find that that internal self is still there from time to time (as it is more fixed), and our brain may default to our internal self during interactions. When our internal self occasionally pops up, it takes energy to override it, and reform our approach to a situation in a way that is closer to who we feel we are. Nevertheless, we can change our self-perception, and it can have a positive effect on our lives.

On the second point, regarding **how much "self" we can pass on**, we can firstly consider this from the point of view of *"focus"*.

Lacking self can affect how much of it we can pass on. If our thoughts and definition aren't centred on ourself, but instead dependent on others, it can be harder for us to make others feel personally valued. If we rely on comparisons and placing to define us, we may not have something core to transfer to someone else. They may feel that we are simply trying to pass on things that aren't really ours.

People with less self can inspire others to follow their own comparisons, and feel elevated and enthused to chase success (both of which have their purpose in a competitive world), but perhaps not be able to make someone feel as if something personal inside them has been recognised and nurtured.

One common relationship where this occurs is the parent-child one. A parent who lacks self may be more likely to raise a child who lacks self (although all sorts of possibilities exist depending on the circumstances). A parent whose focus is on others is more likely to raise a child with greater focus on others.

If the parent's focus is consumed with others, or strongly on those around them, then the child feels less value from them. A large part of value is time and attention, so the more a person is distracted by others, the less we feel important to them (as modern humans, we can't help but be more absorbed in our social lives, rather than be able to give our children the time and attention we want, but some more than others).

The child may respond to this by seeking greater social bonds in their friends and pursuits. But without a centred self, they may find that they get more caught up in those groups, and their self becomes more tied to others. Their focus then drifts onto others more of the time, and the result is that the parent's situation is replicated in the child's.

A Theory of Everyone

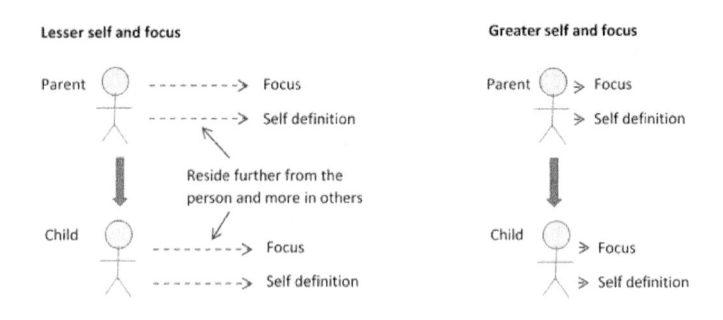

Lesser self and focus

Parent → Focus
→ Self definition

Reside further from the person and more in others

Child → Focus
→ Self definition

Greater self and focus

Parent ≽ Focus
≽ Self definition

Child ≽ Focus
≽ Self definition

Regarding the consistency model, then with less comfort and value coming from the parent, a growing adolescent is more likely to draw the fragments that make up their internal self from whoever is around them. There will be less copying of mannerisms, gestures and interactions from the parent, and instead more copying from role models that they come across. It is therefore more likely that their internal self is less consistent with their external self.

In terms of what it feels like for self not to be imparted, then sometimes we can feel that other people (parent or otherwise) look at us, but don't really see who we are. We don't feel recognised, or valued for our individuality. Without that, we are more likely to seek (or be swayed by) definition from others instead. From the other side of the interaction, sometimes we can be reticent to really take notice of the depth of another person. Or we can be more consumed by our own personality, or own headwinds, and simply not have space to be able to show recognition to others.

We all lack self one way or another, and most of this is largely irrelevant in our day to day lives. Providing we have places in our life where we can use reciprocated behaviours, be treated how we like, then we can *feel* most ourselves.

Nevertheless, against all this background, where self is difficult to find, and our focus can get drawn away from us, it can affect each person's grounding. With our focus on others, we can often forget who we are. It can be hard to think of our own needs, and act for ourselves, sometimes very hard.

The modern world is not as conducive an environment, compared to our evolutionary one, for developing a strong sense of self. How our self works will have evolved in a tribe environment, for which it is well suited, however nowadays we live in a different environment, and this can cause some side effects, and difficulties in self.

These are merely a result of the social environment we live in. As the world becomes fairer and more equal, all of this will become easier.

6

Modern Society and our Self and Web

We've now looked at our fundamental drivers, and the key aspects of modern life.

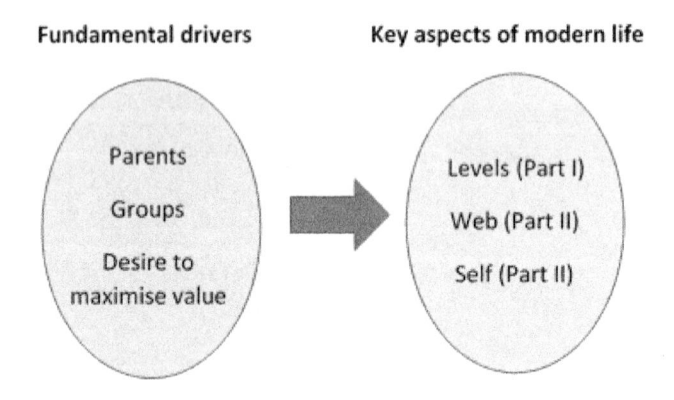

Fundamental drivers

- Parents
- Groups
- Desire to maximise value

Key aspects of modern life

- Levels (Part I)
- Web (Part II)
- Self (Part II)

We've touched on some of the consequences of living in our large modern societies, but with a programming suited for small isolated tribes. With our Levels, Self and Web described, we shall explore four more consequences of how our modern societies affect us as individuals:

1. **Personality type:** How the *type* of group in our web, that most defines us, and that we feel most ourselves in, impacts our self;
2. **Narrow values:** How being diverged affects our values and self-belief;
3. **Negative acceptance:** How being diverged affects our ability to accept negative feedback or criticism, warranted or otherwise;
4. **Unusual self-belief:** How levels can warp our internal self.

There is of course another modern issue to talk about, which is social media, and this will be covered in a later chapter in Part III. However, even without social media, our modern social environment can cause added difficulty, produce strange results, and affect our experiences as human beings.

Personality type

We looked before at how people can be very tied to a single group. They may be very sociable outside of that group, but all of their definition, comparisons and focus are strongly linked to that *one* group, even when away from it.

We all do this to some extent. We are a member of many groups, but one or two will be more important than others. It is partly a coping strategy for dealing with a spread-out social lives, and partly because our programming is looking for something tribe-shaped.

We feel most association with that one (or two) groups. Our identity gets drawn from there, and we feel we are a reflection of the people within it. Our behaviours were forged there, and we feel most ourselves when socialising there.

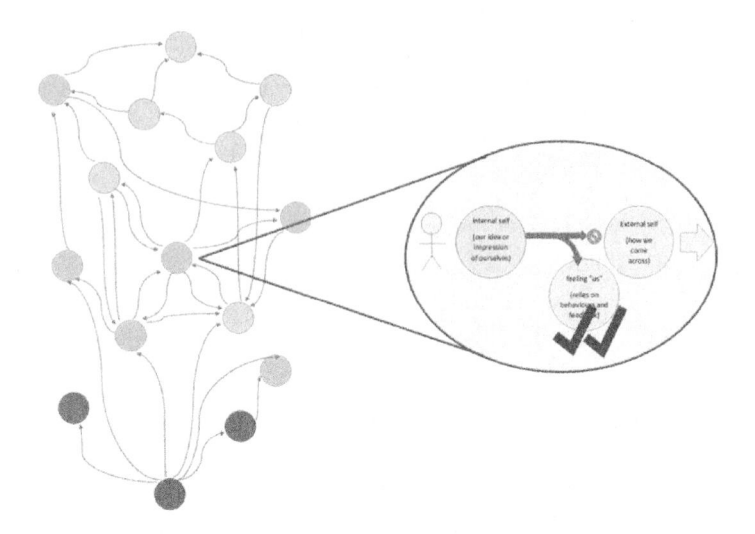

This is because it's unlikely we're treated how we like across our social spectrum, and so we deal with those situations where we aren't treated how we like, by knowing we can return to a group where we are, and so the bonds deepen.

For some people, it is just one group. For others it can be two groups, or sometimes three, but even if we have lots of friendship groups, we tend to focus on a small number for our core definition and identity.

For some people, they find this group early in life. For some people, it is their family group, although this is rare in modern civilisations. Others find it with a social group during adolescence. Others find that one group, that defines them well, later in life, in a job or role.

With our focus and definition residing a small number of groups, but our daily lives spread over many more varied interactions, then the **type** of group that we draw our definition from affects our behaviours and experiences.

Family groups are about our personal bonds. In social groups, we are often acting with contemporaries for friendship or enjoyment. With our role groups, which are often related to jobs or organisations, we need to perform required tasks, or achieve objectives, and we must adopt behaviours to be able to perform that role. Those behaviours are a reflection of the organisational culture, and often quite defined, perhaps with implicit (or explicit) rules or guidance about how to perform different interactions.

Broadly speaking, we can simplify the groups of our web into these three categories: family related, social and role.

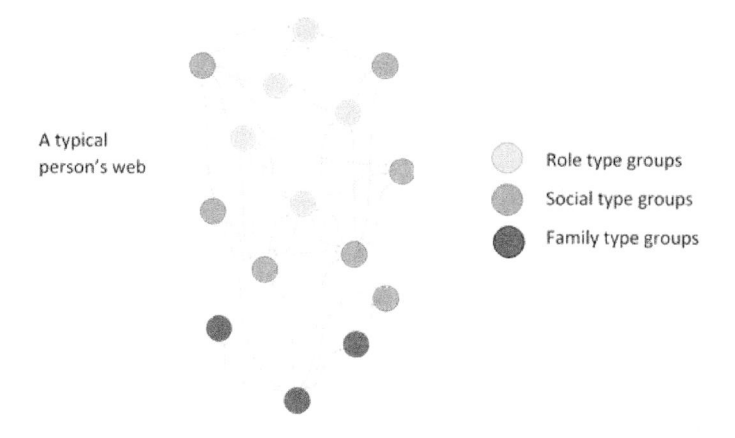

A typical person's web

○ Role type groups
◐ Social type groups
● Family type groups

Any group can become someone's main definition, but we tend to go for the earliest one that works, as well as one that mimics our parent's type of group (however much we do or don't want that to happen).

As an aside, when there is greater inequality in society, there is greater difference in levels between ourselves and those around us. People become more stretched, more likely to be diverged, and so have greater reliance on role type behaviours, and strong cultures for protection.

The type of group that a person uses as their primary definition will be associated with their level of divergence.

The further away our main group is from our parents, the more diverged we are likely to be. The closer our main group is to our parents, the more we are able to see similarities with, and draw definition from, our family group.

If a social group is where we most feel ourselves, we are likely to be somewhat diverged. A role type group (where our behaviours, and sense of belonging, are generally taken from an organisation) is likely to be associated with greater divergence. The more diverged we are, the narrower our focus and area of comfort, so role type groups (where the sub-culture is more defined) suit us.

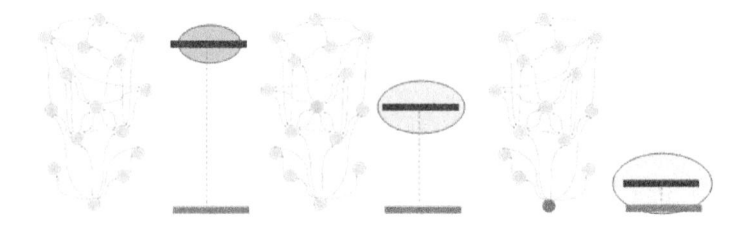

Even the family type person will be diverged a little. This is because of the "social delta": which comes from the need for parents to reduce their children a little more than they'd like (for example to ensure they don't "out value" the parent); and due to the variety in sub-culture from group to group, in our spread-out social lives.

There are exceptions to the above three cases, most notably when someone is largely diverged but strongly tied to one social group, but otherwise the general trend above appears to hold.

Whether our main group is role type, social type or family type impacts us in a few ways:
1. The types of **behaviours** we use in our daily lives
2. How we feel **valued** and how we encourage others to value themselves
3. Where we go for support and **dependency**

The following brief sections explore each of these, as well as discussing some of the resulting traits and characteristics in people.

Behaviours

We take our behaviours from many different places in life: our friends, our role models, our job, and our family and parents. We copy and learn behaviours from others, and this results in a situation where each human learns a set of behaviours that integrates with those around them. Using those behaviours then makes us feel ourselves.

With our spread-out social lives, where we can come across such a large range of behaviours, we tend to zone in on one or two groups, and our behaviours are drawn from those groups, and reflect their sub-culture. We then only fully feel ourselves in those groups. Our behaviours outside of this group then become shaped by it, and our whole personality can form around it.

The "type" of group that we zone in on, that most defines us, can affect our behaviours as a whole. For example, if we are role type, we feel most ourself, and most comfortable, using behaviours that are appropriate for that role.

In general, the behaviours we copy from our parents are the easiest to do. We do them even without thinking. We don't have to consciously try them out, test them, or think too hard about doing them beforehand. Even if we don't like our parent's behaviours, we may often find that we end up using them, because when we are challenged, we sometimes have to respond quickly and naturally, and those behaviours that we subconsciously copy from our parents are the most at our fingertips. It has to be this way in order for humans to favour copying behaviours from their parents, so that our parents act as a social anchor, whether we want them to or not.

When a person diverges, they tend to copy behaviours from their social and role groups instead of those of the parent. The more diverged we are, the more different our behaviours are likely to be compared to our parent's. They feel entirely natural to the person using them (even if they are very different), because when they are in their main group, they feel accepted, and their behaviours are reciprocated by others. However, when we view others, we can often tell whether someone is using more natural behaviours, or whether they are using behaviours that they've copied from a group in their web further from their parents. They use them trying to appear natural, but it just doesn't quite come off, or there are inconsistencies, that the person appears to disregard. This is just one of the side effects of how being diverged affects behaviours.

The set of behaviours we end up with as an adult can be quite fixed. We can change them, and adapt to different circumstances, but we are bending our personality, away from what makes us feel most ourself. Towards the end of adolescence, as we become an adult, our behaviours become interlinked with our web, and our main bonds and comparisons.

Therefore, as adults, we tend to have fairly fixed behaviours, and they tend to be drawn largely from a single group. How diverged we are, and the resulting type of group that we draw our behaviours from, can have a big impact on what they are.

Value

We can feel valued whatever type of person we are. However, our type: whether role, social or family; can have an impact on *why* we feel valued.

Humans are very good at sensing value. Sometimes someone says something supportive, and we don't quite feel it, and other times all we get from someone is a smile or nod, and we can feel very valued. We know what kind of value we want, and we can sense when we get it and when we don't, even if we can't always articulate why.

There are two main types of value, personal value and comparative value. Personal value is more about us just feeling valued as a person, whilst comparative value is us being valued in comparison to other people. Both can feel equally good, and perhaps comparative value can even feel better. However, comparative value is more likely to come with highs and lows. It makes us feel good for a while, but then it passes, and we want more of it. In contrast, personal value leaves us feeling content and satisfied.

The further away from our parents that our main definition is drawn from, the more we have to rely on comparative value. The closer we are to our parents, the more personal value we are likely to have, and the less we are affected by comparative value. We can still compete and succeed, but there is less on the line for us: we are happier in ourselves as we are.

If our parents are role type people, or strongly rely on comparative value one way or the other, then there will be greater distance to the child, and the child will likely replicate the parent's situation.

A role type person may find it hard to give personal value to their children. They may try to act rewardingly towards the child, trying to pass on value, but to the child it just feels as if the parent is trying to pass on value from their role group, rather than it coming from themselves. This is often confusing and frustrating for the child, who feels both valued and not valued at the same time, and who then distances themselves from the parent, and seeks their own comparative value. Alternatively, the parent may directly try to encourage the child to seek their own comparative value. Either way, a role type parent will likely result in role type children (although efforts to try to pass on personal value are normally beneficial in the long run).

If we are around role type people, it's likely they will try to encourage us to be valued in a similar way to them, i.e. valued because of our role. To them, they believe this is how people should be valued. This is for a few reasons. Firstly, it is difficult to understand that others can feel valued without the role, if we haven't felt that ourselves. Secondly, if we lack personal value, we may find we wish to deny it in others, so that we aren't disadvantaged. Thirdly, encouraging others to be valued in the same way we are, reinforces our own value. If others value the same things we do, they are more likely to see us according to our identity level. The same is true of social type people, who will encourage us to seek value because of our friendships and associations. Everyone tries a little to encourage others to be valued in similar ways to themselves.

Perhaps personal value is what we really want, but it's rarely given to us as much as we'd like. To feel it we'd have to have a parent that felt it from their parent, and theirs from theirs etc.

Modern Society and our Self and Web

In reality, most people feel valued by comparing themselves to others, to some extent.

The hunter-gatherer tribe environment is much more favourable for us to receiving personal value, not least because there is no greater comparative value to be had outside of that group (like becoming a rock star or famous athlete).

In the modern world, our lives include much more comparative value. However, some people rely on comparative value more than others, and it can be traced to the type of group, whether family, social or role, that most defines them.

Therefore, the *type* of group that someone uses as their main source of definition, and comparisons, will indicate the *way* they feel valued.

Dependency

Our type also affects our dependence.

Our dependence is who we rely on, who we turn to, or simply how we go about sorting our problems, when and if they arise.

Generally, we seek dependence in our group type. A role type person will be more likely to use their role environment. A social type person will use their friends more, and a parental type person will feel more able to turn to their parents. It may be that, even if we don't talk to someone about our problem directly, it can be sorted simply by being in the group where we feel most ourselves.

The most effective way of solving problems is with our parents, theoretically at least. But often it isn't possible. It can be terrifying and brave to turn to our parents with a problem, especially if there is some conflict between us.

But it's not just overcoming this. If our parents are diverged, and, say, role type, they may be less good at giving advice, relating to our emotions or situation, or saying something that makes us feel better. Some people are just better at this than others anyway, but the role type parent may be more likely to encourage us to seek dependence from our role, or someone related to our role, instead of them.

If our parents are diverged, then it's less likely that they received good dependence from their own parents, and therefore may struggle to give it to us.

Add to this the fact that the closer we are to someone, the more we see their inherited level, i.e. how they're reacting to people around them, and how they really feel about their situation. This is none truer than when a child wants to be close to their parent for support. If the parent is diverged, and trying to protect their identity level, and prevent people exposing their inherited level (which will be fairly apparent to the child), then they may be more distant and less personally supportive to their children.

Therefore we seek dependency in the area of our life comfortable to us. Mostly, this won't be our parents. It may be a social group, or it may be the place where we get to use role-type behaviours, depending on which is our main group in our web. This reinforces that group as being the main source of our definition, and, with the behaviours and values, generally cements one or two groups as forming the basis of ourselves.

The type of group we use as our main source of support, in feeling ourselves, therefore affects how we go about dependence. Perhaps we'd all like more supportive parents (and perhaps our children will want us to be more supportive), but in the modern world, the social environment can make this difficult. We should always try to do the best we can with what we've got, but nevertheless if we look at all the people around us, they all solve dependence in different ways.

Personality type conclusion

In conclusion, different people use different types of groups as their main definition. This is related to our level of divergence, and the more diverged we are, the greater the difference there will be between our main group and our family group.

The **type** of group that we adopt as our main group can have a big impact on our personality, whether through our *behaviours*, the way we feel *valued*, or the way we go about *dependency*.

This section also shows the different ways that, one way or another, children tend to follow similar patterns to their parents. Some of the ways this happens are unintentional, most happen whether we like them or not, and some happen even when we believe we're going on a different path.

Narrow values

On the second point about modern life in this chapter, we can consider how different people in large societies may have broader or narrower values.

We all have a set of values, and we all have influences that constrain our values more than we'd like.

Some have a narrower set than others, and show approval to a smaller range of values and behaviours, compared to others. They may show less acceptance, and more disapproval. Other people may have a broader set of values.

Whether our set of values is narrower or broader can come down to a range of factors. One of them is our level of divergence. When we are more diverged, we are more stretched, and can become more constrained, and find it harder to be ourself across a broad range of experiences.

However, as we shall see, even if our values and beliefs are narrower, our internal self (which is trying to feel like a proud hunter-gatherer) works around this, and disregards a lot of what happens in our lives, in order to feel like we are broader in our life context regardless.

In terms of how levels can cause a narrowing of our values, then the further our identity is away from our parents, the more we have to deepen our focus and interactions with the people around us, in order to prevent feeling any negative consequences of the dynamic between us and our parents. We are in a situation where our link to our parents, and their link to us, is at odds with our need to fit into a social group. The more diverged we are, the more we rely on that group to define us, and the more we absorb from it. Then, expressing or contemplating a broader set of values is harder.

In terms of our interactions, being more diverged means we are more affected by conflict. We have to deepen our convictions, and find we have less freedom to be ourselves, because we have more to lose, and a greater need to maintain associations and support of the people around us. Our beliefs and values therefore become narrower.

For example, in the following diagram, persons A and B are more diverged, and therefore have less freedom in their experiences. They are more stretched, and face greater consequences from not being treated according to their identity level. They may also have to resolve more challenges, which narrows beliefs, due to it placing greater importance of what they have to use as defences to those provocations. In order for persons A and B to get along, they have to be more aligned in their beliefs, in order for them to overlap.

Persons C and D have broader freedom in their interactions. They have less to lose, and so can interact more comfortably with people more distant, or different, to them.

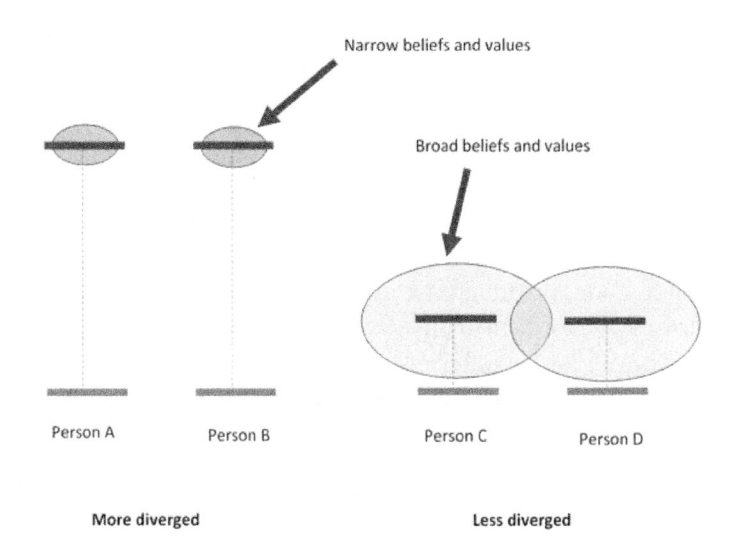

Narrow beliefs and values

Broad beliefs and values

Person A   Person B   Person C   Person D

More diverged   **Less diverged**

Narrow beliefs are often most felt, or noticed, by those close to us, and particularly our children. Our children are tuned to pick up and replicate our inherited level, but pressure to meet our identity level. The narrower we are, the narrower the set of values that we approve of, which can be restrictive or frustrating for our children, and in turn this causes their own narrow context.

As stated already, the more diverged person, to them, still has only one level: their identity.

So, to them, even if they are narrow in their experiences, they may still believe they are broad. When they have interactions outside their narrow area of comfort, that don't quite fit with their identity, their brain just ignores or disregards

A Theory of Everyone

these, even if other people notice. To that person, they know that under certain circumstances they can be themselves, and behave how they want, and since our conscious thought only has space for one level, then humans just don't consider those other negative interactions as important. We know they happen, but they just aren't "us". "Us" is where our behaviours fit, and we are treated how we want, and where we feel ourselves.

This is an example of our hunter-gatherer programming trying to be a complete, content human, in an environment where it isn't possible (for us, or anyone else really). This causes our programming to use some common coping strategies, in order to try to feel like that proud hunter-gatherer, and ignore (or fail to believe) that we may have narrow values, no matter our circumstances. A few common examples of how this plays out are:

Situational

The person finds they feel "themselves" in certain environments, interactions, situations or topics of conversation, but not others. Perhaps the environment is socialising in a particular location, or, the situation is a group that has a strong set of rules, or the topic of conversation is one that favours them, such as sport, music, politics or technical topics.

Other people notice their behaviour when not in their zone of comfort, but whilst that person doesn't quite feel themselves then, they disregard it. It's simply not who they are, and it has no weight in their personality, because when they return to their area of comfort, they can meet their identity. To others, they are seeing that person's inherited position (when not in their area of comfort) and their identity (when they are). But to the person, they are disregarding those interactions where they aren't behaving according to their identity, and not giving them importance. To others, perhaps both seem important.

This can cause strange results, for example where we observe someone behaving with hesitancy or nerves, but when we interact with them, they interact with us on the basis that that hesitancy or nerves didn't happen. This is mostly not a problem, and everyone does it to some extent.

Compensating

The person has a group where they feel most themselves, and this group forms a large part of their identity. However, whilst the person interacts comfortably in that group, they can only do so with some compensation from the other group members. Perhaps it is mutually beneficial to provide this compensation, or there is a strong sub-culture or cliqueness that allows the person to interact comfortably.

Outside of this group, the person's identity is still there, and they still expect to be treated according to it, but they can't generate it on their own. They are reliant on others to provide some compensating feedback. But they have disregarded this compensation. To them, they are simply themselves, and fully associate with, and feel a part of, their identity group. They view people outside the group from that viewpoint. They disregard the idea that others are compensating their identity.

This can produce a strange result when people outside the identity group don't provide the compensation. The person then struggles to achieve their identity, feels threatened and provoked, and responds by reducing or rivalling those that don't provide the compensation.

Isolated group

The person finds a group of like-minded people, perhaps with similar needs, and levels of divergence. Together, they provide an environment where each person treats the others according to their identity. They can do so because it is mutually beneficial: they each raise the others up. These groups then tend to become quite cliquey or isolated, because if someone who is less diverged joins, they may find some rejection or dismissiveness, because that new person may break the illusion.

The person who is a part of these isolated groups then deepens their interactions within it, and disregards those outside of it. They have found their belonging, and place of security; it's just gets a little more fragile, and a little more isolated, the more diverged we are. These groups tend to have very narrow values, that require strong conformance.

* * *

Everyone uses one of these three strategies: situational, compensating and isolated group, one way or the other.

All of us are trying to feel like we would in a tribe, when our modern spread-out social lives doesn't allow it. Our programming is urging us towards feeling complete, regardless of the obstacles in the way.

We likely don't really notice it in ourselves, or people we come across, it's just the status quo. However, we may notice it in our parents, where it can be a source of frustration. Our subconscious brain is trying to copy the parents, but it finds inconsistencies in what the parent believes, and how they come across. It can lead to a little confusion and frustration. If the child placates the parent, and supports their identity level, they find it harder to maintain their own, against all the places where it doesn't quite fit. If the child doesn't support the parent's identity level, then the parent often shows annoyance.

A balance is often struck however. A natural compromise often happens without any logical thought, and the child develops their own coping strategy, for feeling their identity as often as possible.

Negative acceptance

On the third point, we shall consider negative acceptance.

We all face criticism, negative feedback, or challenges trying to reduce us, from time to time. Some people can brush them off easily, whereas other people find these types of interactions much harder.

One common factor, in how we receive negative feedback, is our levels, and how diverged we are. The more diverged we are, the further we have to fall, so we become more sensitive to negative feedback or provocations.

Our web and self can also play a role. If we have rivalries in our web somewhere, then we may find negative acceptance harder, due to the tied thoughts of how our rivals will respond to the negative feedback we've received, if they were present.

Similarly, our self can play a role too. For example if the fragments of information, memories, feedback, interactions, and snapshots, that make up our internal self, are inconsistent with how we come across, then it's quite likely we've disregarded many things about us. Our internal idea, or impression, of how we come across, may not include some realities about us, and when people point them out, it can be frustrating.

Negative acceptance is when someone criticises us, points out a flaw, or gives us negative feedback (or sometimes merely a lack of positive feedback). This can be warranted, constructive, or simply trying to provoke us.

Negative acceptance, of our less favourable traits, attributes and behaviours, can be very difficult for human beings anyway.

We all have them; we make mistakes, we have odd behaviours, and we are all odd shapes and sizes. We're human beings after all. We try to be more accepting of them, but it's often not our fault that we struggle to do so. Negative aspects of ourself can be exploited, focussed upon, or used to undermine us, even when we accept them ourselves. Someone pointing out a negative trait can simply be a provocation or challenge, unrelated to the actual words that were said.

However, if we're diverged, we take any challenge or provocation harder. We looked at this earlier, as shown in the diagrams below.

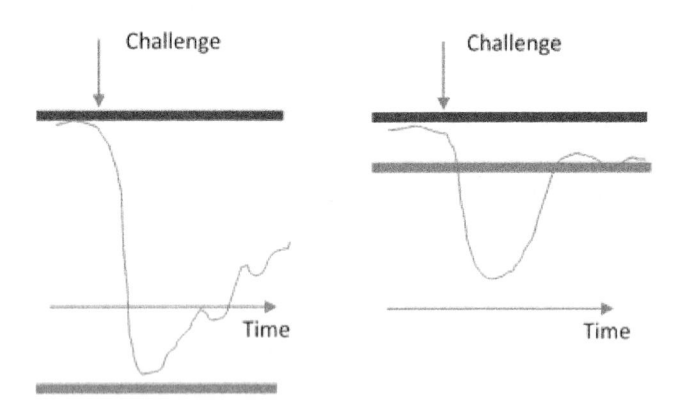

[Two diagrams showing "Challenge" arrows with curves plotted against Time axes]

The person who is more diverged has to work harder to maintain and recover to their identity after being provoked. Therefore, negative acceptance is harder, because provocations are more difficult to brush off, and we have to rely more on our defences in order to resolve challenges, which in turn causes those defences to become more engrained in us.

There are a few more reasons why being diverged makes negative acceptance harder.

Firstly, the more diverged we are, the more obtrusive our behaviours are likely to be, in order to bridge the gap between our inherited level and our identity level. This obtrusiveness may ruffle other people's feathers, and this can lead to retaliation, where we then face criticism and negative feedback more often.

Secondly, the negative feedback, and "denial of self" (where people don't treat us according to who we feel we are), reflect the dynamic with our parent. If we're diverged, it means that our parents are less likely to recognise our identity level (and us theirs). They may provide some resistance, for example not fully recognising our achievements, or pointing out our inconsistencies (which we all have). We tend to see ourself according to our identity level, but others according to their inherited level, and this is true in families also. When people in society do this, it strikes a chord with us, because it echoes our dynamic with our parent. We may get tied thoughts to our parents, and find that we then have to fight that battle in our minds, as well as the one in front of us.

This relationship between divergence and negative feedback is another reason why: the more diverged we are, the more obtrusive we become. For example, we may learn to head negative feedback off at the pass, and try to avoid receiving it. Or we may react strongly to negative feedback if we do receive it, and retaliate. Both responses become stronger, and more obtrusive, the more that negative feedback affects us.

The more equal society becomes, the less diverged that people will be, and the broader people can be in their life circumstances. The level of provocations, rivalries and pressures will decrease, meaning negative provocations will occur less often. Self will become easier to find, and more consistent and realistic. Negative acceptance will become both easier, and less important.

Self belief

On the final point, we looked before at how a close integrated tribe, with no external influences, or external possible greater value, produces humans with self-surety, and a greater appreciation of human core needs.

In contrast, in our large unequal societies, our self-belief can become unconstrained, deluded, unrealistic, and with fantasies and expectations. This can be because whilst we are all interlinked, there is the possibility, however small, of making big leaps over people, and raising our status towards the top. The mere possibility of this happening can cause our self-belief to latch on to ideas of grandeur.

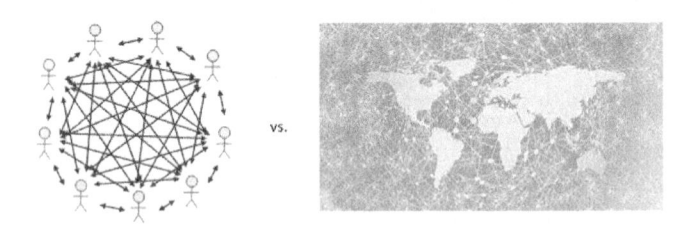

Everyone might get thoughts of greatness from time to time. For some they are momentary, but for others they can be long lasting, and embedded in our personalities in adulthood, even amongst those who otherwise come across as normal. We get a sense of other people's thoughts, but we will never know where they think they're heading, and what they believe about themselves, or their future expectations.

However, when levels are involved, it is not just greatness that can change our self-belief. The need to be our identity level (who we feel we are), against the headwind of our inherited level (how we respond to the world around us), and compete with others doing the same, can cause some unusual conclusions of self-belief, as our brains try to resolve it all.

The following three examples show ways in which our self belief can become a little distorted due to levels. Each is dependent on the feedback we get, and our experiences and possibilities in life.

Unconstrained

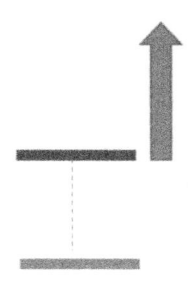

Sometimes, when there is the possibility of attaining greater value, we think about it. We wonder what it must feel like. The more realistic the possibility, the more we feel an urge to chase it, attain it, and feel elevated and lifted up. We dream, we imagine, we want. Our programming is in a large part driven by a desire to maximise our value.

However, the problem is that our programming is also anchored to a point, which represents where we started from in life. This comes from our parents: i.e. our inherited level.

It's actually our parents that, in theory, provide the realism of self-belief. I say in theory, because if they don't have realism themselves, it may be hard to pass it on.

An example of this is the possibility of people becoming **unconstrained** from their parents. Perhaps the child has fitted in at a level the parent feels powerless to impose themselves against, or something has happened in the parent's life that prevents them holding any authority at all.

If we become unconstrained, there may be little downward balancing force coming from our parents, and so our self-belief sees no bounds. We become freer to imagine the heights we could achieve, and there is no restoring force. Perhaps these heights are even somewhat achievable. However, we are still linked and bonded to our parents, so we find frustration in this circumstance. Our unconstrained beliefs can become uncomfortable, especially when, after a while, we need to find an *actual* place to fit in, and it might not match where we thought we might.

Being unconstrained may sound desirable, but there is a catch. Without parents feeling authority over us, they aren't able to show pride and support. Our parents feel a driver for us to be a reflection of them, and look up to them, no matter the actual circumstances, and if the circumstances don't allow this, it can be a source of pain. If the parent has lost the ability to impose themselves on the child, then the child may feel less love and comfort as a result.

Luck, chance and success

If we achieve a comfortable, secure jump up in value, so that we're not unconstrained, but just fitting in at a higher level, our self-belief wants to find reasons why *we* made that happen. Perhaps we did make it happen. However, there are 7 billion people on the planet, and a huge range of circumstances, opportunities, coincidences, personalities, behaviours and situations. When these align, and fortune smiles on us, or a series of chance events gives us an open door, we can find ourselves secure at a higher level. For everyone this happens to, there is someone else who it didn't.

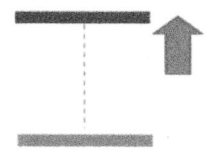

However, it affects our self-belief, because of competition and purpose. We can't say it is all just chance, because we need to maintain our identity level. We are challenged and provoked by those around us, and see people getting ahead in life by acting with strong purpose or conviction, at least in some places. To interact in this environment, we need to find some purpose and conviction ourselves. As a result, our success was down to us, solely. We find something positive about us, perhaps a trait or attribute, and we say that is why we got where we are. It wasn't circumstance, fortune or chance, it was us. And after a while we really believe this. Occasionally we consider the possibility of otherwise, but then tied thoughts come into our mind, of people that compete with us with purpose or conviction, and we find we have to resolve back to our narrow beliefs.

Plus, if we promote ourselves, we can come across as more attractive, compared to someone who takes no personal credit for their successes.

This is all very well, happens a lot, and generally doesn't cause too much conflict, but the reality is that the beliefs we have probably aren't wholly true. There will be complex, nuanced, and possibly entirely random reasons why, out of 7 billion people, we got to where we are.

For most people this isn't a problem. However, for those close to us, in competition with us, or our children, this can cause some frustration. We are acting with purpose on a half-truth, and ignoring circumstance, which puts pressure on them to do the same, in order to maintain a position with respect to us.

Lack of positive feedback

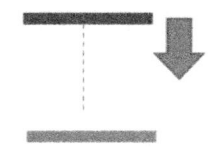

Finally, there is the other side, when we aren't meeting our identity level, or are below where we want to be. This also affects our self-belief.

If we aren't treated according to our identity level it can be frustrating. If our interactions aren't acceptable or comfortable, we tend to try to disregard them in favour of ones where we do meet our identity level. If there aren't any around us, often we look to the future. We think about future interactions where we have the success we want, and people treat us how we like. This could be realistic or unrealistic. The present is difficult and hard to accept, but the future is how we want it. We have hope, and we have a driving force for getting to our identity level, and making things better.

This is all well and good, but now we interact with others on the basis of who we might be in the future, rather than the present circumstances. Again, this isn't a problem, and may help us to get to where we want to go, but it creates a more confusing social environment, where other people have self-beliefs, based on things we aren't aware of.

The more we don't meet our identity level, the harder our brain works. If our interactions aren't acceptable, sometimes our brain can even create fantasy interactions in our thoughts. Our brains are trying to feel like a proud hunter-gatherer. As we have seen, they can disregard a lot of information right in front of us, in order to do so. When pushed a little more, our brains can even create fantasies, future or present, where we feel more complete.

We imagine others treating us how we want to be treated. We imagine a scenario where we find success and are adulated and accepted. These fantasies can feel real, and affect our emotions. The world around us isn't quite how we want it, but in our fantasies it is. Some of these may be tied thoughts to people we know, however some of these are more creative.

Everyone does this to a certain extent. You sometimes get a sense that someone is imagining or reacting to something not there, which could be a tied thought to an actual interaction, or a fantasy interaction.

Essentially, our brain is trying to feel fulfilled, like it would do as a hunter-gatherer. It wants our key drivers to be satisfied, but our modern world throws obstacles in the way. Despite this, our brain is trying to ignore those obstacles, and form an internal self that is good regardless. It can disregard information, and fill in the gaps where necessary.

In a hunter-gatherer tribe, we would have our needs met, feel comfortable, and feel belonging and approval. Even after 12,000 years of leaving our hunter-gatherer past, our brains are still trying to feel like we would in that environment. We can't ever replicate it, when there is more apparent value out there, but we can understand how it affects our own perceptions, and those of the people around us.

Modern society and self & web summary

In a large unequal society, with possibilities of greatness, our social lives spread over several groups, and with everyone a little diverged, we can be more or less, future or past, unconstrained or ignoring circumstance, or living in fantasies or possibilities.

Our self can often be elusive. It is trying to exist against a backdrop that is different to the environment it is suited for. Some feel greater self, some less. On average, self is harder to find than it should be.

Through our spread-out social lives, we often have to focus on a small number of groups more than others, or focus on an idea or purpose, to solidify our self, and our brain then tries to work out the rest. Often our brain disregards quite a lot, which can produce some interesting results.

A hunter-gatherer tribe allows a good self to form, and doesn't test that self often. Our modern social environment is less conducive to producing good self, and tests that self more often.

Compared to a hunter-gatherer tribe, where our self is like a well-oiled machine, in a modern world our self is like a machine that has some parts supercharged but other parts missing, and some parts with too much oil and other parts not enough.

Nevertheless, providing we have places where we feel ourselves, and are treated consistent with who we feel we are, most other things become irrelevant. The more diverged we are, or the more inconsistent our self is, perhaps that place is harder to find, but when we find it, the rest is inconsequential.

Part Three

Interactions

Part Three Introduction

So far in the book, we've looked at the three fundamental drivers, and the three key aspects of being a modern human being.

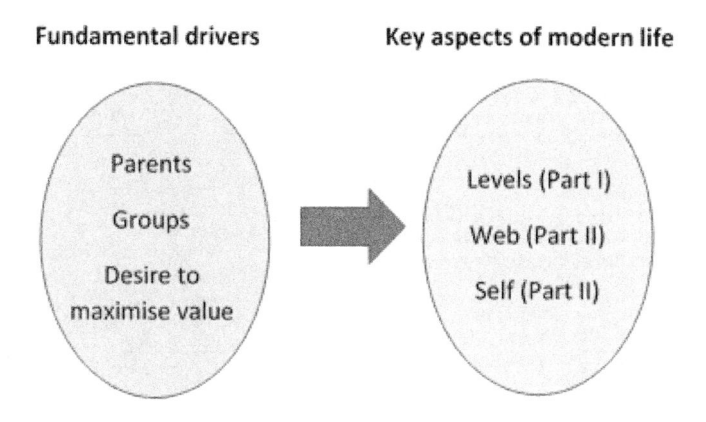

Fundamental drivers

- Parents
- Groups
- Desire to maximise value

Key aspects of modern life

- Levels (Part I)
- Web (Part II)
- Self (Part II)

As we discussed in the previous chapter, we don't really experience the world this way, even if they're the driving forces. We tend to view the world through our interpersonal interactions, and it is often hard to remove ourself from a situation, in order to be able to understand why it's happening.

Life is supposed to be this way, where we get caught up in social interactions, good and bad, that consume the majority of our focus. Through this process we are linked to others. If we weren't affected by what others did, and how they behaved towards us, then we wouldn't be able to create integrated social groups, where people work together, and look after each other. If we didn't feel compelled to change our behaviours, actions and motivations, depending on the influences of others, then we wouldn't be able to create groups that move as one, with a common culture and purpose.

As beings, we are more front-line troops in our lives, rather than generals surveying the battlefield. Or, even if we understand the state of the battlefield, we still have to fight at the front line of our own particular circumstances.

Therefore, whilst we can consider the cause of behaviours; Part III is about how we actually experience interpersonal interactions in our daily lives.

7

Simple Rules for Understanding Human Beings

The first aspect of interactions to look at is two simple rules.

Human behaviour can get very complicated. Our mind can get snagged on what people say, rather than why they said it. People project one thing, but mean another. People get frustrated at others for reasons we can't relate to. People seem convinced they come across one way, but we just don't see it.

Everything else in this book is about trying to explain all that complexity, but this chapter is about really simple rules.

You can forget all the complexity by considering two simple rules. These rules are the basic building blocks of interactions.

Rule 1: "...people try to make other people feel like they do..."

Rule 2: "...every behaviour in some way reflects an aspect of a person's relationship with their parents..."

They are perhaps an exaggeration, and the second rule may raise an eyebrow or two, but bear with me. So, lets dive into the first of these rules, and look at them in a little more detail.

1. "...people try to make other people feel like they do..."

We are not telepathic beings. We aren't able to transfer thoughts and emotions directly into someone else's brain. And yet our emotions are interlinked. They need to be so that, in groups, each person's needs are accounted for. If one person's needs aren't accounted for, then this affects the others in the group, which provides motivation for a social group to integrate and look after each other.

We feel compassion and empathy. When we feel good, we may want to cheer others up. But if we feel bad, we need to communicate that too.

We transfer a lot of our emotion to other people, not through telepathy, but through behaviours. How we behave towards someone causes their brain to interpret this, and produce an emotion. And the emotion produced in that person will be somewhat similar to how we feel. The two are connected.

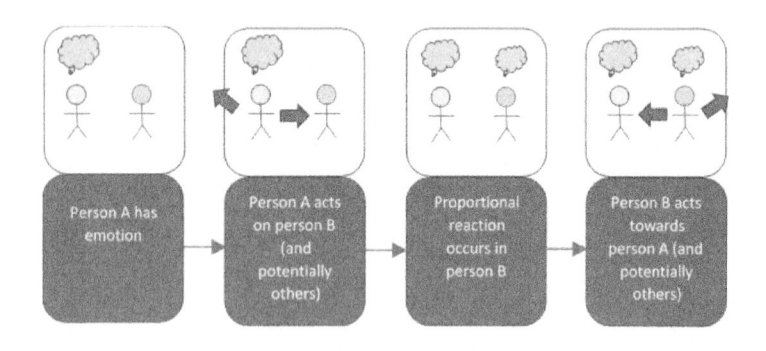

Person A has emotion	Person A acts on person B (and potentially others)	Proportional reaction occurs in person B	Person B acts towards person A (and potentially others)

Simple Rules for Understanding Human Beings

Social beings across the natural world, whether humans or otherwise, don't communicate how we feel through complex reasoning and explanations. We don't articulate exactly how we feel, and eloquently explain the reasons for it, good or bad. Even if we did, it's possible that another person could just ignore it. Instead, we do it through our actions.

Positive emotions are most easily shared. When we feel good, we tend to feel more enabled in socialising, and want to spend time with others, and cheer them up too, or at least have a good time with them, for ourself.

In terms of negative emotions, we may not want to act on these, but it's just hard not to sometimes. If we didn't, we'd simply be left with those unwelcome emotions by ourselves. Part of us wants someone else to feel (at least a part of) how we do, so they can understand our current difficulty.

Making others aware of our difficulty means they are connected to us, and emotions are shared so that, in theory, each person's emotions are accounted for. This allows beings to create social groups of individuals. Each individual participates in the group, and each individual's needs and emotions are shared, and we create connections with those around us.

There is a second side to why people make others feel like they do. When we feel positive, we feel more enabled and confident, and when we feel negative, we can feel a little more reserved. When we feel negative emotions, we can feel a little weakened. We're more likely to feel threatened by those around us, and we are more likely to challenge them to level the playing field, to ensure that they can't take advantage of our slightly weakened state.

We therefore make others feel like we do in order to create connected social groups, and in order to level the playing field.

There are of course many difficult emotions out there, borne in unusual and varied circumstances, that aren't able to be fixed simply by sharing them. This is the crux of living in large societies. Nevertheless, like the move to equality, there is somewhat of a move to equal emotions. The end point is with everyone content. At the moment, many people chase excessive pleasure and gain, which often comes from getting ahead of others. Clearly therefore not everyone in society can feel that excessive pleasure. As the dust settles on our slowly developing societies, emotions will become more spread out and evened out, with less highs and lows, and greater contentment.

In both cases, making someone else feel like we do, good or bad, also gives us an internal reward in our own emotions. When it is good emotions we're sharing, the reward is for spreading our current fortunate circumstances. When it is bad emotions we're sharing, the reward is for lessening of our own burden, although it will have some side effects of guilt and regret. Nevertheless, by making others feel some of our negative emotion, we have increased the likelihood of others being aware of a predicament we are in, giving them motivation to try to resolve it, and levelling the playing field between ourselves and them. In the modern world, there are of course many more constructive and successful ways of resolving difficult emotions without simply taking them out on others (especially when the complexity of modern society can prevent full resolution of difficulty), but that is the base programming mechanism. The behaviours prevalent in a society, and across the world, are indicative of the emotions and circumstances felt by people living there.

Therefore, according to this rule at least, if someone challenges us, and makes us feel a certain way, it's likely that they feel that same emotion, or are trying to avoid a similar emotion (or the same thing was done or said to them in the past). Behaviours are indicative of the sharing, transmission, and interlinking of emotions. We may not know *why* they feel it (although we can try to think of reasons why they might), but we may feel the impact of their behaviours regardless.

2. "...every behaviour in some way reflects an aspect of a person's relationship with their parents..."

Considering the second rule, this rule is perhaps a little of an exaggeration, but then perhaps not. We are so bound to our parents, throughout our lives. They are often at the core of our thoughts, even if we don't want them to be, and avoid them. They sit at the foundation of our web, and can have an impact on how each of the other groups, that we come across, are formed. We can certainly find ways to deal with difficult parents, and find support and love elsewhere, but it's hard to avoid them completely.

For social beings such as ourselves, who maintain lifelong bonds with our parents, and who we spend roughly a quarter of our lives (the first part), dependent upon, and in close proximity to them (however fortunate or unfortunate you may view that), they tend to underly our lives.

But we actually spend the vast majority of our lives socialising with friends and colleagues. Our minds tend to get drawn in to *those* bonds, and we feel most ourselves in their company. This split, where there is an underlying driving force, which is separate and outside of the place where we most feel ourselves, causes transference, as we looked at earlier:

Modern web

Transference

Place to use our behaviours, group security, feel ourselves

Anchor for human programming and source of emotions

As a rule of thumb, you can actually say that this transference is almost complete, and that everything someone does reflects an aspect of their relationship with their parents, in some way. It could be a way they behave towards their parents, or a way their parents behave towards them. Having parents are one of the only sureties in life, and so are the source of some of the fixed nature of our programming.

We project annoyances from our parents onto others. If something our parents do annoys us, when someone else does it, it annoys us too. We follow similar paths to our parents, as we looked at earlier with personality type, whether it is family, social or role based. If our parents are diverged, we will likely diverge. The frustration we feel at having to maintain our identity level, in our daily lives, mirrors the frustration in the respective parent-child dynamic.

Simple Rules for Understanding Human Beings

When threatened, our parent's behaviours are the easiest to use to defend ourselves, even if we don't want to use them. This is because behaviours we copy from our parents are most at our fingertips, and the easiest to use without thinking.

If a parent isn't nice to a child, they are less likely to be nice to other people. If a parent is controlling over their child, the child will more likely be controlling to other people. If someone feels undervalued by their parents, they're more likely to make others feel undervalued.

This isn't about blame, and it doesn't really help with resolving disputes, but it simply allows us to understand. Parents are bonded to their children through very strong forces and often do *all they can in the circumstances*, whilst wishing they could do more, or explain themselves better. Our current arrangement of society simply doesn't allow parents to do everything they *could* do. That being said, any genuinely positive effort that parents make for their children generally helps.

This simply explains some of the more unusual or unexpected behaviour. It doesn't mean that the parents are the cause of that behaviour, or that everything about a parent gets mirrored in their children. It just means that as we head out into life, whatever circumstances we find ourselves in, we still maintain a tether, or link, to our parents, and how we interact in those circumstances is some reflection of that tether. This rule is perhaps a way to step back from our circumstances for a moment and understand why things are happening, and then to re-engage with it.

And of course, every parent has their own parent. If every behaviour represents an aspect of a human's relationship with their parents, then our parent's behaviours were borne from our grandparents (and so on), and emotions and behaviours flow down generations in a cascade.

At the core, this also explains: what someone didn't get, or finds difficult, with their parents, they will find difficult to do with their own children.

What someone didn't get with their parents gets caught up in their social lives and interactions, and then, when faced with their own children, they face tied thoughts, influences and conflicts, from multiple directions, affecting their feelings.

We've been Homo Sapiens for 200,000 years, and our common ancestors date back millions of years. We've been living in large societies for thousands of years. Yet there are still many difficult parental relationships in the world. It's unlikely therefore that we are getting better with each generation. If we were, we would be perfect parents by now.

In reality, there are strong forces at play determining the relationship between parents and children. Difficulty in society is mirrored in difficult parent-child relationships, and difficult parent-child relationships are transferred into society. The two are linked, with one underlying the other.

This rule is perhaps an exaggeration, because of course we have our own individuality, our own personality, our own uniqueness, and we head out into the world, and experience our own story and direction. But, we aren't completely untethered beings. We have a fixed side and a flexible side, and some of that fixed side comes from our parents and our DNA.

***

These two rules can provide a simple explanation for most behaviour. We can forget the complexity in life, and instead understand it from the point of view of these rules. They can allow us to take a step back and explain people's motivations, when this can be hard to do.

We spend so much time in the foreground (given that conflict often draws us into it), and our lives are often consumed in battling a variety of words and provocations, that hide true motivations. These simple rules allow us to see the wood for the trees, and understand the background a little better.

These two rules can help us understand other people, but there is one more simple rule to consider in this section, that can help us understand ourself:

> **"...if you were the last person alive, and you would still do what you are about to do, you are doing it for your "self"..."**

The final rule can help us gauge, or understand, ourselves, and the people around us.

It doesn't have to be just us either, you could replace "the last person alive" with "in the last group alive". The point is to consider a completely different set of circumstances, that remove the pressures and constraints of society, in order to get closer to our own personal motivations.

"Self" isn't about being selfish. We are interlinked, social beings, who will always do things for others, to some extent. We look after and care for our children, and look out for our friends. However, in every action we do, there will be parts we do because of comparisons, rivalries, or conflict with others, and parts we do for ourself. Separating out the two, and being able to understand and focus more on the parts that relate only to us, can help us understand ourself.

"Self" is about having personal freedom and direction, in balance with those social links. It is about finding our own motivation, and being able to act on it. It is about being able to take the influences, provocations and constraints that other people impose on us, and still do (what we consider) the right thing, and take actions for our own fulfilment.

Trying to develop a greater sense of self can help us to navigate a world where we are still acting as hunter-gatherers, looking for small tribes, friendship groups, and family units, whilst living in large societies, in close proximity to other similar sized groups, that have slightly different behaviours and values. Having "self" allows us to still be ourselves, despite influences pulling us in different directions.

It may be that we can only nudge ourselves towards having a little more self, because especially as an adult, our behaviours, bonds, and what makes us feel most ourself, become more fixed. The world is also a competitive place, so we may have to compete at times, and act on comparisons, rivalries and conflict. Against that, self can be hard to find. We have our underlying amount of self, but developing greater self can be difficult. It requires energy, but it can be worthwhile, because it is easy to lose ourselves in competition of life, and find that later we are too constrained by other people's influences and pressures. If we can only nudge ourselves towards having greater self, then perhaps having *much* greater self will simply be a result of growing up in a world that has become fairer and more equal, as wealth and power are evened out.

Nevertheless, the third rule allows us to consider parts of our lives from a personal and comparative perspective, in order to point us in the direction of greater self.

For example, our interactions, and those of others, are an intermixed jumble of motivations, and often it is not obvious what is causing us to do the things we do.

Say we are a race car driver. We enjoy racing, but there is more to it than that. There are some parts of it that are **personal**. We enjoy driving at speed, and the skill required to feel the movements of the car, and turn it through a corner whilst carrying momentum. However, there are parts of it that are **comparative**. We enjoy racing because we beat other people, and we enjoy the fact we are better at driving than others. We enjoy driving in the rain less, but we like the fact that we can drive in the rain better than others. We like the feeling of winning, beating other people, gaining money and fame. We like being number one because it makes our social interactions easier, and people treat us more favourably.

Separating out the parts we do for ourself, and those we do in relation to others, requires a test.

This test is a little extreme, but it nevertheless works.

We can ask ourselves: if we are the last person alive (which I appreciate is a slightly morbid question) how would we fill our time?

Or, if we were in the last group alive (be it friends or family, or others), how would that group fill their time?

We wake up one morning and everyone else has disappeared. It is heart-breaking, but we feel an urge to survive. Nature takes over the once bustling towns and cities, and we engage in a similar struggle that our hunter-gatherer ancestors used to face. In this hypothetical situation, there is plenty of food, in tins (in warehouses and supermarkets), and so we have some spare time.

We live near a race track, and we enjoy racing. There is a car there, and plenty of petrol. Would we drive it, and how often? Would it form part of our routine? Do we feel the same enjoyment (in whole, or in part), or do we find that we actually don't find it satisfying when there aren't other people to race against, or a crowd to support us?

Of course we are social beings, so nothing would quite feel the same. But there would be some things we do, in this post-apocalyptic wilderness, that we'd take personal pride in. We'd feel proud of ourself for those activities, regardless of the fact that no-one was there to see them. *We* did them. Our ancient hunter-gatherer ancestors wouldn't have needed a chanting crowd, or a thousand "likes", every time they lit a fire, and so if we found ourselves in a similar situation, neither would we.

In our actual lives, there are some things that are more likely to make us feel pride in ourself, rather than because of the effect it will have on other people. If we approach tasks and activities from the perspective of our "self", i.e. to draw satisfaction from the parts that give us personal fulfilment, regardless of who else is participating, then we are less likely to get into conflict. Our focus will be more likely to be closer to ourself. We can still win and be the best, and enjoy all the accolades that go with that, and we can still work hard to achieve those things. But if those things are a side-show, and the main event is us doing things for our personal fulfilment, then we are more likely to live in balance, and find personal satisfaction in our lives. The things we do because *we* enjoy them, regardless of who else is involved, or present, are more likely to be representative of our individuality, and give us greater contentment.

Our modern social arrangement is unnatural compared to our evolutionary one. We live closely, side by side, with people from different factions, with different views, and different backgrounds. There is no more room on planet Earth to expand, and the top of society doesn't live too far away from the bottom. As social media shrinks the world, we are more interconnected than ever. We have to expend energy and focus in order to make it work as best as it can, when our natural behaviours and instincts often encourage us to do other things, that often aren't in balance when applied to this modern social environment.

Simple Rules for Understanding Human Beings

We can't really change the modern social environment. We can't have a single, isolated, secure group to live entirely in. Therefore, if we can nudge ourselves towards having greater self, it can become an asset, and give us an element of self-determination (despite other people's influences), and perhaps the modern social arrangement can then work a little more smoothly.

Our lives can often be a kaleidoscope of social interactions, and it can be easy to lose sight of ourselves, when bombarded by societies' pressures and competition. But, if we consider what life would be like if our circumstances were very different, and what we'd do then, it can be an avenue for exploring our own personal motivations.

8

Challenges and Provocation

Modern humans provoke and challenge each other a lot.

We do this to make others feel like we do, or act on a difficult parent-child relationship, or because we are all diverged and our positions are less secure.

Challenges and provocations can therefore form a large part of our interactions. In this chapter, we shall consider their nature. This is less about the different ways we experience them (which is considered in the next few chapters), and more about what happens in our brains, and how we respond according to patterns.

As modern humans, we're constantly testing each other: provoking, sending barbs one way or another, or competing with a rival in a power struggle.

This happens even amongst friends and family. Entire conversations can be less about what is said, and more about the dynamic between the two people. Sometimes it can be enjoyable to be trading blows, for example in a friendship group, but sometimes it can be exhausting and frustrating. Sometimes we just get a difficult challenge from someone,

Challenges and Provocation

which was perhaps intended to hurt, limit or define us negatively.

This chapter looks at, as an individual, how a challenge affects us, and what we do in response.

Firstly, what is happening in a challenge or provocation?

It is a balance of emotions, from one person to another. As touched on in the chapter (on simple rules), emotions are transferred through our behaviours, as a method of communicating how we feel, and it allows each person's needs to be accounted for, even when our emotions become complex and hard to understand.

Humans aren't telepathic, and yet we need to live closely in groups where a social structure can be formed, and positions organised. Emotions therefore need to be transferred and shared in order for each person to be a part of, and influence, the group dynamic. This is done in the following process, as shown before:

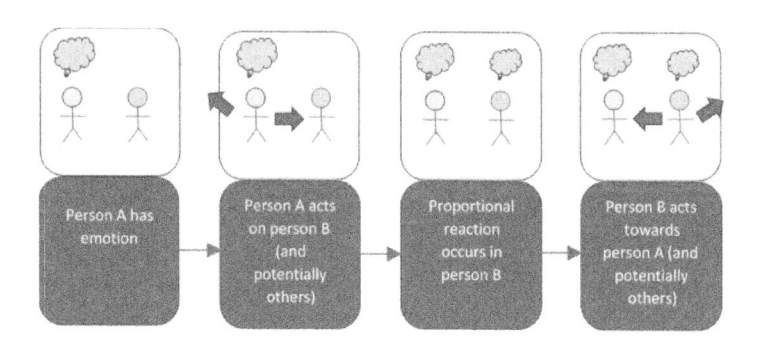

| Person A has emotion | Person A acts on person B (and potentially others) | Proportional reaction occurs in person B | Person B acts towards person A (and potentially others) |

This is a key part of our programming in that how other people behave towards us, i.e. what they say and do, creates emotional responses within us, good and bad, whether we want them to or not. This mechanism is how beings that aren't telepathic can live closely in groups with each other.

For hunter-gatherers, challenging or provoking each other would have been infrequent. It would only be required in order to resolve a rivalry (which would be rarer given the established hierarchy and sub-culture of the tribe), or to become aware of an issue a member of the tribe felt, and to adjust the group dynamic accordingly.

In that tribe environment, occasional difficulty would be like ripples from a drop of water, reflecting around the group, until they are absorbed, and the water becomes more still again.

However, in modern society, there are often groups where a large number of provocations occur regularly in the dynamic. The social pond experiences more constant agitation. This is because our positions are less secure compared to if we spent our whole lives in one small tribe. We are often a part of several groups, and have a position in each, and they are all interlinked and sometimes a little like a house of cards. There is the possibility that group dynamics can change, or that those that we compare ourselves to find greater success. There are also a much greater range of difficulties that modern humans face in our current way of living. As a result, we are less secure in our positions, and so often need to challenge those around us, in order to maintain them. This results in fairly constant choppy waters, as difficulty is splashed around, but can't always be resolved.

We behave towards others principally through voice and words, but also through non-verbal communication such as body language and actions. Often the *way* people say something is more important than *what* they say, because it represents the dynamic. Our subconscious is very good at picking up on the intention of others, and producing emotions based on it, however we aren't always consciously immediately aware of it, there can sometimes be a delay. Our brain can get caught up in what was said, and we find ourselves trying to resolve that, when the real reason for an interaction was someone trying to establish positions or dynamics.

The feeling of being challenged can sometimes be very deep. What people say and do can create a strong emotional reaction, that compels us to act in response. This emotional response happens deep within us, and is effectively a reflex action, and is a core part of our programming.

The emotional response is uncomfortable, and a negative reaction, until we can resolve it. Most often, resolving the challenge requires other people. In this way, challenges can reinforce our social behaviour. A challenge between two humans causes them to seek support or conflict in others. This is representative of ripples of difficulty spreading around groups, in order for the group structure to try to solve the problem, as best it can.

Responses to challenges

Each person has different methods and strategies for resolving challenges. Some people seek help and support of other people. Some people use superiority, and some people just oppose every challenge.

Each person's methods will match the behaviours they have, be similar to their parent's methods, and be quite difficult to change. Learning to seek help and support, learning to oppose challenges, or learning to feel superior, when that behaviour doesn't come naturally to us, can be hard to do.

Sometimes our circumstances dictate what strategy we use. Seeking support in others is normally the most non-confrontational, but sometimes we simply have to oppose challenges, for example to prevent further ones, or in competitive environments, or when there is no-one to validate with.

Therefore there are three main evolutionary responses to challenges:
- Validation;
- Superiority; and
- Rivalling.

Each one can be used successfully to resolve a challenge.

Rivalling, where we take direct action against the person who challenged us, and challenge them back, is the oldest response, and is seen across the animal kingdom, being a key part of survival of the fittest.

Superiority, where we resolve the challenge by reducing how we think about the other person in our minds, is a side effect of large unequal societies, where there are different levels of value.

Validation is a very social behaviour, that is the least confrontational, and most likely to result in peace, resolve differences, and minimise stress. It is part of living in groups, whereby we can use alliances to be able to deal with confrontational behaviour from others. It is also a fairly essential part of large societies, where we can resolve conflict in one group in a different group, and vice versa. In this way, it allows the difficulty of having spread-out social lives to be managed.

Superiority

Some people use superiority more than others, but we all use it from time to time on a small scale. We have derogatory words for other people. If someone is mean to us, we think of them as "nasty", a "hater", or a bad person. If someone bumps into us on the street, we might think of them as "rude" or an "idiot", even if it was our fault. We can resolve challenges by thinking of that person in a way that is less than us. If we convince ourselves they are less than us, we are less affected by what they say or do.

We use our achievements or attributes as superiority. For example we won that golf tournament a few years ago, so we are a better golfer than our friend, even if our friend is beating us right now, and rubbing it in. Our brain holds that golf tournament in our mind as a defence. Or, perhaps we have a love rival who is finding success, so we reduce them in our mind because of one of their flaws, and instead focus on our positive attributes. Sometimes, when we are challenged, our brain starts searching around for ways that we are superior, even if we don't want it to. If it finds an achievement or attribute that the other person doesn't have, then it builds a picture around this, and any challenges from the other person can be resolved. However, unfortunately, our personality becomes a little more dependent on that achievement or attribute, and, next time we are challenged, it might seek it out more quickly.

The other person isn't involved in this process (otherwise it'd be rivalling, i.e. taking action to oppose a challenge), it simply happens in our mind. If we don't ever see the person again, then they are none the wiser that we have reduced them, so no great harm is caused. However, humans are often irked and annoyed by the mere thought that someone else has reduced them in their minds, or felt superior to them. If they act aloof, even if they haven't said anything, it often makes us feel like we want to oppose them. We don't like the idea that someone thinks of us in a way that is inconsistent with how we think of ourselves. We all need integrated definitions. We can feel compelled to challenge them, and to get their thoughts out in the open, in order to prevent them feeling superiority over us.

Sometimes we tell our derogatory words to our friends, in order to reinforce them in us, so that we can use them to reduce other people more effectively, when they challenge us. If we hear others, for example our parents, talk in derogative ways about other people, we are more likely to be able to feel superior to those people. Sometimes, if we're struggling to resolve challenges at that time, then we may use an aspect of superiority as a defence, even if we don't want to.

Therefore, often, our personalities are not forged in who we want to be, but in how we respond to challenges.

Knowledge about how and why people do the things they do can help prevent superiority. In young children, often they simply wouldn't understand complex social behaviours, so we simply have to describe other people as good or bad, and behaviour that upsets them as wrong. But as people grow older, they can better understand why other humans are behaving the way they do.

Rivalling

Sometimes we just have to take action against someone in order to resolve a challenge. We have to in order to prevent them making further challenges, to prove them wrong, or because they've challenged us in a way that is related deeply to our self-definition. However, sometimes people have whole personalities based on opposing others. It keeps life simple; you don't have to think too hard about challenges, you just oppose all of them.

Rivalling is also a side effect of competitive environments. Nearer the top of groups, or society, there is simply less people to validate with, or to feel alliances with. If we're competing with someone else for the same thing that we both want (for example to be the leader), then it's harder to feel superior to them because of something else.

Rivalling creates winners and losers. For the winners, they feel good, believe that society should be about winning and getting to the top, and encourage others to do the same. For the losers, they feel bad, and wish things were different.

However, rivalling in the modern world is a little out of balance. For example, it can cause escalation. Two rivals can trade blows, but in doing so they become more focussed on each other. This makes the challenges more important to them, so they have to increase the strength of their challenges, to ensure they are the winner.

In the modern world winning also doesn't have the long term affect we think it should. Our rivals can always come back. Perhaps they'll try to change the playing field, and compete on a different set of values. A common change of values, based around our key drivers, is a change in the competition from being less about money and success, to more about how good a parent we are. After that, perhaps it changes to something else.

In society, rivalling will always be present to some degree. However, minimising the amount of rivalling creates more harmonious and less stressful groups and societies. As discussed previously, one way to do this is by greater equality across society, rich and poor, and across each person's value.

Validation

Validation is where we seek out support in someone else. In doing so, we know they have our back, would be on our side, or can say things that replace the challenge in our mind, and so the challenge can be resolved. Sometimes, even if we don't mention the challenge, spending time with people who are on our side, who treat us according to how we want to be treated, can resolve or lessen challenges we received from elsewhere.

Validation can be a very effective method of resolving challenges. It can also provide a defence or barrier against further challenges. For example, if we're in a difficult situation, where we're getting repeated challenges from someone, validating with someone else can allow us to deal with this. Because we've got support, or someone on our side, then if the person challenging us does it again, we have tied thoughts to the person who is on our side, and it is as if they are there with us in spirit. As a result, the person challenging us has less effect on our definition. Alliances within friendship groups can be used to deal with a more obtrusive friend, and alliances with colleagues can be used to deal with a difficult boss.

Sometimes with someone else on your side, counteracting, or listening to the challenge, our minds can resolve the emotions associated with challenges. Sometimes even just talking about something gets it off our chest. There is a powerful impact on our self, and our emotions, by involving and communicating with other people. Interdependency is part of socialisation.

Validation doesn't actually require understanding. We may not appreciate or understand why someone has behaved the way they did to us. But if someone else validates our position, then the challenge can be resolved. If someone is on our side, even if we both know we were in the wrong (note: being wrong, and less than perfect, is unavoidable at times), it helps us not to feel wrong.

But it's often better with understanding, for the person giving it to understand the situation the person is describing, and think of an appropriate response that will make the person better able to take productive actions.

Validation sometimes uses superiority or opposition. For example a friend might help us to reduce the other person (e.g. why we're better and shouldn't have to worry about them), or encourage us to stand up to them (e.g. oppose or rival them). But in these circumstances, because at least a part of the process has involved someone else, the result can be more harmonious: we rely less on superiority or rivalling. The ripples are allowed to spread out a little, and lessen in height, rather than being immediately bounced back.

However, validation can require some caution and skill. For every time it works, there are times when it doesn't. Someone may take advantage, and we have to regain some ground.

Part of the problem is when we're diverged. Our difficulty, or the strength of how a challenge affected us, can be influenced by our inherited level. We can therefore face a crux. We want to validate, to be open and share our emotions, but we can't if the result is that people won't see us according to our identity level.

People who both are open and supportive of us sharing our feelings, and yet are still supportive, and treat us according to our identity level regardless, are quite rare for anyone. The more diverged we are, the rarer they become. This is why so much of human difficulty is discussed behind closed doors, in private, and only with someone we can trust like a life partner, whilst outwardly we present our identity level without that difficulty.

Another issue is that *everyone* is diverged. Everyone, to some extent, is facing that crux. Everyone is following the core human driver to be their identity despite the headwind of their (mostly unwelcome) inherited level. We can come into conflict with others, each trying to be identities that are incompatible. In some rivalries, each person is trying to find reasons why the other person isn't their identity level. Then, opening up to anyone is much harder, incase the rival gets wind of it.

Finally, validation can be difficult because, whilst everyone has a social moral to want to help each other, we also have a driver to maximise our own value. Having someone open up to us can inflate our own self-worth. Sometimes, having someone open up to us can make us feel better about our own problems. Sometimes people want to focus on other people's problems rather than their own. Sometimes people want to be a source of strong dependency to a friend, for their *own* feeling of value, rather than trying to help the person help themselves. Sometimes people don't want other people to solve problems that they haven't.

In more equal societies, there is less to gain, and we will be less diverged. Our driver to maximise our value is tempered and more in balance, and we'd grow up in a world where it's easier to be content with what we have, and what we have gives us everything we need or want. In this world there is less conflict and friction between people. And, when conflict does arise, it is easier to validate, and be interdependent on those around us, because those around us are more content with what they have.

However, on the whole, this isn't the world we live in at the moment. Therefore learning how to use validation, if our circumstances make it difficult, can be very useful, but prickly. Some people we can trust, some we can't. It's not that they are untrustworthy per se, it's just that they have needs, and their own life and difficulties, that might conflict with ours. The results of using validation can be an unknown, and it can be uncomfortable at first. Sometimes someone might take advantage, and we may find we have to work hard to regain position, to get back to where we were before.

Challenges and Provocation

Generally though, validation is the most effective way of resolving challenges, and resulting in peaceful social environments. It is an essential part of living in large societies. Difficulties we have in one group can be validated in another. This allows us to deal with the complexity of a society where everyone is being influenced by multiple different groups of people.

As a final note on validation, there is one key aspect of it – it requires some degree of separation from the person provoking or challenging us.

The more we can get away from that person, the less we have to rely on rivalling or superiority. The more we can get away from that person, spend time in different social environments, talk to other people about it, and have our focus drift away from that person, the more effective validation can be. This separation allows our brain can learn, rationalise and consolidate our experiences. We can then switch off from that conflict, and be able see the wood for the trees.

This will happen fairly naturally as we move around and socialise with different groups. However, it's worth making a point about social media here. The bulk of the discussion on social media is later in Part III, but as it is important in relation to validation, here is a quick side note.

Social media can play havoc with it. Being constantly connected to people means that we can feel other people's influence on us at any time, and our focus can't drift away from them. They can contact us whenever, wherever, and it's harder to forget about conflicts and put them out of our minds. Because of this, we can feel greater social stress, and have to rely more on superiority and rivalling, instead of the more peaceful and harmonious validation. If our brain can't drift away from people, and momentarily forget about them, then we have to be mentally prepared for potential interactions, with provocations and defences. This means there are more winners and losers, greater fear of being on the losing side, and social environments become more obtrusive and less friendly. There is more to say on social media in a few chapters time.

Whether you use validation, superiority or rivalling, everyone is doing the same thing. We are all trying to resolve challenges in a large, complex, often difficult, and interlinked social environment, that differs from the hunter-gatherer one that Homo Sapiens emerged into, 200,000 years ago.

Variety of challenges

As modern humans, we have to face more challenges than we should. Our social environment isn't a snug fit to our programming, and our spread-out social lives produce a greater number of provocations, as we try to resolve more complex issues than a simple tribe.

However, it is not just a greater *frequency* of challenges that we face however, the *variety* of challenges that we face has also increased.

As described at the start of the book, our social environment isn't a simple straightforward one anymore, as it would be in a tribe, and we now compete over what the prevailing cultural behaviours should be. We have groups whose hierarchy is based on posturing (through behaviours, or sometimes physicality), we have groups based on value (perhaps money, intelligence, attributes etc), and we have groups based on defined roles of responsibility. We are not playing a simple boardgame. Instead, in each group, we compete over what the rules should be, and everyone is suited to playing a slightly different play-style, based on their backgrounds.

Challenges and Provocation

Throw in the fact that society can be unequal and stretched, and therefore have deeper groups, and greater variation in subculture from one group to another, then the situation gets a little tougher still.

Modern humans tend to have one or two groups that they are more closely bonded to, that they associate with, and that defines their identity. These groups will have their own subculture and set of values.

Our behaviours are linked to our one or two core groups. Even when away from those core groups, we likely behave consistently with them. Then, we may find that, as the social landscape around us varies, the behaviours we use, to give and defend challenges, may not be a good fit from time to time, and may be unacceptable or inappropriate.

Sometimes we may find that we're frustrated when we can't use behaviours that we feel are right, i.e. the behaviours that make us feel "us". We may become dismissive of a group, because, in that group, the behaviours we'd use to attain our identity position would be deemed unacceptable.

Also our behaviours have things that we feel compelled to do, and things that we feel blocked from doing. We may find that these compelled behaviours, and blocked behaviours, whilst fitting well into our core group, may leave us with a vulnerability or two, or provoke others without meaning to, when outside of that core group.

All this leads to situations where we may not always recognise the challenges going on around us. We can become blinkered, or be on different wavelengths. We can find we get unexpected challenges in new environments, and have to learn or adapt our behaviours to better deal with them.

An implication of this is that sometimes an emotional response can be delayed.

An example is when we have a conversation, and it seemed friendly and non-confrontational, and then later on our mind focusses on something they said, that we didn't realise at the time, that actually annoys us, and we wish we'd responded differently. Another example is when someone tries to define us, for example they might compliment us and say that we look like someone famous. We like that, it makes us feel good. But later on, we realise that actually we don't want to be defined by that person, even if they define us positively, and then we might feel about it differently.

When there's such a variety of sub-cultures out there, often we have to change our behaviours a little, and adapt to each group. However, this can be hard, because our "one tribe", hunter-gatherer psychology is more set up to integrate into *one* core group: our tribe. In that tribe we are interlinked, so that we intuitively recognise the challenges and posturing going on. In the modern world, we are often less in tune, or on a slightly different wavelength to the goings on around us.

It results in competition within groups, where each person is trying to instil their behaviours as acceptable and "right", so that they can challenge and defend others using the set of behaviours they have available. This normally happens without incident or difficulty, but if groups become tighter for some reason, for example due to social media, this competition of sub-culture can intensify.

Some people more intuitively recognise challenges, whatever sub-culture they are in. Or, perhaps they are simply less diverged, or they are just more obtrusive on those around them, so that they try to steamroller over everyone. For those with less of this intuition, recognising and adapting to different environments and challenges requires some skill and thought.

Challenges and Provocation

It also requires some self-trust: we know when we've been challenged, because we feel it (even if it's delayed), but others may not have recognised it.

There are some universal patterns of different challenges however. Challenges can be trying to do one of the following:

1. Trying to define us
2. Disapproving of us
3. Giving us commands ("you should", "you need", "you must")
4. Offer dependence when it's unwanted
5. Controlling interactions

There are also ways that people can either strengthen a challenge, or provoke someone simply through the way they say things. These involve:

1. Stressing syllables in words, either with volume, sharpness or elongating them
2. Saying things in a melodic or moving pitch
3. Adding aggression to words
4. Talking in a domineering tone or talking over the top of us
5. Adding stressing facial expressions, flaring the eyes or nose or body language

Certain people that we look up to, respect or value, we don't mind challenging us, and obviously some of the above are leadership behaviours. However, we can tell when someone is using these methods responsibly, to take the lead from a position we feel they warrant, as opposed to someone challenging or provoking us.

We can't stop all challenges, and often have to accept a certain amount of cross conflict, where rivalries can't be resolved. This is why validation is so useful, if it's available.

Proportionate & disproportionate interactions

The model of human transfer of emotion through behaviours, introduced at the start of Part III, shows *proportionate interactions*.

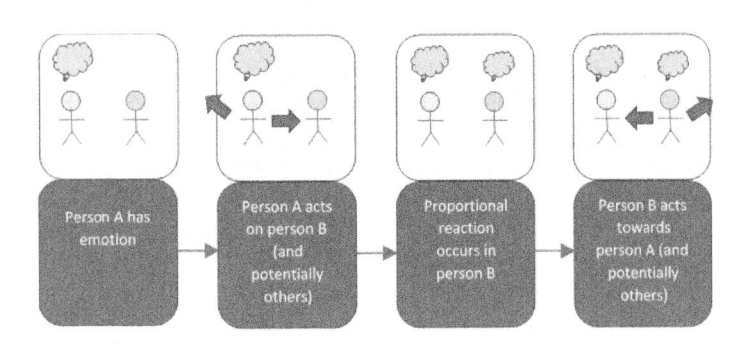

| Person A has emotion | → | Person A acts on person B (and potentially others) | → | Proportional reaction occurs in person B | → | Person B acts towards person A (and potentially others) |

Person B gets a lot of information from person A, that includes what is said, their body language, their tone, and their expressions. From seeing someone move, how they look, and how they interact around other people, our brains make quite a detailed assessment of people. We can judge their social position, read facial expressions, and have information to be able to judge the nature and intent of behaviours.

Challenges and Provocation

The emotional reaction in person B is therefore normally interlinked and connected with person A because of this. The reaction in person B is *proportionate* to the situation.

In a tribe environment, this will cause each member's emotions to be interlinked, and accurately represented with the rest of the tribe. Behaviours cause emotions to transfer around the group like ripples across a pond, reflecting back and forth until they are absorbed and accounted for.

However, in recent times, humans have developed technology that allows us to interact in new ways. Often these new ways are *disproportionate*. This is because challenges occur in ways where the person being challenged lacks information from the challenger, such as body language, facial expressions, or seeing how they interact with others. Without this information, the response generated in them, from the challenge, is disconnected from the emotions in the person making the challenge.

One of the first examples of ways humans interacted in disproportionate ways was the car. When viewing a moving car, we often can't see the driver, who they are, their state of mind, their intentions, and why they might be driving the way they do. Yet, if they drive in a way that provokes us, we can become annoyed, frustrated or angry.

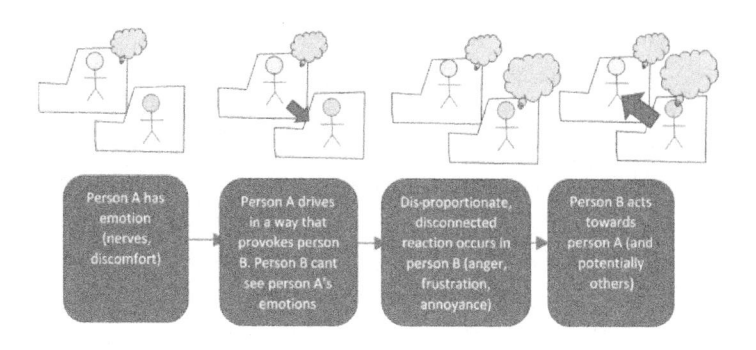

| Person A has emotion (nerves, discomfort) | Person A drives in a way that provokes person B. Person B cant see person A's emotions | Dis-proportionate, disconnected reaction occurs in person B (anger, frustration, annoyance) | Person B acts towards person A (and potentially others) |

If you drive, perhaps you've found this. You might have someone driving in a way that obstructs you, perhaps too slowly, or driving erratically and blocking your path, which makes you feel provoked and annoyed. Yet, later, you see that they are actually an underconfident driver, and that their driving was through nervousness rather than intention, and perhaps you feel a little guilty for being angry.

This was a *disproportionate* interaction. because the response in you, from the perceived challenge, was not linked to the emotions of the person in the other car.

Part of the problem with disproportionate interactions is that they can lead to escalation. We see this in cars with road rage, where there is an escalation in the disproportionate interactions that leads to anger spilling over. This escalation is much less likely to happen if the interaction was face to face, for example simply walking down the street, where the full range of information is available, and the interaction was connected. If we are blocked walking along the street by someone nervous or uncomfortable, we would feel less provoked, because our emotional reactions would factor more information in. The interaction, and our emotional response, would be more balanced, and any emotions transferred more linked.

The escalation comes from the fact that, when we feel challenged by someone, but lack information on them, our brain fills in the gaps. Our brains can be quite cautious, and often our emotions are representative of what *could* happen. Someone could be provoking us, or trying to attack us, so our brain acknowledges this, and our response can be more than what was intended.

The escalation also comes from the fact that, if we feel challenged, and respond to the other person, we often don't actually see any impact of our response. If it was face-to-face, we'd see a change in their expressions, or shift in body language, so we can gauge how our response has landed, but when that information is missing, we can feel like we need to respond again. Both of these reasons can cause a disproportionate interaction to escalate.

A second example of early disproportionate interactions, that are still prevalent today, is the use of photographs. When we see a photo of someone, we can feel provoked or challenged by their expressions. They might appear aggressive, happy, smug or superior in a photo, and our brains interpret this as a challenge, as if they were behaving like that in front of us in real life. However again, this interaction is *disproportionate*, because the photo is just a snapshot. It doesn't represent how the person is feeling, and their true emotions or intentions. As a result, the response in us, from seeing a photo that provokes us, is disconnected from the actual emotions of the other person.

The impression we can make on others, through posing in a photograph, can be different than the impression we make on others in real life. The impression we make in real life is more proportionate to our levels, and how we socialise and integrate into groups. In contrast, the impression we make in a photograph can be a snapshot, a distorted image, and other people's reactions to it are disconnected and disproportionate.

In the modern world, many more disproportionate interactions have crept into our lives. Text messaging and emails are also *disproportionate* interactions. Our brains interpret the text words with intention as if they were being said to us in person. However, what is said in the text may not be representative of the person's true emotions, and how we respond to it may not be representative of a transfer of emotions, that would occur if the interaction was face to face.

Perhaps the worst culprit for disconnected interactions is talking to random people on the internet. Often all we get is a username and perhaps a picture. Yet what is said can elicit a response in us regardless. If someone is hurtful or boastful, we can feel provoked as if they were acting like this in person. Yet we have absolutely no idea the emotions and intention behind the provocation. Yet, regardless of the intention, or source of the provocation, the response in us is the same. This is truly *disproportionate*. It can lead to online flame wars, bitter online rivalries, we can get drawn into arguments on topics we never knew we cared about. There can be significant escalation of emotions, as people's brains are making poor assessments of who the challenge has come from, and why it's happening, and, if they respond, then it doesn't have any immediate effect.

These interactions are a bit like being in a competitive social environment but with the lights off. It's pitch black, and we will therefore be more on edge, and find it a little more stressful, because we don't know where provocations are coming from, and we have less information to understand them.

In resolving disproportionate interactions (which we still need to do; using validation, superiority or rivalling), often we need to come to some conclusion and about the intentions of the other person. In doing this we inform our understanding of human motivation, and human nature, since our personalities are often forged in how we respond to challenges. Unfortunately, because the interaction was disconnected, we can be wrong or misguided. We can come to conclusions that "people are...", when actually there is something else going on, that would be more apparent if the challenge was face to face, in a more proportionate way.

Spending too much time or focus on disproportionate interactions, for example if we communicate excessively through text, photos or with random people on the internet, can therefore be stressful, cause escalation, and lead to misconceptions about human motivation. These disproportionate communication mediums aren't all bad, but we just need to approach them with some scepticism and caution.

Challenges and provocation summary

In the modern world, we can be challenged and provoked much more than we should be as human beings. Instead of challenges being occasional ripples in a pond, the social pond is much more agitated.

We rely on our evolutionary responses: rivalling, superiority and validation in order to resolve challenges. Each can be used successfully, and different people rely on different responses more than others. Validation is the most effective at resulting in a balanced and harmonious outcome, and is fairly essential for modern humans, where we can resolve difficulty in one group by validating in another. However, validation requires some level of separation, to put the person that provoked us out of our thoughts, and social media can compromise its effectiveness. As a result, we then have to rely on rivalling and superiority more.

We can find ourselves in sub-cultures where we're challenged in ways we're not used to. Our behaviours, forged in our key social groups, may be on a different wavelength to the people around us, and we can feel blocked or compelled to behave in certain ways, that may be a slight mismatch to the group in front of us.

Finally, in the modern world, we face many different types of disproportionate interactions, which interfere with the way that behaviours cause emotional reactions in others. The emotions felt in the person challenged can be disproportionate to the emotions in the challenger, and escalation can occur. The common factor in disproportionate interactions is that they're not face to face. Then, body language, expression, and tone are missing from our brain's assessment of the provocation.

Essentially, challenges and provocations are complex in the modern day, and often require a little more thought and focus than they would otherwise. Instead of them being natural, and an occasional part of a hunter-gatherer tribe life, they can now be more of a constant back and forth, and a skill that we have, or need to learn, depending on the environments that we find ourselves in.

9

Individual's Behaviours

With challenges and provocation described, we can now explore different relationships and dynamics.

This chapter looks at an individual's behaviours, and the next few chapters look at group dynamics, societal dynamics, and social media.

Each of the three main aspects of our lives: our levels, our self, and our web, have an impact on all of our interactions. However, some perhaps have more of an impact on certain parts of our interactions than others. In this chapter, looking at an individual's behaviours, we shall mainly be considering levels.

In Part I we looked at how the difference between our identity level and our inherited level causes us to be obtrusive. We are obtrusive in order to overcome reactions caused by our inherited level, as well as to warn others off exposing our inherited level. In being obtrusive, we are able to feel more our identity level. However, the more obtrusive we are, the more we are likely to come into conflict with others.

A Theory of Everyone

In this section, we shall look at some very common ways that humans are obtrusive on those around them, whereby they challenge and provoke other people.

Levels are a big influence on how obtrusive we are because, whatever we think of ourselves, and, whatever we believe about the world, when someone is standing right in front of us and we're interacting with them, our behaviours come down to three things: how we feel; how we want to come across; and what we do if those two are different.

How we feel in that interaction is determined by our inherited level (which is often unwelcome for everyone, including our parents), at least until we can establish a secure dynamic based on our identity level.

How we want to come across is our identity level.

What we do if those two are different is what we shall look at in this chapter.

In this book, I've said that if our inherited level and our identity level are different, we are diverged. Most modern humans are diverged, but some more than others.

We can be diverged on value, for example where we have attained greater value or status in our lifetimes (or our parents did):

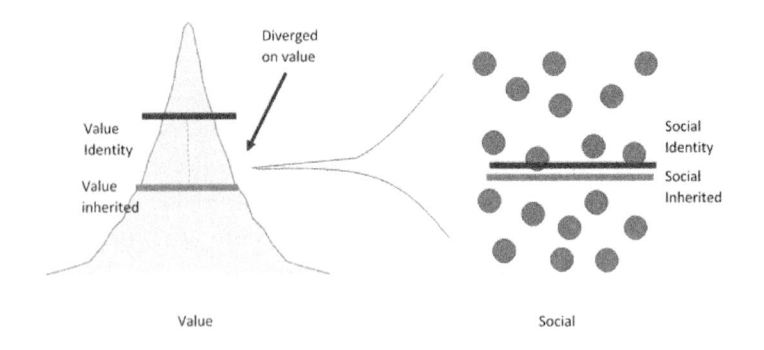

Individual's Behaviours

Or, a person can be diverged on social, which occurs due to finding circumstances where we can take on a more socially important role. This can come from, for example, attaining a role in an organisation, or having favourable attributes:

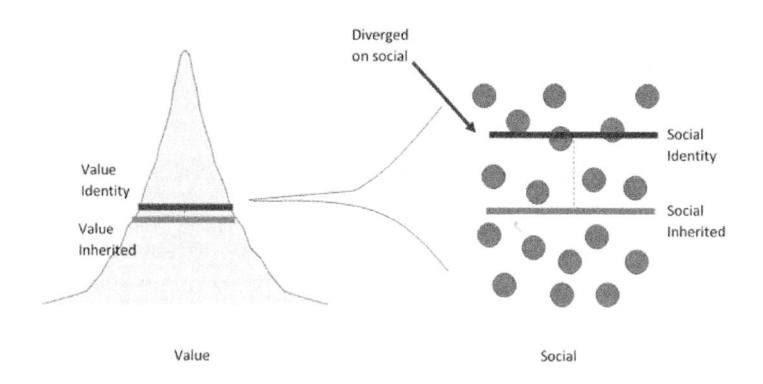

Whether we are diverged on either "value" or "social" doesn't really matter. In each case the same situation occurs: we face an additional headwind, from our inherited level, that makes it harder to maintain our identity level. As a result, being diverged on "social" or "value" will have similar effects on behaviours. We can therefore simply consider whether someone is diverged or not, and why they are diverged is less important.

Each person who is diverged learns a set of behaviours that adapt around the fact that they are diverged. These allow the person to feel their identity level, avoid themselves feeling their inherited level, and prevent others exposing their inherited level.

There are many different strategies that humans learn in order to do this. Some are more passive or socially constructive, and some are more provoking. Whether someone uses one or the other comes down to a range of factors. For example we copy behaviours from our parents, and also from our peers and role models. As we grow through adolescence, we are constantly trying out different behaviours. Some of those behaviours are too strong, some not strong enough. Some fit, and are approved of, and some aren't. We find a nuanced set of behaviours that matches our circumstances. Even our tone, the way we stress certain words, the sayings we use, the types of jokes we make, and what we find funny are all influenced by (and representative of) our situation.

Our behaviours, during adolescence, adapt to our circumstances, and allow us to deal with those circumstances.

The passive or more socially constructive behaviours are more about working together to raise our status, whilst the more provoking interpersonal behaviours are more about lowering the status of those around us. Whether we like it or not, both are playing some role in moving towards a common point.

Regarding the passive, or socially constructive behaviours, these can take many forms. For example we can form strong alliances with someone, so that together we provide a united front, and achieve our identity through strength in numbers. Similarly, we can form isolated, cliquey groups with a number people in a similar position to us. In that cliquey group, we each treat each other according to our identity levels, and exclude people who might not.

Alternatively, we can placate others, giving them what they want, so that in return they give us what we want. We treat others according to their identity level, and in return they treat us according to ours.

These tend to be more socially constructive, but rely somewhat on finding the right people, and having the right

Individual's Behaviours

environment. This can narrow the range of people or environments the person feels comfortable in. Outside of those environments, difficulty can emerge. Even within those environments, there can be some frustration somewhere. When levels collide, they create a difficulty that cannot be avoided completely. Whilst they are socially constructive, there is still an element of overcoming a difference in levels, and there is likely to be some obtrusiveness somewhere in those behaviours. Perhaps that difficulty only manifests itself into specific friendships, or only in a subsequent difficult parent-child relationship. Alternatively, the difficulty gets transferred onto those excluded, or disapproved of, by the alliances or cliques. However, with socially constructive methods, that people develop for overcoming levels, perhaps, on average, the obtrusiveness can be spread out more evenly.

The more provoking, directly obtrusive behaviours are generally where the person more actively imposes themselves on others. They make those around them feel in a similar way to themselves, in order to level the playing field, and feel comfortable.

In this chapter we'll look at the more provoking behaviours, because they can be more difficult to understand in our own lives. Social alliances seem, at least on the face of it, more natural and normal. On the other hand, the more provoking behaviours normally involve challenging and reducing others, and the fallout, from that, causes the motivations to become hidden. It therefore becomes harder to link those behaviours to what is driving them.

For example if we see someone nervous, but comfortable when surrounded by their close friends, it is easy to understand. However, if we see someone being hurtful to someone else, we tend to get caught up in that conflict, and generally have to see that person as wrong or unacceptable. It

A Theory of Everyone

is, and I'm not condoning that behaviour, but I'm just illustrating that it is harder to understand the circumstances that lead to someone behaving in such a way.

In both cases, passive or provoking, the behaviours are about how a person develops strategies for matching how they feel, with who they feel they need to be. If you are on the wrong end of them, they can be very frustrating, stressful or hurtful. This shows the power that levels have, and how important they can be. Levels are the driving force for these behaviours, and we experience them through interpersonal conflict, difficult parent-child relationships, and transference of difficulty from one place to another.

There are general ways a person can be provoking, for example unkind, aggressive, stressing certain words, or invading personal space. However, we shall look at four strategies that can develop into a person's personality, and that can result in them behaving obtrusively. There are many more, however the discussion of these examples is intended to show a link between behaviours, motivation, and levels (whereby our levels are generally drawn from circumstances outside of our control). In each case we can look at the impact and the cause.

The four types of obtrusive behaviour we will look at are:

1. Define and control
2. Narrow competitiveness
3. Manipulation/coercion
4. One person/scapegoat

This chapter is merely about explaining why. It is neither condoning nor judging. Every person should aim to be as least intrusive as possible, but we are limited by our circumstances.

Most people that do these behaviours are unaware of their impact, or sometimes unaware they are even doing them. Or, they couldn't not do them even if they wanted to. To not do these behaviours would be to face deep personal difficulty, and to not be able to level the playing field, and therefore lose the ability to feel like an equal. Ultimately, when someone uses these behaviours, they are trying to make other people feel like they do.

Define and control

Being diverged makes us feel more exposed to definition.

People try to define each other all the time, saying "you are this" or "you are that". Sometimes it is helpful, and we like it, but sometimes it is a provocation, from someone trying to reduce us, or give us a negative reputation. If it comes from someone we look up to and respect, we are more likely to feel comfortable with it. If not, it can make us uncomfortable.

The more diverged we are, the more we are affected by provocations, because we have to work harder to maintain our identity level, and have more to lose.

The more diverged we are, the narrower our set of values. As a result, there is a smaller number of people that we feel comfortable with defining us verbally.

We are therefore more sensitive to others defining us, or giving us reputations that we are uncomfortable with.

To combat this, some people develop a strategy of going on the offensive. They repeatedly define others, control their reputations, and perhaps provide an undercurrent that they have the power to give people negative reputations, if they upset the apple cart.

Through these behaviours, they have made others feel like they do, i.e. concerned or vulnerable to having a negative reputation.

They have also reduced the risk of others exposing their inherited level, for example when they feel a little down, or weakened. They have established a dynamic where they can define others, and they now have an avenue to retaliate.

There is another, more personal reason why we do this behaviour. The more diverged person needs more support from their friendship and social groups, rather than their family. They need deeper social relationships, and as a result, they are more vulnerable to changes in their social links. To combat this, by developing a set of behaviours that more strongly defines others, the person has greater leverage to prevent how changes in other people can impact their deeper social ties (for example if someone they know finds success and wants to be treated differently).

These types of behaviours will have been (most likely) copied from a parent during adolescence, through which they become part of the child's personality, whether they want it to or not. This is partly due to the way that our parent's behaviours (whether we like them or not) are most at our fingertips, and partly due to the way the parent makes the child feel, and what that causes the child to do. If their parent has these "define and control" behaviours, the child may feel weakened from the way that parent tries to strongly define them, which will likely feel restrictive. As they feel weakened at different points in their life, they find that defining others eases the burden. Over time, this simply develops into a set of behaviours.

Narrow competitiveness

Being diverged means we face a greater headwind meeting our identity. If life is a running race, then a strategy we can employ is to make sure that we, and those around us, only race on paths, and in environments, that favour us.

If we have a lower inherited level than those around us, we feel challenges harder. It takes more energy to maintain our identity, and we find frustration and conflict more often.

We can develop a strategy where, in the groups we are a part of, we narrow the group's values.

If we impress our own values (which relate favourably to our attributes or skills), on the group, and the group adopts these, then we are on safer ground. We can play to our strengths more often, and are more likely to achieve our identity level. We are less likely to face challenges or negative feedback that we are uncomfortable with. If a person establishes this behaviour in the group dynamic, then they will feel more enabled in preventing the group pursuing different interests, or going to unfavourable environments.

For example, we can make the group about a sport we are good at, a skill we are good at, or approve or disapprove of others based on attributes that we have in abundance.

If someone learns these behaviours from their parent, then it's likely that their family unit has narrow values, and an element of competition. If a parent is competitive with their children, then the children won't get the approval they'd like. This makes it harder to be themselves in their family, and find their own path. As a result, the child will balance this difficulty in their own social lives, by narrowing the values of their own social groups.

This can be obtrusive on others, because it is now harder for those friends and colleagues to be themselves. They find they have to adapt their behaviours to meet someone else's values, which can cause opposition, conflict or frustration.

The discomfort we feel, with someone narrowly trying to compete with us, mirrors the discomfort the person feels, or would feel, if the group had more open values. In that situation, the diverged person would feel more exposed. They would feel more vulnerable to someone else changing the group's values to be something that isn't favourable to them. It would make it more difficult for them to achieve their identity level, which in turn causes negative emotions in the diverged person.

Manipulation of emotions

The more diverged we are, the greater distance there is between ourselves and our parents, and the less our parents are likely to approve of, and recognise, our identity level. In the more extreme case, this can lead to situations where the difference in levels causes us to feel undervalued, unable to be open with our parents, or sometimes unloved.

We perhaps learn to get these things (that are missing from our parents) from the part of society we come across instead. We form deep social bonds, or develop a deep focus in our work. But, we are now very vulnerable to how others treat us. If the people around us pull away, or change allegiances or friends, we lose something that, for us, was providing core emotions, the loss of which can be deep and painful. Some people find they deal with this by causing other people to become dependent on them. They can cause others to deepen their focus in them, to prevent the loss of something important.

In order to get that control, a person can draw others in. They can coercively control how someone thinks of themselves, or values themselves, and offer them strong approval, dependence, or even love. They can exploit emotional vulnerabilities, giving people what they need, but only to further their own needs.

All of these are to force another person's focus and emotions to be on them, so that they then have greater purchase and control. The emotions they convey are more about motive, and trying to achieve an aspect of manipulation, rather than being reflective of the emotions they are actually feeling.

A person may do this quite blindly. This can be because they may be receiving this type of behaviour from the parent. For example, there may be difficulty in that relationship, but the parent is ignoring that difficulty and projecting positive intentions. The parent is effectively being coercive and controlling against unusual modern circumstances, and without allowing the child to resist.

When this behaviour is simply wrapped up in someone's personality (so that they try to draw everyone in too strongly), or when this type of behaviour is received unwanted, it can be very hurtful. The person is being very obtrusive, in order to overcome their divergence, and pulling strongly on the strings around them. When people pull strongly on our strings, in a direction we don't want to go in, it can be deeply uncomfortable.

Humans tend to know this, so there would always be some level of guilt and regret in the person doing it. However, we develop behaviours and beliefs that reflect our situation, and, want to make others feel like we do, at least a little.

One person/scapegoat

The more diverged we are, the more pressure we feel to be our identity, and the more we can fear being the odd one out, or the lowest social position. There is no harm being in this position, if it suits us, but if someone's identity is that they are a higher position, but against a strong headwind, they can fear being singled out, and lose any opportunity to be their identity level.

We can even feel we need to be positioned in a group near the top, but our inherited level is below everyone else's.

In certain circumstances, the difficulty can be projected onto one person, or scapegoat.

There is power in how we perceive *one other person*, both good and bad. It can be good because, sometimes even though *only one person* supports us, it's enough. If *one person* believes in us, that's all we need, even if it's a fight with everyone else.

The negative side of this "one-person effect" is that even when a large number of people support us, we can focus on the fact that *one person doesn't*.

Similarly, in groups, if *one person* is more nervous or out of place, or worse than us at a skill, we can feel more comfortable in the group. There is no harm in being that person, and there will be a group in the world where everyone is the worst at something, but it is just the human nature of how people respond.

This leads to an unfortunate side effect where someone can isolate and suppress *one person* in order to make them be the worst, or the scapegoat, in order to prevent themselves being it instead.

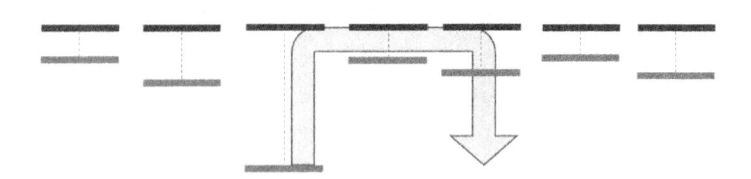

Individual's Behaviours

This can lead to bullying or oppression. That can be established and, unfortunately, tolerated because, when a social group forms with this dynamic, people can become afraid of the focus shifting onto them, and becoming the scapegoat instead. Alternatively, if someone is nervous or uncomfortable in that environment themselves, they may be secretly slightly pleased that the focus isn't on them.

This can come from a family unit, because, if their parent has these behaviours, they may find they can't not use them on their children. Laughing at others misfortune, or singling out others, may simply become part of their personality. The child may have no defence to this when it comes from their parent, so their only outlet is to victimise someone else, in order to offset their own difficulty.

If no-one stands up to them, then the person using these behavioural traits may even feel it is justified, or that the behaviour is acceptable. They may not realise how they are making someone else feel, partly because that is exactly the feeling they are trying to avoid.

This is perhaps the most obtrusive strategies a person can develop for being diverged. It is quite destructive on other people, and, if we find ourselves on the wrong end of this behaviour, it can be very hard to stand alone to prevent it happening. There is always support out there however, and socially able groups generally work together to try to discourage and avoid this behaviour. Bullying and oppression should never be tolerated, and everyone needs to find the extra strength to prevent it happening.

This behaviour doesn't just happen in individuals, but also at a group level. Certain groups may be treated as scapegoats. Like with individuals, when a group feels oppressed or restricted, they can seek an outlet.

For example, in the late 1600s the town of Salem faced a series of hardships. The Massachusetts Bay Colony had its charter revoked, and this was on top of the fact that disease was rife at the time, and that there was the threat of war. The people of Salem started blaming others for witchcraft, and the victims were jailed or burnt at the stake for the relief of the masses.

When a person or group is suppressed, squeezed or pressured, they can take a course of action that offloads this onto a different person or group. This isn't constructive behaviour, but it happens.

It happens even on a global scale at times, where entire countries may feel squeezed, and react by finding scapegoats, and single out other countries or groups.

It can be hard to stand alone, but we all need to at certain points in our lives. In a more equal society, there simply would be fewer people who feel out of place, threatened or vulnerable in certain social environments. There would be fewer people who fall into the hidden pitfalls of society while jostling for position, and everyone would feel, on average, more secure, and able to manage and compromise in social situations.

And, there wouldn't be such a driving force for these types of behaviours, that humans develop in order to meet an identity level, against difficult modern headwinds.

10

Group Dynamics

In theory, groups should be simple and comfortable for human beings. After all, they are one of our main behavioural traits. They allowed us to survive and thrive in the wild.

As a result, there should be mechanisms in our behavioural programming that instinctively allow us to create harmonious groups. Without even thinking, these mechanisms should sort out problems, and find commonality, as they did for millions of years for our ancestors. And, as they do for other social animals on planet Earth, who perhaps have limited methods of communication, yet still manage to form stable social groups, and resolve conflict.

These mechanisms exist, but there is a problem. No longer are we a part of just one group, as we would have been as hunter-gatherers, that included all our family and close friends.

Nowadays, everyone has "other" groups. As we've looked at, everyone has a whole web of "other groups" by the time they reach adulthood. We have spread-out social lives, and we each form a part of society's giant social web.

When we join a new group, each of the other groups in our personal web will be having an influence on how we perceive and behave in the new group. This happens through our tied thoughts, as well as the fact that our behaviours and beliefs were forged in those other groups. As a result, in modern groups, a lot of what each person wants and needs is being dictated by people outside of the group. Those external influences could be very different from person to person. They could include influences from different sub-cultures, for example different appreciations of what behaviours that they find acceptable or rude. These influences can include competition, or difficulty, with people outside of the group, that pressure or constrain people to act in certain ways within it.

These external influences can create conflict in the group, through different people wanting different things. A group can become stretched, as the external influences, of different people, pull it in different directions.

The external influences obstruct our social instincts. Those social instincts, that allowed us to fulfil our main survival trait (groups), now find something holding them back. Our social instincts give us emotions that should compel us to take actions that resolve conflict. However, when conflict is being caused by influences external to the group, those emotions can't find resolution.

We are being pulled in two directions in a group.

We are being pulled away from the present group, by our web of other groups. These "outward forces" include influences and pressures from other groups, as well as representing the fact that our beliefs and behaviours were forged in other groups, and therefore are drawn to them.

We are also being pulled towards the present group, by our social instincts. These "inward forces" represent the fact that, in a group, our focus is on the people and conflict around us, and our social instincts are giving us emotions to help resolve any conflict, in order to create harmonious groups.

However, due to the outward forces, the inward often can't resolve, and are left in a state of limbo.

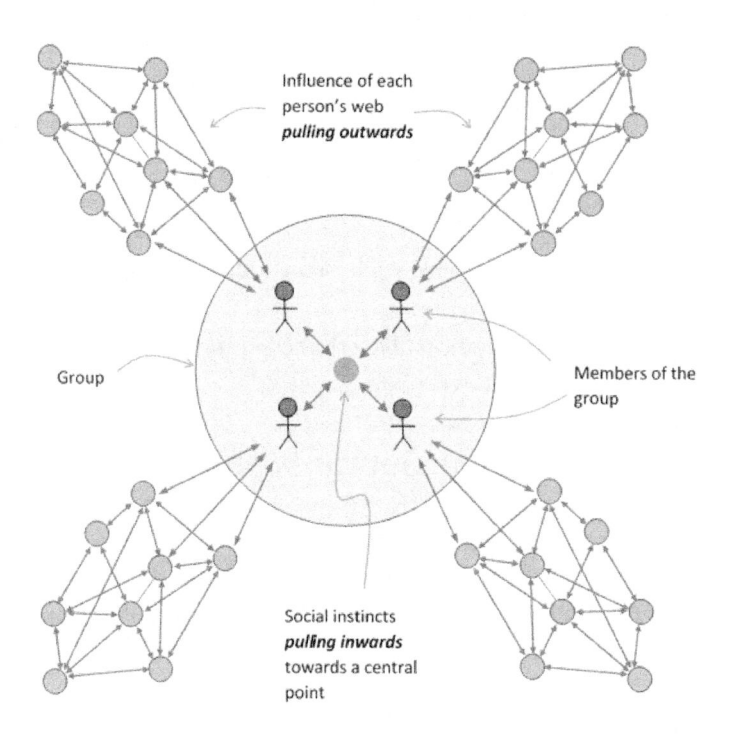

Influence of each person's web *pulling outwards*

Group

Members of the group

Social instincts *pulling inwards* towards a central point

This process will happen in every group we are a part of. It will happen in each friendship group, as each person feels influences from their other friendship groups, colleagues and family. It will happen in families, as each family member feels influences from a different set of friends and colleagues. And, it happens at work, as each person feels influences from different friends and family.

In every group we are a part of, despite those external influences, our focus tends to get drawn into the social dynamic going on at that time. We find interest in gossip, we experience and try to resolve conflict, and also try to position ourselves based on our identity. The more important the group is to us, or to someone else in it, the tighter the grand social web of society bunches up around that group, and the stronger the respective inwards and outwards pulls.

Therefore, inward forces represent our socialisation instincts, and outward forces represent our spread-out social lives. As they pull against each other, difficulty can arise in a group.

We shall now look at those forces in more detail, starting with the outwards force.

The outwards pull

When we're with a group, how we interact in that group will be influenced by other groups we are a part of. This happens through many different avenues, a few of which are described below.

We may feel pressures or constraints from other groups. We may be reminded of frustrations in other groups, which can affect how we feel at any one moment, and can make it harder to interact in the group in front of us. Difficulty elsewhere can be transferred in to the group in front of us, to some extent.

We may feel uplifted by tied thoughts of other groups, and feel an encouragement to behave in certain ways. We may interact using behaviours and values that have been forged in other groups, perhaps the groups where we feel most ourself in, and we simply feel compelled to act that way.

Perhaps we feel some resistance to coming across how we'd like, due to thoughts of someone else in our web, outside of the present group, who isn't supportive of our identity level. We imagine something they'd say, and it affects our emotions, so that we have to find a little extra strength, to be able to still act how we want.

If we face embarrassment or insecurity, it may be a reflection of how someone, outside of the present group, may react towards us if they were there in person.

We may try to shape a present group to be a certain way, because of how someone in a different group might view our participation in it.

We might compete with people in a group in a way that is more representative of a rivalry elsewhere. Losing in any situation makes us think of how that rival might respond, if they were present.

Essentially, in many ways we can be conduits between our wealth of social bonds, and the people in front of us. We of course have our individuality, but we are also social beings that are tempered and shaped by our social ties. We have our own thoughts and ideas, but our emotions are largely interlinked and shared with others.

A large part of how we interact in a group is based on the influences, associations, behaviours and values of people from across the whole of our web. We rarely think of it this way, but in each group we are a part of, each person is carrying their web of other people into the group.

Other people form part of our web, and we form part of others. We may resist them pulling away from us, and changing to fit into a new group, and so they do us. We are important and interconnected with each other, but often geographically separated.

All of this is the outwards pull on a social group, felt by each member, to their respective social webs.

The inwards pull

There are many different types of forces that pull groups together. They each play a part in facilitating the sharing of emotions, in order to resolve conflict, and create a group structure that takes into account the needs of each person in the group. Our instincts try to reach a common point in a group, where each person is integrated and feels belonging.

They come in a variety of types. Some make us feel good, and others make us feel bad until we take action to resolve them. Some are more nuanced. They each play a role, in our reactions to those around us, that causes us to be drawn together.

The ones that more obviously make us feel good are the shared bond of having a secure group. It can give us defences and security against other groups around us. Groups often therefore try to create a sense of togetherness, as well as reasons why they are better than groups around them (or often, in complex societies, reasons why they are the best group). Groups can give us commonality, reciprocated behaviours, shared humour, the enjoyment of group activities, and a sense of belonging.

The ones that make us feel bad until they're resolved are less obvious. This is partly because, in the way our groups and webs form, we can't always resolve them, so they just persist. We can't always see what they're trying to achieve, and they lead to stress and frustration, so they just seem negative.

We shall look at two forces, empathy and bristling.

Bristling is more of a negative force, because it can be a little uncomfortable to experience. Bristling relates to our need to establish hierarchical positions, preferably without resorting to fighting.

Empathy is more nuanced. It is of course our ability to understand, sympathise with, and to some extent feel the emotions that we see in others. It shares emotions, even without interpersonal interactions, and the result is that it provides motivation to care for each other.

These forces are a key part of our social instincts. They produce emotions from deep within us, in ways that can sometimes be quite powerful, so that we simply have to try to solve our social relationships. Because they are instinctual, they worked for us before we could communicate with complex language, millions of years ago. And, they work in other social animals in the natural world, who have limited methods of communication, but yet still form harmonious close groups.

Empathy

We aren't telepathic, and yet we feel other people's emotions.

We feel the emotions of others based on the way they behave towards us, as we've looked at in previous chapters. However, even without an interpersonal interaction, we pick up on other's emotions.

We pick up on them through our senses, mainly sight and sound. Through how we see and hear other people, some emotion is transmitted, and a reaction occurs in ourselves.

We then empathise with the other person. We see them express and experience certain emotions, displayed in their body language, tone and facial expressions, and it has some effect on us, even without any interaction occurring.

However, without any interactions, the transfer of emotion that occurs is based on fairly limited information. When emotions are transferred through behaviours, it is based on a huge range of nuanced, subtle information. When emotions are transferred through empathy, without interactions, our brain has to estimate the emotion the other person is feeling.

To do this, our brain interprets what *we* think *they're* feeling.

But it is only that: what *we* think *they're* feeling. We have no way of really knowing exactly how they feel. What our brain is actually doing therefore is using our experiences and emotions to approximate how we think the other person is feeling.

We do this in two ways.

When we see **emotions** expressed in *others*, we think about what **events** would cause *us* to feel those emotions, and project that onto the person. We feel, subconsciously, they must have experienced similar events to these, in order to feel the way they do.

Secondly, we see *other* people experiencing **events**, and we project onto them the **emotions** *we* would feel if we were in their shoes. If we see someone crossing the finish line in first place, we conjure up how we would feel, if we were in that position. If we see someone being picked on, we get a feeling inside us of how we would feel, if we were in that position.

Sometimes we get it right. Sometimes we under empathise, where we don't realise someone is finding difficulty, when they actually are. Sometimes we over empathise, when we feel someone should be experiencing certain emotions, yet they aren't.

In general, the closer our experiences to others, the more likely we are able to empathise effectively. When we get it right, we can take more helpful actions. If we don't get it right, our actions can often be rebuffed.

Group Dynamics

This works very well in a group in nature, because animals in that group all tend to have similar experiences. For example, in a tribe, each human would have their parents, their children, their tribe, their home, the need to mate, and the need to survive. Therefore, what makes each member feel good and bad will all be quite aligned. When there is interpersonal conflict, and one of the members experiences and displays a negative emotion, then the other members see that emotion, and their brains interpret it from their own experiences. Because their experiences are similar, the interpretation is correct, and how it makes them feel, and the action they take, are often helpful in resolving the situation.

In comparison, modern humans can have very different experiences. For example, for some, winning makes them feel ecstatic. For others, something else does. Some have close families. For some, friendship groups are everything. For some work is everything, for some a sport or hobby is everything. For others it is their partner. Our core needs get transferred and imprinted onto the world around us, rather than being all aligned to our families and tribe.

Not only that, but people can react to the same environment in different ways. Due to our multi-layered societies, and huge range of circumstances, and different social environments, there can often be large differences in how one person reacts to a situation compared to another. This can be difficult to fully appreciate, when we ourselves have only ever reacted to an environment one way. For some a situation is intimidating, for others it is relaxing.

Therefore for modern humans, empathy can be harder, and less accurate. Our brains still empathise with other people in the same way, but now those people may have had very different experiences to us, and be feeling different emotions to the ones we think they're feeling, or the emotions stirred in ourselves, on viewing them.

There are more reasons why empathy is difficult for modern humans. For example, when we take actions based on our empathy, if we are diverged, how we come across, and how we think we come across, can be very different. Our actions are rebuffed, and we may not understand why. The actions may, on the face of it, be correct, but the other person doesn't see us the way we see ourselves, and so doesn't feel our intentions. This can cause us to doubt our ability to empathise. We often can't accept that we were rebuffed because of our own abilities, so instead we just assume the person is wrong, or feeling the wrong emotions, or being unreasonable.

Also, we tend not to really appreciate emotions until we've felt them. However, there will be many emotions, or circumstances, that we will simply never experience, so we are always at a slight disadvantage with being able to empathise accurately with others. People can live their whole lives in a bubble, or be so tied to a particular group that their emotions aren't affected by anything outside of it.

Finally, levels tend to cut through empathy. We struggle to empathise with difficulties of people who have much more than us, and, in the reverse, we struggle to really appreciate what it's like for those with much less.

This leads to modern situations where we expect others to feel a certain way, or act a certain way, but they don't, which surprises us. At times, we (or other people), may say "do you feel this, or that", but actually they don't (or we don't, if it's someone saying it to us). Someone can make assumptions about what someone else needs, based on what they need themselves. What people need, or feel they need, can vary a lot from person to person, having transferred their core needs onto the world around them during adolescence.

Empathy is a very core part of our programming. It would be extremely rare for someone not to be able to empathise. Some people have more awareness, or simply an ability to facilitate solutions to problems, but everyone has the ability to empathise well. It is our modern social environment that obscures our ability to empathise, and it produces many situations where it doesn't appear to work, because of the unusual circumstances discussed above. This is part of the reason why we can be so obtrusive towards each other in modern societies, because we have to make others feel like we do, otherwise they may simply never appreciate it.

In groups, empathy is an inwards force, pulling us together.

It facilitates the sharing of emotions, even without people behaving towards each other. We see others experience events and emotions, and it makes us feel a little of that. Those feelings compel us to take action, to share successes, and help others avoid difficulty.

In tribes, this pulls the tribe-members together. If one person is mistreated, then it has a knock-on effect on others, so they resist that oppression. This helps the tribe move as one, and take account of each other's needs. This facilitates our interconnected social nature.

When empathy can't resolve

In modern groups, when people are being pulled away from the centre of a group by the influences from the rest of their web, empathy often can't resolve. We find, for some reason or other, we can't take the action that would resolve difficulty in others. The difficulty persists, and we are left empathising with other's difficulty, but unable to help them, which can be uncomfortable.

There is also frustration at people's different experiences. For example, frustration that others aren't empathising with us, or that they aren't able to help us, or frustration that we have to explain to others why we feel certain ways. There is frustration when we feel something is blocking us taking an action to help others.

Sometimes we can't take the right action because the source of the difficulty, in someone else, is in a different part of their web, a part that we have no influence over. Sometimes we can't take the right action because other people, in our web, might disapprove of us taking that action. Sometimes we are so tied up in our core social groups we are simply unaware of how people with different circumstances feel, or are unsure what the right action is.

All of these situations can cause unresolved empathy somewhere within groups.

Empathy needs to be unavoidable; it can't be a choice. When empathy can't resolve, when we can't take the actions that resolve it, discomfort can build.

The reason for this is so that there is a backstop. It makes the process of empathising, and taking action, an unavoidable part of our programming. If we try to ignore it, it can build until we can't ignore it. We can even feel guilty for not taking action to help, even if, objectively, we can't really do so.

This doesn't always happen; it depends on the situation. However, sometimes we simply have to find ways to resolve that unresolvable empathy, and guilt, without action. Empathy pulls groups together, but in the modern world, where groups can't reach a common, central point, it will regularly not be able to resolve.

We resolve the unresolved empathy mainly in one of four ways. We may not want to do these, but sometimes it is unavoidable. We convince ourselves that either:

- We shouldn't have to help them;

- Somehow, the little we have done, the other person experiences as if we had taken action;
- If things work out ok, we believe we did the right thing (even if this was very little) and take some credit for it; or
- They deserve their predicament (this is clearly the most unhelpful way of resolving it)

None of these resolutions are ultimately helpful. We should always try to do the best we can, and break our personal boundaries to help others. However, the reality of our modern lives is that there are often strong forces preventing us taking action sometimes, so we simply have some empathy and guilt left over that we have to resolve. We can only do the best we can in the circumstances, and find ways to live with our limitations, whilst trying our best to overcome them.

Essentially, empathy tries to pull groups together, but our webs prevent empathy pulling the group in front of us to a common point, where it can move as one. This results in a tug of war: inwards and outwards. We are left with our emotions compelling us to take actions that we can't, or find resolutions that aren't possible in the context of that group. Then, some frustration and difficulty remains.

If the world was more equal, we'd all have more similar experiences, and we'd be able to both empathise more accurately, and take action more freely.

Bristling

Looking at the second inward force: bristling; it is also part of our social instincts, and plays a role in pulling groups together.

Bristling is the feeling we get when there is a stand-off to someone else, or when there are unresolved hierarchical positions. It is a little uncomfortable, and can persist until the pecking order has been established. It is normally low-level,

A Theory of Everyone

and generally goes unnoticed. It is a minor feeling that is simply part of modern socialisation. If you'd prefer not to read about it, by all means skip this section.

It's actually easiest to describe in relation to other animals.

For example when a cat is performing its daily prowl of its territory, if it spots another cat in its way, it will bristle. It tenses up, and stands up taller, with legs more straightened. It arches it's back, or adopts a defensive pose. The two cats will engage in a stand-off like this for a while, perhaps without even moving, until one of the cats backs down. Then, they relax and both move on with their daily routine.

Bristling allows the resolution of hierarchy without conflict. Those two cats were able to establish hierarchical positions (i.e. which cat had the upper hand), without resorting to physical interaction. This reduces the risk of injuries, which, especially in wild animals, can result in being unable to find food, or defend themselves. Having social mechanisms that avoid the risk of injury is beneficial for a species. Resolving conflicts without fighting is in both cat's interests.

In order for bristling to work, whilst the two cats are in a stand-off, there must be some transfer of emotion. There must be some battle of minds.

Since there is no physical interaction, and often no verbal interaction, this battle of minds occurs individually, in each cat's brains. After this occurs, some tension is relieved, and some order is established.

The feelings of bristling aren't necessarily dictated by will or desire, but by our core programming (for example our inherited level and our identity level). The feelings have to representative of something real, i.e. how the conflict would occur if it was more direct. The result of bristling, who wins and who backs down, has implications on the social dynamic, so it has to be realistic.

In humans, whether we bristle more or less can come from many sources. One is how diverged we are. The more diverged we are, the more we rely on communication and interaction to indicate to others what our identity level is. We have to work a little harder to establish our identity level, and prevent others exposing our inherited level. As a result, bristling (the stand-off before communication) doesn't favour us, and the feelings we get can be more representative of our inherited level (i.e. how we emotionally respond to others, before we can establish our identity level).

In nature, there will be some feeling of reward for the cat that wins the bristling, and some frustration for the cat that loses. But this will be short lived. Bristling isn't supposed to persist in social dynamics, it is just there to force social beings to form hierarchies, with relative positions. It rears its head when positions are unclear, and stays until the positions are sorted out. If it takes a while for these positions to be ordered, the feeling of bristling will stay, until that feeling is actually more uncomfortable than accepting the lower social position, at which point that becomes the more palatable option, and doesn't seem so bad.

Cats tend to compete for physical territory, but humans tend to compete for groups. Just like a cat is programmed to want a territory, we want our groups, both to give us security, against conflict with other groups, and to define who we are. If a new member joins one of our groups, or someone is trying to change it, so that our position within the group is threatened, we feel some bristling towards them.

Like the cat, we tense up a little when in close proximity to someone we might have conflict with, or against someone who our position isn't secure and established. We may feel that bristling, until one of us signals that we back down. Sometimes this is purely non-verbal, but sometimes we bristle until we are able to interact, perhaps use our behaviours on them, verbalise our identity (and therefore how we want to be treated), and establish some sort of hierarchical order.

Those feelings are there to establish hierarchical positions in a low risk, non-physical way.

Bristling is an inwards pull on a group because it forces our focus onto those around us. We can't ignore those people; bristling compels us to interact and establish positions. Bristling will cause a group of social beings from different backgrounds to create an ordered group, find a common subculture (that the group can be positioned against), and thus create a group that can move as one. To resist this may cause discomfort.

When bristling can't resolve

In modern humans, it is quite common for bristling not to be able to resolve.

This is perhaps because there are so many different subcultures in societies. Every friendship group will have people positioned according to a different set of values. Mixing of people in new groups therefore creates greater cause for conflict.

Or, it is because most people are diverged, and no-one has a completely secure position. Everyone has to work a little to establish their identity, and be positioned how they want.

However, these are difficulties for creating hierarchies in groups, but not obstacles. The real obstacle is the outwards pull we feel, to other groups in our web.

If you took a group of people, some significantly diverged, some with very different values, they would eventually form an acceptable hierarchy, if they were the only group in the world.

Group Dynamics

The difficulty comes because our personal webs are interlinked. Our position in one group is supported or propped up by our position in another group. The position we need to achieve in any group has to be consistent with the positions we achieve in other groups in our web. This is because we feel influences, and tied thoughts, to those groups, and we know that at some point in the future we will be with that group again, interacting on the basis of that group's hierarchy. Our webs can be a little like a house of cards.

As a result, the part of bristling that allows it to resolve, where one person backs down and accepts the result, can't happen.

We may find this in our own lives from time to time. We may get into a conflict with someone else, where we're closely competing, perhaps on different values, and occasionally we're ahead, and occasionally behind. It's stressful, and sometimes when we're behind we just try to think "ok, you win". But it's just not palatable. We just can't accept being positioned lower than the other person. It wouldn't fit with our values, or the other groups that we're a part of. So, we find we simply have to jump back into the ring, and continue fighting.

There are many circumstances where there is no pecking order palatable to everyone's needs, and everyone's outwards pull from their webs. Therefore, there is often some residual feeling of bristling that can't be resolved. No group can truly move as one, because each person in the group has other groups that they feel allegiances to.

Two more specific interpersonal situations that can cause unresolvable positions are "cross conflict" and "leveraged conflict", that we looked at earlier:

Cross conflict:

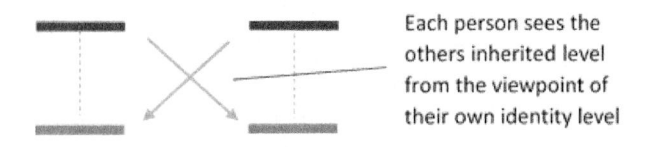

Each person sees the others inherited level from the viewpoint of their own identity level

Leveraged conflict:

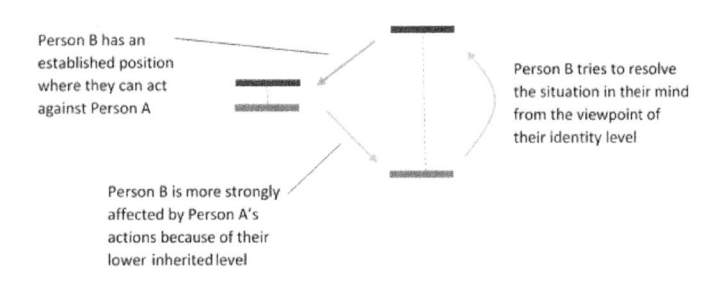

Person B has an established position where they can act against Person A

Person B tries to resolve the situation in their mind from the viewpoint of their identity level

Person B is more strongly affected by Person A's actions because of their lower inherited level

Bristling, like empathy, often can't fully resolve in modern societies, where people have social lives spread over several groups. This means that our groups are often left with a little residual difficulty. This is, in part, what causes all the strings that connect us to be a little jumbled and knotted. We are trying to maintain slightly mis-matched positions across our web, which can add a little stress. The feelings from the unresolved bristling and empathy can create difficult tied thoughts, so that whilst tied thoughts are supposed to innocently maintain positions, and bonds, with people not present, they can instead become uncomfortable.

Hence, being a modern human, with a whole web of groups and influences, is harder than being a hunter-gatherer, with only one group. This difference gets more pronounced in large unequal societies, where there is greater difference in positions, and inwards forces and outwards forces pull harder.

Group dynamics summary

We have many groups in our lives, though some are more important to us than others. Our groups are interconnected with each other, and our web is interconnected to others.

Our groups can be complicated. There can be people from different sub-cultures, different parts of society, different problems or difficulties, and where each person has different filters. Different members of the group can have wholly different views of what appropriate values and behaviours should be, and believe that theirs is correct, see the world only through their eyes, and struggle to understand how someone else could feel differently.

We have our social instincts, that happen whether we want them to or not. They try to move each group to a common point, so that the group can move together. But when our lives are a balance between several groups, no one group can reach that commonality. When the inwards pull (our social instincts or programming), can't resolve, it can be frustrating or stressful.

Of course in many cases this isn't too much of a problem. Some groups are important to people and just work, and are relatively free of drama and conflict. Some people are very good at just getting on with anyone. However, for every harmonious group, there is one with conflict. For every person that can get on with (almost) anyone, there are others that can't. On average, because of the way our large societies conflict with our programming, our social lives are more difficult, and it is harder than it would be living in a small tribe.

Part of the stress of groups comes from unequal societies. In these societies, there is greater difference in sub-cultures, people are more diverged on average, and people need greater security from groups, as there is more to lose and more to gain, making those social bonds deeper. All of these can increase both the outwards and inwards pull, creating greater conflict.

The inwards pull is levelling the playing field. It is what is drawing us together. Empathy is compelling us to look after each other, and bristling is compelling us to find common ground.

In a more equal world, there may still be some inwards and outwards forces at play in group dynamics, but they will be much less. People would feel less threatened by adjacent groups, and covet status less. Everyone's web would be less constraining. We'd find less conflict in the groups we come across, and our mind would get caught up in tied thoughts less. The strings that link us all across society, through our social bonds and comparisons, would be smoother and vibrate less energetically, and, we'd all have more personal freedom.

11
Societal Dynamics

We've looked at an individual's interactions, and the interactions within a group. This chapter is one step bigger, and looks at the interactions within society. This chapter is about how an individual fits into a society, and how a society functions when made up of a huge number of people, most of whom have little knowledge of (and no interactions with) the majority of other people in it.

The first half of this chapter looks at how an individual views society from a "tribe-sized" programming. The second half of this chapter looks at the nature, and impact, of levels in the overall societal dynamic.

Societies are vast. Even a reasonable size town can be several hundred thousand. Countries can be many millions of people, all the way up to the largest, China, with over 1 billion. The global society is over 7 billion.

Our societies are larger than the largest ant, termite or bee colonies, or the largest schools of fish.

Yet despite their large size, we only form social bonds with a tiny fraction of those societies. We live surrounded by neighbours, and often not far from local towns, but many of the people around us we know little about, and have no link to, other than geographical colocation. We live alongside people from all walks of life, with different cultures and behaviours, and, in some places in the world, great wealth lives next to great poverty.

We experience society mainly through our web of contacts. We can see the larger picture, but what we see is different for each person. If our societies are paintings, then we each see different fragments of the painting, and different hues, textures and colours. How we feel about the wider painting, i.e. the people that make up the wider society outside of our web, often gets skewed. The wider painting is blurred: we don't know those people, we often can't fully relate to their positions in life, and we only see small portions of the way they interact. As a result, we tend to view them as figments, good and bad, above and below. We give them labels. Different people produce derision, superiority, aloofness and pity.

In contrast, the people in our web we share some bond with. We have similar viewpoints, experiences and behaviours. Our emotions are interlinked. Because of the bond between us, we have some motivation to resolve relationship difficulties and conflict, because the bonds prevent us heading off in an entirely different direction. We try to understand each other, in a web, and we feel some of each other's ups and downs, whether we want to or not. These are the people we compare ourselves to, and feel a part of.

The people in front of us, in our web, are in focus. The rest of society is behind that web, out of focus.

This is representative of our "tribe-sized" programming. Within a tribe, we have intuitions that allow us to accurately assess people, absorb realistic impressions of those people, and understand the interpersonal dynamics, and social landscape. We have an intuition about expected behaviours

Societal Dynamics

and consequences. Our programming is set up to deal with a tribe-sized layout. Our "tribe" (our web) is more in focus.

In contrast, with the wider society, we have no way of gauge the nature of it, from our habits or programming alone. The emotions, and viewpoints, of people across society, are therefore out of focus to each individual.

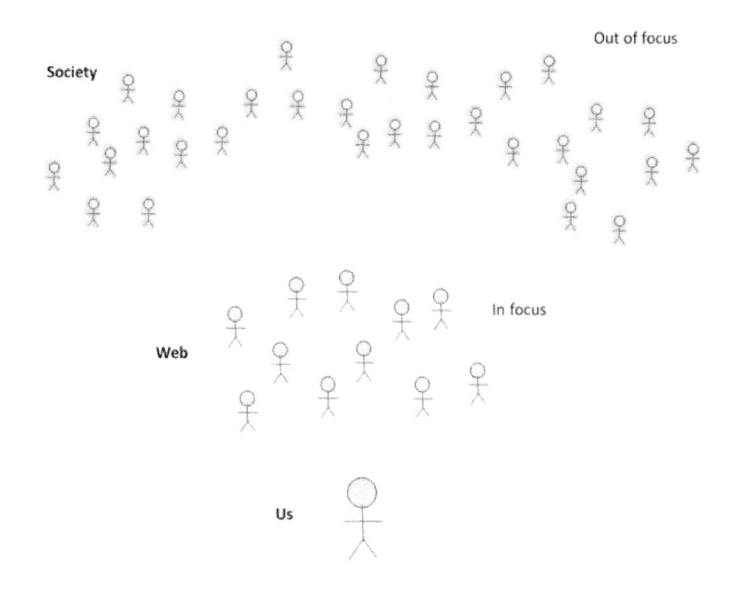

Because of this, society is a bit of an enigma. Different people can feel about it very differently. Our programming doesn't naturally interpret and understand it well. As a result, we can find the wider society quite emotive, and our impression of it can change based on the small fragments of it we see and hear. Sometimes we can over-react to what we experience of wider society, and sometimes we can under-react.

Sometimes people from society come into focus for a time. They can join our web, and we share common experiences, form groups with them, and find some level of linking and competition. Some stay, whilst others disappear out of our lives, back into society, and out of focus.

This arrangement is representative of the fact that, even 12,000 years of after we stopped being hunter-gatherers, our programming is still "small-group" in nature, despite our large societies.

We of course have views of other parts of society. As we view different fragments, on TV, or on the internet, or in our local town centre, we form impressions, and have interactions, here and there.

Yet because those people are blurred, our social emotions aren't closely interlinked with them. We tend to interact, with people from the blurred part of society, whilst keeping our focus in our web. We interpret interactions, with the blurred part of society, from the basis of our core friendships, and groups.

If everything in our web is good, and our web is secure, we feel society is good. We see difficulty around us, but it doesn't stay with us: we can put it out of our mind. Perhaps we don't feel society needs to change.

If everything in our web is bad, and we have much conflict and difficulty, then we feel that society is wrong, and needs to change.

Our web (that includes all the different groups that are important to us), is the basis of our programming. Our web provides the filter through which we view society. The dynamic in our web affects how we feel, and we then project that onto society.

For example, what happens in web tends to colour our overall mood and views, and then, when we think of the wider society, the remnants of those emotions get transferred onto

Societal Dynamics

the part of society we're thinking about. Our view of society is influenced by our experiences in our web.

To complete the link, our web is influenced by society. Through the interactions that our friends, colleagues and family have, and those that we have ourself, we will get inputs from society, that will have a knock-on effect on the interpersonal relationships within our webs.

As a result, how each person views society looks something like this:

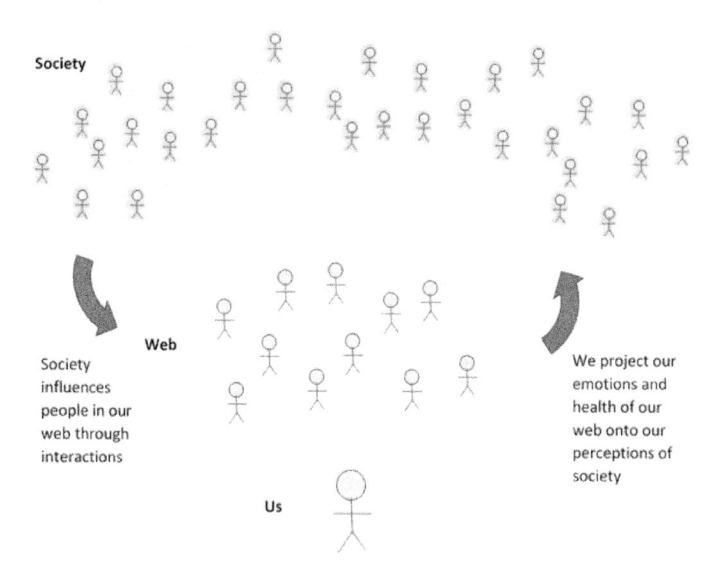

Society

Web

Society influences people in our web through interactions

We project our emotions and health of our web onto our perceptions of society

Us

This is how modern humans experience large societies, and how they are constructed. Each human being has their own web, much like the size of a tribe, of people that we share bonds, experiences, groups and emotions with, and that forms a part of the larger society.

We do feel large scale allegiances, whether by town, city or country, and this gives us a feeling of shared culture and belonging. We also feel threats and oppression based on allegiances and rival cultures. But the majority of the way we experience the larger society is through the interpersonal interactions and emotions in our own webs.

Societies therefore move as one through the summation of all of these individual experiences. We aren't like bees or ants, who are directly linked to the hive mind. We aren't even like a large herd of animals, for example emperor penguins or buffalo, who are directly linked to the whole herd pecking order and movements. Instead, we are like many small prides of lions, or groups of elephants, all collocated in a safari park. We are still our old hunter-gatherer selves, that we were for millions of years. We are still largely dictated by that programming, and needing groups and webs that represent the size of the tribes. It's just that now we find ourselves surrounded and interlinked with other tribes.

Some people have good experiences of this, some bad. Those that have bad, feel compelled to try to change society. Those that have good, probably understand less why society needs to change. On average, each individual will view society in a way that represents the health of society. In unhealthy societies, there will be a greater number of people finding difficulty with their web. In healthy societies, there will be a greater number of people finding secure and comfortable webs.

The two perspectives

Whilst the majority of our emotions are derived from our web, we are occasionally pulled above that, and find ourselves focussing on the bigger picture.

Societal Dynamics

When focussing on our web, our emotions are interlinked, and representative of the interpersonal and group dynamics. Our brains are set up to absorb and manage the goings on in the groups in our web. When our focus is pulled onto the larger society, it can become more emotive, because our programming is less well suited to this arrangement.

We view the people around us in two ways. At times, we are focussed on our interpersonal relationships, whilst at other times we are focussed on the societal big picture, and how we feel about it.

These two perspectives tend to be quite separate. We view people differently whether we're thinking more interpersonally, or in a societal way.

We have our web, where we see individuals, share experiences and connections, and are able to empathise more accurately. In contrast we have the blurred society behind, full of people who have very different experiences, people who probably feel about the world very differently to how we do.

On the interpersonal perspective, when someone comes into focus, and we interact with them over a not insignificant amount of time, then we generally see the human being. Differences of belief and opinions can dissolve, and we realise we are just human beings, and not so different.

On the societal perspective, then the wider group, that includes all the blurred people that we live side by side with, is less trustworthy. We can feel threatened or intimidated by the blurred society, behind our web. And with good reason, those people may have little reason to empathise with us, and, as we've seen throughout history, and in the world right now, there can be oppression and subjugation. We rely on people that we share common culture and history with, to defend against the other part who we don't. We also push our own allegiances, because, if we are part of a wider group that is valued, then we become more valued in ourselves. If there is inequality in society, then there is the possibility of some people being more, and others less. The depth of inequality (mostly monetary inequality) in society will generally correlate with the strength of feelings towards the parts of society that are blurred to us.

We tend to flip between these two perspectives. Perhaps at times we feel the societal perspective, and feel broad-brush emotions, and at other times we feel the personal perspective, where we focus on the interactions around us, and see others more as human beings just like ourselves.

The more unequal society is, the more time we spend in the societal perspective. Similarly, the less we feel in control of the prevailing social dynamic, the more affected we are by potential influences coming from the societal perspective. The less secure and stable our web, the more our mind might wander onto the snippets and fragments of information we get from the blurred picture of society.

We are connected to the wider group through our web, but also through the prevailing government, local authorities and news outlets. In the modern world, we are more connected than ever to the wider society, not least due to social media. We get much more interaction with the blurred part of society. As a result, we feel the societal perspective more than the personal perspective. The societal perspective is generally more emotional than the interpersonal perspective. In it, we see others as good or bad, and we see threats and allegiances to our points of view. It is a more stressful and less comfortable perspective to be in, rather than just interacting with the human beings in our web, that we share social bonds with.

The more time that people spend in the societal perspective, the more of society's emotions come out. This can be a good thing for improving a society, as people are focussed and motivated to change how society is, generally for the better. However, it is a personal trade-off, and at times we might find we need a balance, and switch off the news and social media, to focus more on the interpersonal experiences around us. The societal picture is full of unknowns, of incomplete information, and of possibilities. Our tribe-shaped brains, and the fact that our societies are made up of thousands of small interlinked groups, mean that we simply cannot accurately gauge the nature of society, and it will always be somewhat of an enigma.

Resultant traits of the top and bottom in society

Whoever we are, we have two things: our web; and the blurred wider society outside of our web.

We are all just human beings. However, our different circumstances can cause different traits and patterns to emerge in individuals. We see the wider society as figments and impressions, but people do also have certain distinctiveness, based on the part of society they find themselves in.

As hunter-gatherers, we would all have been relatively similar, but in a multi-layered society, the structure affects how each of us come across.

Those at the top and bottom of society, whether in towns, cities, countries, or across the world, tend to have similar traits, but for different reasons.

The traits are:

- An increased number of social rules, so that the breadth of acceptable behaviours is narrower.

- More distinct sub-culture (compared to the wider society in the middle), with greater differentiating features, for example in styles, fashion, and pursuits.
- More obtrusive behaviours.

The reason for these traits is different in the top and bottom.

The groups at the top tend to have these traits for two reasons. Firstly, the people in that group are more likely to be diverged. There is more competition to be in the top of society, and less spaces (since societies are generally a triangle, with less people at the top). As a result, there is a greater turnover of people entering and leaving these levels, and therefore a greater proportion of people that are more diverged. Being diverged leads us to needing to be more narrow, distinct and obtrusive, since this is how we bridge the gap between our inherited level and our identity level.

The second reason is that those at the top are trying to protect their wealth and not lose out. In order to do this, they make it harder for others to integrate into the top of society. They have a greater number of social rules, and become narrower and more distinct, so that newcomers find it more difficult to feel a part of that culture.

At the bottom of society, the same traits are performed but for different reasons. The traits keep people away who may impose themselves on the group with some element of superiority. By creating a narrow culture, they can form a sort-of clique, where those that are integrated into the clique have greater security, and feel elevated in value. Providing others aren't allowed in the clique in a way that might contradict that belief, it can succeed.

There are some differences between the top of and bottom of society, but there are also many similarities if you look at the patterns of behaviour. We are all just human beings, in an alien environment, at the end of the day.

Empathy in society

The second half of this chapter looks at levels in a society.

This section looks at how large differences in levels between people (which are present in large unequal societies) affect our social instincts, including **empathy**.

The next section looks at the nature of levels, and the final section in this chapter looks at the more theoretical question of whether levels become part of a person (so that society imparts something on us), or whether the effect of levels is merely a result of the environment we find ourselves in.

Firstly, we shall consider **empathy** and the wider society.

Whilst people in the wider society are blurred to us, we do still empathise with them. If we see people experiencing different events, or emotions, it can resonate with us. It's likely that how it makes us feel is very different to how it makes them feel, given our different viewpoints and experiences, but we empathise nonetheless.

We see people experience events in society, and we project onto them how we'd respond to those events. We see people experience emotions in society, and we project onto them the events that would cause us to feel that way. We feel they must have experienced something similar. This works, and provides some motivation to improve society. But, given people's different backgrounds and life situations, and the fact we often lack huge amounts of information when empathising with the wider society, how we empathise with them may be in the right ball-park, but not be similar to how they actually feel.

However, there are a few situations in large societies where other factors override empathy.

One fairly obvious one is warfare. If someone is threatening our home, or basic security, then empathy is overridden. In warfare, people can get a rush from battle, slaughter their neighbours, and celebrate the victory. The rush and reward of fighting, and winning, overrides thoughts of how the other person feels about the situation.

Another factor that overrides empathy is levels.

As much as we empathise with the difficulty of the super-rich, we struggle to feel motivated to help them achieve both wealth *and* resolution of any difficulties they have.

And as much as we empathise with the poor, we can only do so much in our lives to help them without detriment to ourselves. We are all interlinked in societies' giant web, and we are somewhat limited in our ability to give up the majority of our wealth or status (should we feel inclined to), to lower ourselves, and raise others up.

In both cases, warfare and levels, the empathy is there, it's just overridden. If someone comes into focus, and we have interpersonal interactions with them, empathy will draw us together, and we can see them more as a human being. For example, soldiers in World War II, when staring at each other in the face, helped out their opposing soldiers in need, or played football across the trenches at Christmas. Similarly with levels, when we are confronted, face to face, by the super-rich or super poor, and feel their difficulty first hand, we are more likely to see past the levels and empathise.

But most of the time levels override that empathy. When those people are more distant to us, and no interpersonal interactions exist, they become more blurred. We have less of a link to their emotions, as well as being reminded of the threat they may pose to us, or the inequality between us. Then, the societal perspective, and levels, override empathy. We can see difficulty going on, but not feel motivated to help those in need. This can often lead those at the top to feel "how can people not care about my wellbeing and emotions", if they are personally attacked. And it can lead those at the bottom to feel "how can others not care about my difficulty; how can they just walk past". It can lead to everyone thinking "how can humans do these things to each other".

The result is that those more distant to us in society, above and below, become more blurred, and we see them as more of just a label or an idea, rather than a human being like ourselves.

But behind our position in society, behind our outer front, behind our mask or shell, under the clouds, is just that – a human being. And that human being everywhere wants similar things. But others don't see the human being, they see the outer shell, the mask, the top of the clouds, or our defences.

All this determines our behaviour towards those in society outside of our web. We are all the same underneath, but we do not have the same circumstances on the surface. We have mechanisms, such as empathy, that draw us together, but they are "tribe-sized" mechanisms, that don't always work in the same way, or in the way we may want them to, when applied to an environment that is alien to our evolutionary one.

What are levels in society?

Whether we are at the top of society, or the bottom, or somewhere in the middle, we absorb aspects of society, and we view the other parts with blurred filters and skewed empathy. Much of how we view others is a reflection of the relative societal levels.

As discussed throughout this book, levels have a large influence on behaviours and interpersonal relations. But whilst levels affect and maintain a social hierarchy, what exactly are they to an individual?

Levels in society are both a tangible and intangible concept. In some ways they represent the pecking order, and perhaps the distribution of wealth and status. However, in others ways, they merely represent how people feel about those around them.

The intangible part means that people experience levels in different ways. To some people, levels can seem more important than others. Some don't even notice them, whilst for others they are far more apparent.

For some, they will hero worship their manager or CEO, or politician or celebrity. Others will see those people as not too dissimilar to themselves, but just in a different position.

Some will see those below them as lowly, or very much beneath them. Perhaps they see them as deserving of their position, or simply lacking the ability to make more for themselves. Others will see them as people similar to themselves, but facing difficult circumstances, without positive starting points in life, and facing forces that resist them standing up.

It would only be if you aggregated each person's feelings towards everyone else in society, that you could construct any sort of tangible structure based on levels.

Whilst how people view levels comes down to natural variation, it isn't random. How a person views levels will be dependent on their circumstances. Like much of our fixed nature, it comes down to our parents, and the distance between us and them.

The reason for this, is that a lot of the views and feelings we have, of people across society, are influenced by the emotions and set-up of our web. In turn, how our web forms is influenced by our family unit. The family unit affects how a person's web develops, and then those deep family relationships underly our web, and transfer onto our social lives. It also comes from our parents because we pick up on, and replicate, our parent's reactions to those around them, which forms the basis of our inherited level. How we view society's hierarchy is therefore affected by the hierarchy in our family unit.

If there is distance between us and our parents, if they keep us at arm's length, hiding their inner emotions, and with a rigid hierarchy, then we will be forced to view them as unattainable. This viewpoint then transfers onto society:

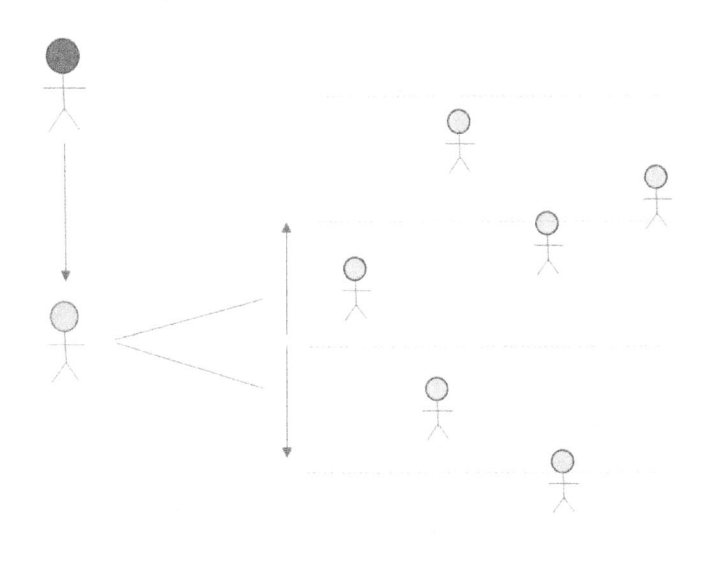

In comparison, if our parents are open, close to us, treat us as an equal (although there will always be some element of the parent being unyielding and not giving up the upper hand), and portray themselves as a human being, rather than a strict authority figure, then we are more likely to see our parents as human beings, and see those in society as similar to us but in different circumstances:

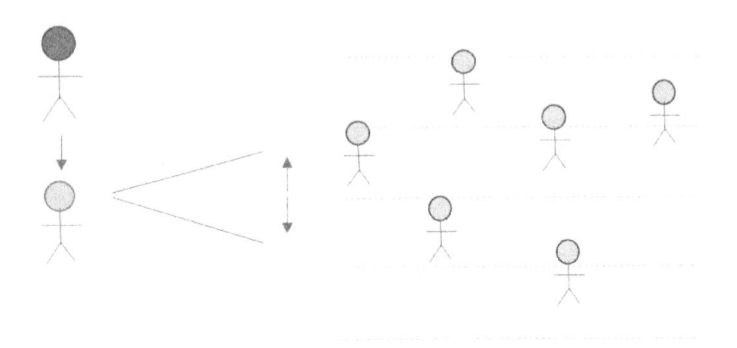

In these diagrams, two people are viewing the same group, but one person sees greater difference between top and bottom, whilst the other sees less.

If the person that sees greater difference between the top and bottom achieves a higher position, they would feel much greater internal reward, a rush of elevation. They would then expect to be treated in a similar way to how they once saw their current position. They would expect to be looked up to and revered, as they once looked up to and revered someone.

This also occurs if they become a parent and have their own family. On becoming a parent, they feel the elevation and reward of finally attaining the level that their parents made unattainable to them. Some part of them expects, or needs, their own children to feel about them the way they did about their parent. As such, a person's perception of levels cascades down generations of their family.

Societal Dynamics

If we all saw less distance between levels, then the need for fame and wealth would be replaced with family contentment. In contrast, the more stretched society becomes, the more family falls by the wayside, against the desire to chase success.

Our perceptions of levels, and the emotional distance in family units, are linked. The greater distance between perceived status levels in society, the greater distance between parent and child.

This will vary from person to person, with some experiencing greater family distance, and seeing greater difference in society's levels, and some less. However, in general, our relationships with our parents affects our views and experiences of society, and the current nature of society affects the myriad of parent-child relationships within society.

Therefore levels are both tangible and intangible. They represent the pecking order, or distribution of wealth and status, but each person will experience them differently. To one person, levels may be unnoticeable, but to someone else they may be very important.

After all, our large societies are like thousands upon thousands of small tribes, each with their own hierarchies (like we see throughout nature), but each interconnected, and muddled, with those around them. We are like a giant jigsaw, where none of the pieces quite fit together, and the overall picture changes over time. Some people will have good experiences of this (and perhaps hardly notice it), and others bad (and find real difficulty, conflict, and crossed-wires). There are some areas of freedom, and some gaps, crevices and pitfalls.

Those experiences then flow down to the next generation, through each individual parent-child relationship, as each person draws some learning of socialisation from the parent, and it forms part of their foundation. The new generation then has their own experiences of our spread-out social lives. It is perhaps no wonder that we all may have very different perceptions of the hierarchies around us.

Much of this book discusses people's reactions to levels, but is largely referring to an *average* situation. Levels have an effect, and that effect is described in this book, but how each person will experience that may be different. Some will feel the effect more strongly, others less so. Some will perceive a greater distance between levels, others will see levels as closer together.

As a final note, this relationship between society and parents, whereby the greater average distance between levels in society results in greater emotional distance between parent and child, actually provides another driver towards equality. This is because, just as we feel some draw towards our parents, and are frustrated by emotional distance to them, so there will be some force acting to close the gaps between each person in society.

How permanent are levels in an individual?

Levels therefore have both tangible aspects, related to the distribution of wealth and power, and intangible aspects, related to an individual's perceptions, and reactions, to those around them.

The first is, at least theoretically, possible to change. Money moves around in society, and the balance of power can shift. In this chapter, we'll consider whether an individual's perceptions of the levels around them can change. For example, could you take a person out of a society, place them in a new hypothetical one with a different structure, and over

Societal Dynamics

time, would they fully change and adapt to that new structure in their lifetime?

Do the levels in society represent something permanent and tangible within us, or are they merely a consequence of the social environment, and would disappear if we moved to different circumstances?

Levels are powerful because they represent wealth, opportunity, privilege, and being treated as more, not less. Across society, they are reinforced by large numbers of people at each level, and the resistance we feel from them is representative of these numbers. Rearranging levels in society is like reshaping a beach: moving one grain of sand is easy, but moving large quantities, so that the beach looks noticeably different, is not.

But take away all those aspects, the wealth, status, and numbers, and how much are levels ingrained in us?

Take two people, from different ends of society (one high, one low), and say they are stranded on a distant planet. There is no hope of rescue, but the planet is lush with vegetation, and there is a breathable atmosphere, and plenty of drinking water, so survival is not an issue.

They were transported there by a chance accident, say an unexpected wormhole, and there is no method to even communicate with another human being.

We looked in the last chapter about how the two would be drawn together by bristling and empathy. Despite one astronaut coming from wealth and privilege, and the other growing up without that, there would be socialisation forces encouraging two humans to find commonality. However, this would be resisted by their own respective webs – i.e. the people close to them from their respective levels in society (one high, one low), that influence them even when not around, through their tied thoughts.

But if they are never to see or hear from anyone in their web again, how much will they be affected by them? Will the influence of levels simply evaporate, as if there is no real permanence to them, or will they still be felt, even after years of the pair being isolated on the planet, i.e. will they still fall back on old habits and comfortable cultures? Will they still see the other person through the filter of old preconceptions, or will all those be forgotten, when they aren't relevant to these two astronauts trying to survive?

Until we develop deep space travel, we'll never know of course, but as a thought experiment, here are some arguments either way. Firstly, arguments that the influence of previous earthly levels will evaporate, and not influence the social dynamic, and secondly arguments that the levels will persist, and have some permanence.

Levels evaporate

A lot of our emotions are influenced by what *could* happen. If something could happen, our brain gives it focus and mentally prepares ourself for it.

For example, if someone, who we have some conflict with, *could* contact us easily, it is harder to put them out of our mind, compared to if they can't.

Therefore, a lot of the influence we feel from tied thoughts, to people in our web, is dictated by the fact that we are likely to meet up with them in the future. We have those tied thoughts to people, where they pop into our mind, because our mind is mentally preparing ourselves for future interactions. If we know we will likely meet up with them, at some point in the future, our programming keeps track of them, and occasionally reminds us of that link.

If we truly have no interest in meeting up with someone we once knew, and they have no interest in meeting up with us, they are less likely to drift into our thoughts. Instead, they drift out of our web.

Time is also a factor. The longer we go without seeing someone, the more likely it is that they drift out of our thoughts. For example, time is a great healer in break-ups.

It's possible then that the two lost astronauts would slowly feel the effects of their respective webs less and less. After a while, knowing that they'll never hear from their close friends ever again, and being consumed in their present circumstances, helping each other survive in the alien wilderness, they may feel the effects of their previous levels in society less and less. They could actually be drawn to a common point, with the shared experiences, camaraderie, and sub-culture, they develop, lost on the planet.

They will be able to see through the levels, see the commonality they have, and see each other as less blurred and just a human being.

If this is true, then the feelings we have towards different levels in society are just an illusion, and could evaporate after a while.

If levels are just an illusion, then you could take humans out of society, place them in a different one, and after a while they would forget why they used to feel their old feelings, towards people previously above and below them.

Levels have permanence

On the other hand, perhaps the two astronauts would continue to feel the influences of their webs, despite time and distance.

For example, people who we lose contact with still linger in our minds a little. They crop up when we do certain activities, or see certain objects, or hear certain sounds, or smell certain foods. Or, for no good reason, we think of a childhood friend, or a time we spent with someone a long time ago. We think about how we used to act together, behave towards each other, and how they made us feel.

When we experience the loss of a friend or loved one, even after they have left our lives, they still have some impression on us. Our thoughts turn to what they used to say, or what they might say if they were still around today. These thoughts can still impact us many years after they are gone, lifting us up, or pushing us down a little. Good and bad, we never truly forget people. What people said a long time ago can stick with us.

With our friends and family, they form an impression on our mind, fulfilling the role of our tribe, that our mind is searching for. These impressions have some permanence, although the strength of each impression waxes and wanes.

In these bonds, which have permanence, our levels somewhat reside. The memories of people, how they made us feel, and how we interacted with them, are all influenced by levels. Therefore because our bonds have some permanence, so do levels. If, say, during adolescence (the time when our mind most readily forms social bonds), someone made us feel not good enough, or we felt a strong superiority to someone, then through our memories of the impression of that person, our levels somewhat persist in us.

If our levels have permanence through our bonds, then this is no truer than through one of our deepest bonds, our parents. We feel levels through this bond in a number of ways, for example how our programming picks up on our parent's reactions to other people, as well as how they treated us growing up, both of which will have been a reflection of their levels. Since this is a deep bond, then, even on the distant planet, each astronaut's memories of their parents, and each astronaut's tied thoughts, to how their parents would react if they were there, will have some influence on the social dynamic between them.

There are other aspects of our personalities that are permanent and traced with levels. One such example is our behaviours. Our behaviours, in adulthood, are quite difficult to change. We find that how we are compelled to act in certain situations, what we find amusing, and what we enjoy doing (that makes us feel most ourself) all become relatively fixed. These behaviours were tuned during adolescence, based on the interactions we had, including the influence of levels. As a result, the permanence of our behaviours causes the permanence of our levels within us.

If this is true, then even if we never saw our web again, we'd still feel some influence from it. The two astronauts would work together, find some shared bond and camaraderie, but even after many years, and with no hope of returning to Earth, they would not be able to find complete comfort and commonality, and they would still remember their respective "roots", which may cause some conflict from time to time.

* * *

In reality, perhaps both are true to some extent. The influence of levels would lessen over time, but perhaps not be forgotten.

This goes some way to explain why the move and momentum towards equality is slow and on a generational timescale. Each generation cannot simply adapt to a changing arrangement of levels. As the levels get closer throughout their lives, their perception of them remains more rigid, and based on the bonds and behaviours that formed during adolescence, as they took in the world around them.

Those bonds and behaviours form a blueprint of how each person perceives and reacts to the world, and how each person feels differences in levels. That blueprint can't easily change, even if the world around does. Humans may resist change that

A Theory of Everyone

is too fast, because it would mean we find ourselves in social situations inconsistent with how we perceive the world.

Theoretically, this contributes to more stable social environments (whether in a tribe, or in a larger group), that are less prone to change, and feature less competition for culture with each new generation. Theoretically, without stabilising factors, then groups, and society, would be more erratic, and lurch from one place to another, good and bad.

Regarding "self", then if levels have some permanence in an individual, so that a person's levels, in life, have made some indelible imprint on their personality, then this also provides a different angle to explain why we can have an inconsistency between our internal self and our external self.

This is because our levels (which we didn't choose) affect how we come across, often in slightly frustrating or unusual ways. How we come across affects the impression we make on other people. Other people see us according to our actions and behaviours. However, to us, we don't see levels as forming part of our personality. If levels cause us frustration, anger, or other unwanted emotions, then we don't see those emotions as coming from us, and being a part of our personality. We see it coming from levels, and we see our personality as how we would act, and who we would be, if levels were removed. Therefore, the permanence of levels within us can cause a difference in how we come across vs. how we see ourselves.

Nevertheless, whatever happens to those two astronauts, on the distant planet, then, if, by a second chance (say, creatively, a second wormhole), they were rescued, and came back to Earth, they will likely find they have to fit back into society amongst their friends and family as before. The influence of levels would be reinforced, and however much commonality they found away from Earth, it would be difficult to find that back on Earth, with the influences of their webs re-strengthened.

When they met up and socialised back on Earth, the difference in wealth, culture and opportunity would be all too apparent. The rich astronaut attempting to act as if they were the same as the poorer one would come across as patronising, whilst the poor astronaut attempting to come across as no different to the more privileged one may be obtrusive.

The result of this is that society imposes a duality on us in the way we view people. We view the societal perspective and the personal perspective. We see both a human being and a label. This is rooted in the structure of society, and the way that our programming, which is still set up for small groups, is merely trying to bend and adapt to the circumstances it finds itself in.

It requires some force and action to change the levels in society to be more equal, but as long as there is inequality, there is motivation in abundance to make this happen.

Societal dynamics summary

Society is a complex structure, which each human only views a part of. We only view one section of the painting, and it is only through the interactions of everyone that the whole picture becomes clear.

Because we only see one small section, we often find we simply cannot understand other people's points of view. Our personal view of society can be completely different to someone else's, because we are looking at different parts of the painting. Each person's perceptions and emotions towards society are influenced by their own respective web, and their family units.

We see society in many different ways. We see people out of focus, and give them labels and stereotypes. Different levels of society cause people to come across differently, and these labels are reinforced somewhat. We find people more different from us are harder to empathise with, whether the top or bottom of society.

We each have different perceptions about the relative status levels in society. Our own perceptions are engrained in us, whether through the distribution of wealth and power, or through our own experiences. We absorb our own perceptions during adolescence, from the world around us, and from our family units, and these forge our personal blueprint for how we feel about society, and the world, that doesn't easily change throughout our lifetime.

It all just about works. Despite it being an imperfect system, that humans aren't really suited to, then over 5000 years, perhaps by trial and error, we have created large societies that find a balance between everyone's individuality, and the collective.

However, societies are still far from perfect, and there are many different motivations to change society.

12

Social Media

A discussion of interactions wouldn't be complete without talking about social media, since it has invaded our lives so much over the past 15 years. It changes the way we interact with our web: with our close friends and family; and it changes the way we interact with the wider society.

As social beings, our sense of self, and our emotions, are derived from our web, and our interactions. Therefore, anything that changes the way we interact, especially with those close to us, and anything that changes the structure of groups, can have a profound effect on the human experience.

This chapter looks at the good and the bad, the positive and the negative. There is no doubt that social media can instigate change for the better. But, it also can affect the individual, with many people finding their mental health and social relationships can be made worse.

Social media has been around for decades. However, it was only in the early 2000s when, in combination with mobile phones, it became very widespread.

Ever since the 1970s, when personal computers first came to prominence, people have been communicating through digital means. Even back then, there were message boards, blogs, and instant messaging, for example the PLATO system developed by the University of Illinois. However, they were only used by a select few, and only in a functional way, rather than infiltrating people's social lives[26].

Throughout the 1980s and 90s, as personal computers started to become a part of ordinary households, interacting through the computers increased. Email and message board use increased, and humans quickly adapted to reading text of a computer. We would read messages from an unknown username or email address, and interpret meaning and intent from it.

In the early 2000s, digital interactions exploded. Mobile phones became widespread, and through them a new form of communication was born: social media. We could now be contacted anywhere and everywhere in our daily lives, exchanging text, news and gossip, and, provoking people, and stoking conflict whenever we felt like it.

MSN messenger was launched in 1999. MySpace and Linkedin launched in 2003. Facebook was launched in 2004, Youtube in 2005, Twitter in 2006, Whatsapp in 2009, Instagram in 2010, Snapchat and Twitch in 2011, and TikTok in 2017, to name some of the most successful.

Each provides a different way of communicating. Each provides different rules, limitations, and ways of interacting and expressing ourself, depending on the features that the companies (that sell them) add in.

For social beings, such as ourselves, who would feel most ourselves, and most fulfilled, in a hunter-gatherer tribe environment, surrounded by our friends and family all the time, it feels almost right to communicate more often. It doesn't seem harmful to communicate by social media. We like to get a text from a friend. It can make us feel good to get followers, feel connected, and to get likes, and amass a number of connections, and digital status.

Platforms were launched without regulation, and simply gained popularity through word of mouth. The more people used them; the more others had to use them in order not to miss out. The more people used them; the more platforms appeared. The more people used them; the more important they become in our lives.

There is an old Ethiopian proverb: *when you pick up a stick, you pick up both ends.*

This means that our actions are often in balance, and that chasing desire and temptation comes with undesirable consequences: take the bad with the good, and they can't be separated.

Soon, people started realising that there were downsides to social media. It affects our mental health. It makes us frustrated, anxious, or pressured and constrained, even by friends and family. The permanence and public nature of interactions leads to greater conflict, humiliation and more impactful provocations. We get angry with newmember299, who we've never met, and know nothing about, because they post conflicting views to us, or disapprove of us online. There have been studies that show social media is a net detriment to our mental welfare.

We pick up the good end of the stick, that appears to make us feel good, to be more connected and sociable, and it appears to add something positive to our lives. But soon after we feel the other end of the stick, and we find social media has had a greater impact on our relationships, and our web of social contacts, than we realised.

Social media is a bit like chocolate. We like it, and unless we eat a lot of it in one go, we don't actually immediately notice any negative implications. It gives us a sugar hit, and we want more of it. Perhaps we'd much rather have it, compared to healthy vegetables. But if we eat too much chocolate, then after a while, we notice that our health is affected. The chocolate, that is enjoyable to eat, is having knock on effects to our physical health down the line.

The reason for the delayed negative impact of social media depends on which type of social media we consider: whether the type that connects us to our web, or the type that connects us to the wider society.

The problem with social media that connects us to our friends and family, is that it gives us the illusion of a hunter-gatherer tribe, to be more connected and ever present with the people that are important to us. However, the reality is that we just can't be in our modern environment. We need space to be able to fit the different parts of our life, which often don't quite fit together, together. We are all pulled in different directions, by our families, by different social groups, and by our work or career. Social media makes each pull stronger, so each person becomes more stretched.

The problem with social media that connects us to everyone else is that the interactions become very disproportionate. We feel good and bad based on the approval and disapproval of people we've never met. We have no information as to why they liked or disliked us, or said what they said, yet we still feel the effects of it. One of those people says something, and we can feel like *everyone* thinks that. Our programming isn't very good at interpreting these types of personal interactions from the blurred wider society.

Social media is affecting the mechanisms and coping strategies for dealing with our modern societies. Our interpersonal interactions are a delicate balance of forces pushing and pulling us this way and that, and social media can disrupt these. It appears to give us something we want, but what we want (a tribe) is something that can't really be achieved in a modern unequal society, with its different levels of value, and our spread-out social lives.

Some people will say that this isn't true, and that the mirage is real. They may say that it is "other people" that are the problem, and the way those "other people" use social media.

Perhaps we could all just be kinder, and just use social media more nicely. Perhaps this is true, and that humanity is facing a learning curve with using it. As we use it, we learn how our social digital footprint affects others, and how they respond. Some platforms we find, after a while, are more beneficial, whilst others leave us feeling less fulfilled, and we move on.

However, the other side of it is that social media is actually bringing out negative emotions that are already there. These are present in abundance in society, where difficulty is everywhere and unevenly spread. There is resentment of those with more, or the feeling of being less, or the feeling that our way of life, or values, are being threatened by those who think differently. In the world, there are huge inequalities, whether monetary, status or otherwise. There is persecution, control and oppression. There is greed, narcissism, and strange personalities and self-beliefs. There is a huge amount of conflict that goes on behind closed doors. And there are those that are facing very difficult circumstances. None of these are issues that can be solved quickly, yet social media allows the difficulty to be expressed. Social media brings out the frustrations of being a modern human, faster than it can solve them (and some it can't solve at all).

Some believe social media is good, some believe bad. Whether you think human nature needs to adapt to social media, or whether our use of social media needs to adapt to human nature, there is one thing that is true: social media appears here to stay. My personal view is that human nature hasn't changed in 12,000 years, given our experiences, emotions and relationships are all still dictated by hunter-gatherer instincts. In my opinion we should be wary and cautious with new technologies that change the way we interact and experience the world. We should respect the human nature within us, rather than imagining it away. Our societies, and our cultures, should be built around wholesome and balanced pursuits, so that children can develop in a grounded way, and adults have the best possible chance of living long full lives.

It is unlikely that large swathes of population will give social media up, even if it would result in a net increase in their mental health. If others obtain closer bonds and more control of group dynamics, through being more connected, then we feel some pressure to become more connected ourselves.

It is therefore important to understand what we are engaging with. There are positive and negative impacts of social media, and we will look at both sides in this chapter. We will start with the negative, which there are more of, and then look at the positive. There are more negatives discussed here, because this book is focussed on individuals, and what it feels like to be a human being.

Negative

Social media has a large impact on ourselves. It has grown into something that is almost a staple of daily life, rather than an optional extra.

The main ways that social media can negatively impact our lives can be split into two aspects: those related to the types of social media that affect our interactions in our **web**; and those that affect our interactions with the **wider society**.

After those two topics, there are three more points to consider: how social media can be addictive; how social media affects our internal self; and how it affects the parent-child relationship.

Web

Firstly, our self gets drawn out, and our focus becomes more strongly on those around us. Our actions are more constrained, and more representative of other people's influences.

Social media therefore tightens our web. It causes everyone to pull more strongly on the strings that link us through our social bonds. Groups become stretched, pulled one way and another, and it becomes harder to be an individual. People then try to find greater individuality by being more obtrusive to those around them, and the whole situation exacerbates. After a while in this state, we can find it can be a source of difficulty, and it can become harder to feel ourselves.

Our focus drifts away from us, and we spend more time thinking of other people.

We can be contacted at any time, and our brain spends longer in a state of readiness, preparing us for all possible interactions that might come in. All manner of social interactions, good and bad, could happen at any moment, and this is reflected in a subconscious state of alertness, making it difficult to switch off.

When we get "thinking of you" moments (when something reminds us of someone we know), we can immediately contact that person, and these moments are then reinforced, and happen more often. Then, instead of being able to interpret our surroundings from a personal point of view, we interpret them from the point of view of being surrounded by people that aren't there.

We find it harder to be alone, or to be bored. Our brain tells us that we should pick up our phone, and spend a small amount of energy getting something that feels rewarding.

This all strengthens our links to other people, and draws our focus away from our self, and onto our social interactions.

So what is the problem with focussing more on our social links? Why can it feel good to be doing it, and why does the negative come down the line, in a delayed fashion?

The problem is not that humans aren't suited to stronger links and constant communication, far from it. The problem is that our modern social environment, where our social lives are spread out, isn't suited to stronger links and constant communication.

Our social lives are spread over several groups, each with different values and sub-cultures, and each potentially being at different levels in society. Each of the people in those groups have further links to a whole range of other people. This environment is different to the one we evolved in.

In order to deal with this environment, even without social media, we need to rely on certain instincts to help guide us through the difficulty. There are many unknowns, a few surprises, and a few pitfalls in our modern social lives, and so we need to have our wits about us. We often naturally find solutions to social issues, but in order to do that we need to have the full social-toolkit available. For example there are some traits and mechanisms that make this environment easier. Two examples of these mechanisms are adaptability, and validation (which was briefly mentioned earlier).

However, with social media, these mechanisms become harder to do. After a while, with less access to adaptability and validation, we can feel more constrained.

On the first, social media makes adaptability more difficult. In our modern social environment, we may have to adapt who we are for each of our groups, using different behaviours, expressing different views, making different types of jokes and being a slightly different type of person. We might act differently with our family, compared to our friends, and compared to our profession. We bend and flex who we are from one group to the next.

Further, what feels comfortable one day may change the next. Or, people may move together and move apart. Groups of people may find commonality and togetherness one day, but what brought them together may change over time, or may only be applicable in certain environments. If people are maintaining more links, then, as they experience new and different environments and directions, and new friends, colleagues and acquaintances, then they can find that those old links make it harder to experience the new ones.

In order to navigate our modern social environment as best we can, we need a certain amount of space, and self. The less self we have, then every time we have to bend or reshape our individuality to appease others, it can be a cause of stress. It's unlikely that any one group really represents us, at least over an extended period of time. Even if it does, we will still be a part of other groups.

Social media makes this adaptability harder. As we are bombarded with messages pulling us one way and the next, we find increased stress with it. As people feel more constrained and pressured, new conflicts arise, which can then play out on social media, escalating the situation. Social media gives us a new tool, but as we pick it up, we drop some other very important tools that we need to use.

Regarding the second mechanism: validation; then as we discussed before, having space allows us to validate. Validation is very important for human socialisation, where we can seek support in one group, for conflict in another, and then put it out of our mind for a while. We can better put up with behaviours that frustrate us, knowing it is only for a short while, and then we can focus elsewhere.

With greater connectivity through social media, this becomes harder. Even if we seek support in someone, for a conflict elsewhere, it's less likely that we can put the conflict out of our mind. As a result, with less access to validation, we have greater reliance on rivalling and superiority.

Our modern social environment is an imperfect fit for our programming. Social media offers us a mirage, and we see an oasis of water in the desert, that we chase after. But unfortunately, it is just a mirage. We are still in the desert, and must learn desert survival skills, and use the tools that best fit our environment (and, as a side note, people did this naturally and easily before social media).

Social media creates difficulty in our webs in other ways too.

For example, not only does social media create a mirage, it also makes the desert environment more hostile. This is because it fundamentally changes the nature of groups. How groups are arranged across society's giant web is a finely tuned balance, where people find nuanced solutions to an imperfect modern environment. With social media defining how digital groups are formed (including how people create, maintain, and join and leave them, as well as what information is communicated within them), then the finely tuned balance can be disrupted.

For example, groups become more standardised. It is harder for groups to be a loose collection of people, or perhaps two or three smaller sub-groups (each having slightly different interests or pursuits), when the whole group is connected together very visibly online.

Also, each group faces greater inwards forces. Groups naturally try to find commonality, where possible, because it leads to less stress, and a more consistent hierarchy. However, it is often resisted, due to the fact that each person is connected to many other groups, across their respective webs. Without social media, a balance is more likely to be reached. With social media, then people can pull others in, despite resisting forces. It results in more constrained social environment, without commonality, which in turn results in greater conflict, for example because of the need to resolve unresolvable positions.

The links that connect people across society, like a giant pattern of strings between people, become more energetic and choppier, and the tension in the strings increases. People chase a mirage, instead of treating it for what it is. The result is that the environment gets harder, and some natural coping mechanisms, for our imperfect circumstances, fall by the way side.

We both feel pulled in different directions, and the need to pull in different directions. People now pull on their strings more harshly, dragging others into the groups they want, competing more relentlessly, and having a greater influence on each other. This all makes finding some semblance of balance in our lives harder.

It perhaps doesn't look like this to an individual. To an individual, it makes us feel like our spread-out contacts can be our own personal tribe. The problem is that other people see things very differently to us. All those people want their own version of *their* tribe, that includes different people, and represents their own, different, individuality. And just as we feel we can achieve ours, through our various groups neatly arranged in our social media profiles, so other people feel they can realise theirs. When each person dives into their own respective digital world, in their phone or computer, they see very different things, and try to achieve different results. This is representative of people pulling more on strings.

With our focus drawn out of us, and onto other people, we can find greater stress, and greater dissatisfaction after a while. We can find it harder to live in the moment, to absorb the world around us at that particular time, and have our thoughts reside closer to us, rather than wandering. We can feel more stretched, and our social links, like pieces of string linking us to others, are being pulled on more strongly. And finally, we still have to interact with people and groups in front of us, in the real world, that can have a big effect on our emotions too.

Society

Social media also changes the way we interact with the society behind our web.

That society is blurred, because we only see fragments of it, and it's largely made up of people who've had very different experiences to us, and who we don't share personal connections with. Social media causes a much greater number of interactions with people who we've never met, and yet those interactions feel very personal.

When we start interacting online with people who we don't know, when we perhaps only have a few pictures, a username, or a short description, our interactions become very disproportionate. The emotions we feel, from messages, or from getting likes, or followers, are often completely disconnected from the emotions of the person who sent the message, liked or followed you. We are more connected to others, in a disconnected, disproportionate way, which can frustrate the mechanisms (that are reserved in our programming) for trying to help us create stable groups.

Social Media

When we get negative messages online, from random people we don't know, they can feel too personal. We often have little information on those people, so our brain just naturally makes up who we think they are. The actual motivation could be that they are a drunk college student who won't remember it in the morning, or someone lonely, or feeling the bad end of society, or someone on the other side of the world just having a bad day, but our brain doesn't know this. Instead of having reasons to disregard them, our brain almost searches for reasons *to* regard them. One bad message among a hundred good can upset us. One negative comment online, can leave us thinking "everyone thinks this about me", because, in theory, that message could have come from anyone.

Our brain is often readying us for what *could* happen. When we have these disproportionate interactions, where we're lacking a lot of information about the other person, our brain becomes quite creative in deciding what just happened, and often comes up with a "worst case" scenario. This isn't because our brain is pessimistic, but because our brain assesses our social interactions, and subconsciously prepares us for potential future ones. When information is scarce, our brain prepares us for a wider range of possibilities.

The emotions we feel, that play a part in our social nature, are acting in strange ways, and producing escalation. When we interact with the wider society through social media, we are effectively wearing an emotional blindfold, and our brain isn't all that good at interpreting the information and communication that we do get. It can lead to greater stress, frustration, and escalation of emotions.

Interacting with the wider society is full of pitfalls that can impact us negatively.

There are two more brief points to consider on social media and the wider society. Firstly, if we are instigator of content, then it can also be hard to gauge the impact of our own digital footprint. Without information on the people we might be interacting with, we have no knowledge of whether we're stepping on people's toes or not. For example, people sometimes find random feedback from members of the public hard to fathom, and think "people wouldn't dare say that to a stranger walking down the street". However, to complete that analogy, positing on social media, to the general public at large, is a little like walking into the town centre and shouting our views to anyone nearby, which, if we did in reality, may actually garner a negative comment or two.

Secondly, online interactions with people we don't know can be disproportionately "good" as well. For example, if we get a follow or like from a celebrity, or we watch a live stream from them, we can actually feel disproportionately connected to those people. We can feel personally approved of, and our brain tries to elevate our status, as if we were actually friends with them. Of course we aren't, so this causes undesirable consequences, like confusion over who we are, or a feeling of superiority that others don't see.

Therefore, interacting more personally with the *wider society*, in a very disproportionate way, causes escalation of conflict, muddled emotions, a deepening of frustration, and more confusion over who we are.

Digital addiction

There are a few other ways that social media affects us more generally, and the first is how social media, and our phones, can be addictive.

We can become addicted to the positives. We get "likes", "views" and "hearts". Our phone beeps and buzzes, and has bright colours like a slot machine. We can be drawn in to needing or wanting more of these things. But, when we pick up one end of a stick, we pick up both ends. Now we need the bright colours and satisfying sounds, and feel a draw to get more of them. We need more likes and views, and feel undervalued if a post doesn't get positive feedback.

Social media, like any digital addiction, gives our brain something it wants: socialisation, information or entertainment, without expending much energy. We can get those things lying on the couch. Our brain is still thinking we're trying to survive as a hunter-gatherer, and likes to conserve energy wherever possible.

Relying more on positive digital feedback isn't a problem in itself. Often the problem, and the addiction, comes when we try to do more energy intensive activities, that ultimately make us feel more fulfilled. Then, our brain provides some resistance. That resistance is because it's learnt to get the things it wants in a more energy efficient, but less fulfilling way. Then, we feel a draw towards our digital world, and the cycle repeats.

With social media being a bit like chocolate, or sugar, we have to learn that too much of it isn't good for us. We have to teach that to our children, who would eat sweets all the time if it was up to them.

As an aside, even positive digital interactions can sometimes feel unfulfilling after a while. For example it can feel like we push the accelerator pedal, but the car doesn't move. This is representative of digital feedback being a poor match to our programming, which is fundamentally based more on our core interpersonal relationships, and our web.

Internal self

Social media can change who we think we are, and how we think we come across.

This can be either by just picking up bad habits, or, if we use it during adolescence, having a greater impact on how our internal self forms.

For example, we can get such a range of inputs from social media. They tend to be more extremes of positive and negative than we might get in real life. People are freer to say things online, without being hindered by face-to-face social dynamics, and it is often easier to say things by text than in person. People are therefore both nicer or meaner on social media than they would be in real life.

We feel most ourselves when we're treated how we like, but social media therefore produces more ups and downs. At times we're treated exactly how we like on social media, and at others we're treated as much less.

With digital interactions being less inhibited by face-to-face dynamics, then our identity can become confused, because we may be able to achieve social positions in group chats or online platforms that we can't in real life. Which are we, our online persona, or our real life one? When we meet new people, which do we project? If we join a new group (in real life), do we need digital interactions in order to establish ourselves how we want? All this can lead to less surety of how to present ourselves when we meet new people, or greater difficulty, and more trial-and-error, before harmonious group dynamics are established.

With less surety of how we come across, then it's likely our self will be more confused. Our internal self forms during adolescence based on a range of memories, interactions and feedback. With social media, these fragments are drawn from a much larger range of unusual sources, and how we feel we come across, when meeting a new person, will include aspects of our digital life that are invisible to the that new person. Perhaps we expect people to see us consistent with our carefully crafted profile page, but others are completely unaware of that, and instead see the human being in front of them. Our interactions become less comfortable and predictable, and it therefore becomes harder to feel ourselves more of the time.

Our internal self now contains digital imagery of how we project ourselves online. Our internal self, and our idea of how we come across, can become distorted. When this happens in large groups of people, we now find it harder to have comfortable interactions, where we're treated how we want to be, and where we get to use reciprocated behaviours. We then have less self to pass on, and the next generation can be even more unsure of themselves.

Regarding creating our own profile pages, this doesn't just affect how we feel we come across, but also the nature of our social environments.

Being able to define our own profile pages is generally welcomed by an individual. However, it can have quite large implications.

For example social media now affects the mechanisms for giving us definition. Instead of each person's definition being interlinked, we now have a greater ability to define ourselves. Instead of relying on positions and feedback, from social structures, we now have more of a say.

We feel this is good, and creating social media profiles is something we like. We can define ourselves, and comes across exactly how we want to, and we appear to not be limited by other people's definition of us. This seems desirable, not least because, in our modern environment, no-one quite gets the definition from other people that they perhaps want.

However, when people start defining themselves, it can disrupt this delicate interlinked social balance. When we see someone, perhaps who we have a rivalry with, or compare ourselves to, projecting themselves positively, it affects *our* definition. We feel compelled to keep that change in check. We feel compelled to have a say in it, because we are social beings who compare, and are reliant, on others, for making us feel who we are. It can be frustrating scrolling through friends' news feeds, where they're trying to shape and project a self-made definition, as we feel an urge to both keep it in check, as well as pressure to promote our own.

The more strongly people try to self-define, the more strongly people will try to oppose each other. This results, in general, in people being more reducing or controlling to each other. Because people behave like this, others try to resist this by defining themselves more strongly, and the situation can escalate.

Perhaps we should work on the structure of societies, to allow our interlinked definitions to be more positive, rather than trying to subvert this process, by defining ourselves too much. This would generally require a mix of greater monetary equality and shared common culture. Whilst striving for self-definition, (and concrete individuality) seems desirable in the modern world, as group beings, we will never have all the individuality we want, because of the need to fit in and integrate with others. Especially as modern humans, we have to make some compromises. We can't be like a solo hunter, like a hawk or leopard, where our lives are solely in our hands, and we have self-determination.

We face a difficult social environment, and need to use desert survival skills, rather than chase a mirage.

The development of our internal self is a natural process, that is reliant on others, and if we confuse it, or subvert it, our internal self can be less concrete.

Some level of self-definition is of course welcome, but we have to find a balance between individuality and being interlinked with others.

Parent-child relationship

Finally, social media also affects the parent-child relationship, which is such a core part of our programming.

From the **child's** point of view, with the greater value at our fingertips, we become less comfortably constrained by our parents.

We see greater value out there, and are less likely to want to follow our parents' path. We can become unconstrained from our parents, or more uncomfortably constrained by our parents. With our minds residing in the possibility of instant fame, unrestricted interactions, and self-definition, we find it hard to be constrained by anyone, for example a parent, boss or authority figure. Perhaps we find ourselves drawn into the perceived freedom we might get from social media success, and then find it hard to slot into groups or hierarchies. All of these make the parent-child relationship harder.

From the **parent's** point of view, it causes them to be less focussed on their children.

Our children are tuned into us, and want our time, focus and attention. If they get it, they feel good, and personally valued. But when they see us reacting to our phones, or our mind is clearly on other people most of the time, for example due to social media, then our focus and attention isn't felt by the child. It is common that, when asked, children say they don't like it when their parents use their mobile phones.

An example of this is when parents take pictures of their children, not for the child, not for themselves, but to show off to people they know on social media. This demonstrates how the parent is taking less actions directly for the child, because of being more connected to their own social web.

With the child having less personal value, they need to seek their own comparative value, deepen bonds with their friends, and perhaps then interact more on social media themselves. Social media has become more than just a new habit, and can become reinforced in new generations. A habit for a parent becomes a foundation for a child.

Social media has both aspects that draw us in to using it, as well as aspects that reinforce our desire to use it, once we've been drawn in.

When social media has so many side effects and unintended consequences, we should certainly approach it with care and caution. It can feel so innocent to use: all we have to do is pick up our phone and send a message, or join in with a group chat. However overall, it is infiltrating and changing our core relationships, and on the basis of trends and desire, rather than thought and planning. It certainly has its negative side (which many people have expressed), and how its use changes in the future will be interesting to see.

Positive

Looking at the other side of the coin, social media has many positives too.

Social media gives everyone a voice. No matter our circumstances, no matter how we feel limited or constrained in our personal lives, we can go online and feel more freedom to express ourselves, and fight for what we believe in.

There is less stopping us online. We can say things we couldn't in person. We can contact people we'd be too nervous to approach in the real world. We can stand up for ourselves more easily, and defend ourselves in ways we might find difficult to do face-to-face. And despite those interactions being easier to do online, they can still have the same effect as if we'd done them in the real world.

We can start movements that others join and follow. We can call out and expose unkind or antisocial behaviour, which might go unopposed without social media.

We can post a problem we have into the ethersphere, and get support or advice from people we've never met. Random positive feedback can make people feel better about a present difficulty. It may not be a long-term solution, but positive affirmation, from the wider social media world, can work in the short term.

But perhaps the most positive thing social media has done, which is a reflection of all of the above points, is that it levels the playing field, and is therefore accelerating the movement towards equality.

This happens in a number of ways, for example by exposing injustice and oppression, or allowing those who feel constrained to resist more confidently, or allowing people to find support and commonality when that can be hard to find. It is harder to flaunt wealth, success and influence when you're in direct contact with a large number of people who don't have that. It is easier to be more disruptive and obtrusive to those around us if we feel oppressed or restricted, which, whilst this doesn't sound positive, is normally a representation of an inequality, or some aspect of modern circumstances, that needs spreading out and evening out, to level the playing field.

Social media therefore has many positives. In its short 15 years or so, it has instigated and allowed different movements to spread, that have improved the lives of many people.

Positive vs. negative

How do we balance the positive with the negative? You can look at this in two ways.

You could say that social media is achieving a more equal world, and that all the negatives, and side effects, are simply a result of the fact that we are now moving towards that equal world more quickly. Before social media, this movement was slow, at a generational pace. This is because each person, each generation, has a defined inherited position, that links us to our parents, and doesn't change throughout our lives. If things change too much during the life of one generation, they are pulled further from their inherited position, either upwards or downwards, which brings its own stress and discomfort, as we are pulled further from our blueprint. It is only a new generation that has a clean slate to absorb a part of the previous steps forward.

Therefore if you accelerate the movement towards equality, however much you do or don't want that, it will cause further stress and discomfort. Our position and environment changes, but not how we feel about it. Society rearranging, even if for the better, is a loud and often hostile process.

It's like we are all trying to move to a single point in a huge, giant field where we're anchored to a point by a piece of elastic. We try to move as far as we can in our lifetime, but the more we move, the more the elastic pulls us. Social media helps us move further, at times unimpeded, but then later everyone feels the effects of our elastic being more stretched.

Also, social media can move our thoughts towards equality much faster than it can move money around in an economy.

You can then say that all the difficulty that social media creates is simply a representation of moving our thoughts

Social Media

towards equality faster, which causes frustration, as the structure of society can't change as quickly.

The second way you can look at this is to say that we are moving towards equality faster, but there are side effects. Our programming often relies on a complex, finely tuned balance being achieved. For example, the balance of a social dynamic in a group, or the balance of the expression of emotion in one human being, and how it makes another feel. The balance of who we feel we are, how we come across, and the nuanced behaviours we develop, that allow us to integrate those levels with others.

Social media disrupts these delicate balances, which causes the stress, frustration, and escalation of behaviours.

It's difficult to say which it is, perhaps a little of both. All we can do is explore this in our own lives. We can compare the experiences we have online, to how they'd be if those experiences happened in real life. Or, we can hypothesize what our social dynamics would be like if social media didn't exist (note: people lived in large societies for thousands of years without it, so it may seem essential to people who use it a lot, but it's unlikely to be essential to the modern human experience). It is up to us, and everyone else, to draw their own conclusions on the matter.

What we can say is that it definitely has positives, and it definitely has negatives, neither of which were necessarily planned when social media emerged. Social media was borne in an almost organic way, but there is very little natural about it.

Either way, social media is here to stay for the time being. And, it will no doubt evolve as the positives, negatives, and pitfalls, become more apparent.

Part Four

Core

13

Emotions

The final part of this book looks at a person's core, and their key relationships and emotions. These go beyond society and socialising, and look inwards to ourselves. The following chapters cover emotions, family, and, briefly, the core needs of a human being.

In this chapter, we shall consider the nature of our emotions.

They play a huge role in our life experience. They spur us into action, compel us to perform certain behaviours, and make us want certain things. All of these cause us to arrive at a set of actions that are human, that we've evolved to do over millions of years. Every emotion we feel is a link to our humanity, and how any human being would feel in our exact circumstances.

We are drawn to this set of behaviours by the carrot and the stick. When we do them, we get the positive emotion: the carrot. When we don't do them, we get the negative emotion: the stick.

This is all very well for hunter-gatherers, in our natural social environment. Their emotions keep them doing hunter-

A Theory of Everyone

gatherer things. This is similar to a lion having emotions that encourages it to do lion things, and a gazelle having emotions that encourages it to do gazelle things. Hunter-gatherers would rarely have to think about their emotions, because they can simply act on them in ways that can largely resolve them.

However, the problem, for modern humans, is that these days our social environment is so different to how it was. There are many things we can't change about our circumstances. There are many things we want, that seem unattainable, and many things we don't want, that we can't stop, or get away from. For example, if you put a lion in a safari park, then it can no longer resolve, or act on, emotions that are based on the idea that it is free, and living on the savannah. It may be left with some frustration, and find it harder to get the positives it would feel if it were in its natural environment, at least at times.

And, as we looked at in the last chapter, our experiences of modern society are not equally shared. Some have more positive experiences, and some more negative. Often difficulty gets moved around, and there are hidden pitfalls and crevices, that we can find ourselves in, from time to time.

The result is that we often can't get as much positive emotion as we'd like. Or, we get too much positive emotion and it becomes exhausting. Sometimes we get stuck with some negative emotions that we need to overcome, or have to live with. On balance, in modern societies, we are buffeted by difficult emotions more than we should be. Our emotions are no longer always being helpful, and guiding us towards human-shaped behaviours, because there are now obstacles in the way. No human can fully reach the hunter-gatherer shaped destination.

How our emotions feel, to us, is often so vivid. They are a swirling pallet of colours. They are so hard to describe, yet they are so real and consuming to us. They often feel permanent, and our emotions at any one time can cloud the future and past. However, whilst they can feel permanent, they aren't permanent at all, and pass, sometimes even from one day to the next. The first time we feel certain emotions, good and bad, they can be amazing or unnerving. But, time always passes, and our emotions can always change.

Emotions are often hard to make sense of, and to understand. For example, like our personal perception of colours, they are ours alone, as we simply cannot share exactly how we feel with other people. This is why we find comfort in people with common experiences, who *know* how we feel. This is why we often can't understand other people's actions, for example when they behave according to emotions we've never felt ourselves. And, this is why we make other people feel a little of our own emotions, because it is the most direct way of sharing emotions.

It's also worth pointing out that understanding our emotions can be completely irrelevant. Many happy people have never thought about why they're happy, or where their emotions have come from, because they've never needed to. It is often when we have negative emotions that we find a need to think about them a bit more deeply. However, whether we need to or not, understanding our own emotions, and linking them to our circumstances, can help us better understand ourselves and other people.

Positive emotions

Positive emotions are what we're all after. We have many words for them: happiness, joy, satisfaction, excitement, pleasure, amazement, awe and celebration to name a few. Each feels different and unique, and is associated with people, events, and our environment. In this section, I'm going to break positive emotions down into three types:

1. Comfort;
2. Contentment; and
3. Elation.

The reason to break them down in this way is because each of these three categories share a range of emotions with common characteristics. The emotions in each of the categories come from similar sources, and cause us to take similar actions. It is a simple list of three that encompasses all positive emotions.

Comfort tends to comes from our environment, and is a homely feeling of when things are how we like them, and things just feel right. We feel ourselves, and the tasks and activities that we have in front of us are the best fit, for the way we like to be.

Contentment and elation tend to come from people.

Contentment tends to come from our secure close bonds, for example our family, partners and close friends. In contrast, elation tends to come from comparison to other people, from being better or worse, winning or losing, or being above or below.

Contentment leaves us feeling secure, ok, and satisfied. We feel content when things are enough, and when we are happy with what we have.

Elation, on the other hand, give us a buzz; a feeling of excitement. It can feel better than contentment, but when we get too much of it, or have it for too long, it can leave us exhausted. We often have to defend it, or face opposition from people that don't have it for themselves. It isn't long lasting, so whilst it feels good, when it goes, we find we want to seek it out again, to get a little more of it.

Contentment is like a tribe celebrating the cycle of life, the bonds of friends and family, and the security and warmth of shared comradery. Elation is like an athlete celebrating victory over their fellow competitors, and getting a rush of endorphins at the triumph. Both are natural and part of being human, but in this section we will consider the nature of each, in the modern environment.

With every positive emotion, you can consider whether it falls within the category of comfort, contentment, or elation.

Comfort

Some things just feel right. They feel like home, and they feel natural. We feel we are where we are meant to be, and our environment is satisfying. It is a feeling that is similar to when a jigsaw piece fits neatly between others, compared to the frustration of a piece that is very similar, but not the right piece, so that we push it and rotate it, but it just doesn't slot in.

To most it is actually physically linked to their home. It is the house, the bed, the living room, the smell of cooking, our garden, our family. It is the neighbourhood we grew up in, the way people behave there, the tree we walked past every day, or the sounds of our neighbours and locals. It is the messy house, or the clean ordered house. It is the noisy house, or the peace and quiet. It is the shape of our environment: the rolling hills, or the flat planes, or the jagged mountains.

When a soldier is fighting a battle, in a distant land, surrounded by unfamiliar territory, they often find that thinking of their home is uplifting. They think of the comforts: the food, a warm bath, or waking up to birdsong they've known all their life. Knowing they will return there, or that they are fighting for that, gives them a sense of grounding and purpose.

The same is true of people who live abroad. They adapt, but they also occasionally like to have something from their home, the place they came from. This could be decorations around the house, or snacks only available in their home country. In this position, we like to talk to people who are in a similar position to us, with whom we feel more natural socialising with.

There is a real link there. It is a bond to our home that resides in our mind, and produces tangible response in us.

This bond develops during adolescence in each human being, depending on the environment they grew up in. What we come across, and experience, are the things that our brain finds comfort in. They will therefore be different in each person.

The distant land, that the soldier feels less comfortable in, is someone else's home. That someone else feels just the same about the distant land, as the soldier does about their home.

How we feel about our childhood neighbourhood, and the familiarity of the street we grew up in, is the same as how someone else feels about theirs. It will be slightly different, because of the different aesthetics and experiences, but behind that, there is the same basic emotion of a link to *our* home.

As a species, we appear to be more adaptable than most other species on the planet. We thrive in deserts, mountains, jungles and the arctic. And to each human, that lives in one of those environments, it feels comforting.

For example, take an Inuit to the Amazon, and they will dislike the crowded trees, the heat, and the humidity. Take an Amazonian to the Arctic, and they will dislike the cold, and the vast expanses of white landscape.

Some people grow up in cities surrounded by asphalt and concrete, and feel they prefer that, whilst others grow up in the countryside.

However, both find that plants and natural textures improve the atmosphere of an office or living room.

Why do we feel these feelings? Why have we evolved in a way where comfort is part of our make-up?

It is partly because we rely on our environment to survive: it provides us with food and shelter. So, we share a bond with it, in order to feel protective of it. We sustain it, so that it can sustain us.

It encourages us to stay in a place where we have the understanding, skills and behaviours to best thrive. Distant lands are full of dangers that our parents and elders can't warn us about, so those hunter-gatherers that stuck to more familiar territory were more likely to survive. Those who headed out into the wild, and never came back, were less likely to breed and pass on their behaviours. Those who explored, but not too far, perhaps just far enough that they could return from their exploring, were more likely to breed and pass on their behaviours. As a result, we feel comfort in order to do just that, not go so far as to be unable to return to the place we grew up in.

We still get some sense of resistance to seeking out those distant lands, and it takes some bravery or adventuring. There is fear and uncertainty. In contrast, our home is comforting. Comfort acts as a homing beacon. We may enjoy adventure or danger, but after a while we may miss our more comfortable environment. Sometimes the adventure is exciting and enjoyable, and the comfort only strikes a chord when we face difficulty in that new environment.

We are urged towards places, groups, and people that are comfortable to us, and away from those that are not.

Managing comfort

Comfort seems an odd emotion that we might need to manage.

However, as modern humans, we can often find our circumstances are different to ones that we feel comfortable with.

Also, there's greater possibility that the things we feel comfort to, that our brain searches for, and bonds with, as we grow up, actually contain difficulty and conflict. Then, when comfort acts as a homing beacon, it doesn't take us to somewhere we necessarily want to go.

We can manage comfort because part of it is deep, but part of it is high level. We can change and adapt the high-level bits, and learn to better accept the low-level bits. We can learn somewhat to find comfort in what we used to think was uncomfortable.

Comfort also contains many residual, fringe aspects too. These result in small preconceptions that we have for no good reason. For example, perhaps we never used to like a certain food, place, activity or aesthetic, but when we consider it with a more open mind, we find that actually it's ok, and we can't remember what we didn't like about it before. The homing beacon part of comfort contains these biases and dislikes, and they encourage us towards things we like.

There are many sources of techniques out there for managing comfort. Some are as simple as a quote, such as "it is what it is", or Sinatra's "that's life".

One source of techniques that's been around for a long time is Stoicism. Stoicism is merely a set of teachings and philosophies that originated in Greece around 300 BC[27].

Stoicism aims to create virtuous humans, who find acceptance of their circumstances (even if they fight to change them), and the rejection of temptation and excessive pleasure.

One technique that Stoicism teaches is negative visualisation. We can imagine our circumstances as worse than they are, and imagine ourselves being ok with those, and then when we open our eyes, and are faced with our actual circumstances, they don't seem quite as bad. Our programming naturally wants things to be better and more comfortable, but when we can't achieve that in our present, we can trick the brain into being ok with them as they are. It doesn't work for every circumstance, but it can do.

There are tricks and methods out there, that have been around for thousands of years, that help with the human experience, but yet aren't well known. The people of ancient Greece, Egypt, China or Mesopotamia had to grapple with the same difficulties we experience in the present day, so there are relevant teachings throughout history. Around 500 BC was a golden time for unravelling wisdom on the issue, whether through Greek philosophers, Buddha in India, or Confucius in China.

Contentment

Contentment is a feeling when our social position is secure, we feel good enough, and we are happy with what we have. It feels good, but not excessively so. As a result, it can be steady and long lasting.

Hearing positive, supportive things from our parents or close friends (if we're lucky enough to hear them), gives us a feeling of warmth. That feeling is not one that could escalate, or be difficult to control, it is simply more grounding.

Contentment can be a difficult emotion to find however. There are so many pressures and difficulties in the modern world, that feeling good enough, and happy with what we have, can be elusive. We are bombarded with so many influences that make finding contentment harder. With social media, we see celebrities projecting what great lives they have, and we feel pressure to aspire to that. We see our friend's news feeds, projecting they are "living their best life", and we feel pressure to do the same. We compete with our friends for who went on the nicest holiday, who had the best Christmas, and what we do for a job.

Contentment can also be difficult to find because the places it tends to come from: close friends and family; often don't have the security they could have. Our friends can drift away, make other friends, find success, or change their preferences or allegiances. Modern families often involve more distance between parents and children than we'd like. Sibling hierarchies and social hierarchies have the potential to rearrange, all of which makes it harder to be content with what we have.

Finally, contentment is difficult around inequality. How can we be happy with what we have, when people around us have more? Finding contentment and acceptance whilst having less than others goes against our human instincts. Or, if we have more, others around us want what we have. Having more than others, and having to defend it, leaves little room for a steady and long-lasting security of emotion.

Nevertheless, it's somewhat possible to find a balance between accepting what we have, and fighting for a more equal share. We have to find the best way to live our lives, in our circumstances, whilst making sure that those that follow us face better circumstances.

Managing contentment

If we desire greater contentment in our life, then we can pursue this by focussing our thoughts on finding acceptance, affirming that we have enough, and, instead of comparing ourselves to others, focussing on our self. In doing so, we are using our own self as the source of contentment.

This can be quite hard. Unlike comfort, contentment resides a little deeper in us, as it is linked to our core relationships. It may take some change both within ourself, as well as our relationships, in order to feel more content, but there are always things we can do, and techniques we can try.

Every human deserves to feel content, because every human is good enough. We may have to fight to not be treated unfairly, but, even if others try to make us feel less, we can never be less than the fact that we are a human being, just like everyone else in the world. We are all just human beings at the end of the day.

Elation

The other type of positive feeling is elation. Elation gives us a buzz, and we feel a little euphoric or ecstatic. It is less a feeling of warmth and steadiness, and more of a short-term gain. It can feel very good, but it isn't long lasting.

Elation comes from comparisons to other people. It is the feeling we get when we move up and others move down.

It can come from all sorts of sources. The main sources of elation are:

1. Winning, or demonstrating prowess
2. Something that improves our position in a hierarchy, or lowers someone else's position
3. When we have someone depend on us or need us (other than our children)
4. Receiving approval or praise for a comparative achievement or attribute
5. Success in finding a partner, especially in the early stages of relationships

Different people will experience those sources of elation differently. That is because elation is linked to our comparison to others, so we develop a pattern of things, that make us feel elated, based on what gives us our particular advantage in life.

For example, if someone is very good at athletics, the idea of getting down to the running track might get them excited or give them a buzz. To others, it may not. If someone is good at chess, that might make them feel elated. If someone is successful and efficient at work, and enjoys the culture and tasks, then their work environment may make them feel elated.

What makes us feel *content*, on the other hand, is the same in everyone: secure bonds of friendship and family, and feeling good enough. What makes us feel *elated* differs much more from person to person. Contentment is linked to our core, whilst elation is linked to our transference onto the modern society we come across.

Elation is obviously a natural emotion, but in our modern world it can often play out in unnatural ways. Because it is enjoyable and looks good, we can become a little pre-occupied with it, and see it as the benchmark for happiness, rather than contentment. However, just as our driver to maximise our value becomes out of balance in large societies, so elation becomes out of balance too. Elation can escalate, and we can get a little addicted to it, or not appreciate the consequences of it.

Elation is a little more complex than comfort or contentment. Because of that, there are a few more things to say about it.

The first is to do with the downside to the apparent upside of elation. The second is how other people perceive elation, and how feeling elated is different to watching someone feel elated. The third is how elation and empathy interact.

The good with the bad

On the first, our driver to maximise our value can leave us stretched, compared to our friends and family. As a result, elation often isn't long lived. The idea that we can have endless elation is unrealistic, when we have many social ties across the web of society.

Whilst elation feels good, it generally isn't long lasting. We have to maintain the advantage we gained, in order to keep feeling it. If winning made us feel elated, it will only last whilst we are winning, and when someone else wins, we no longer feel it. We tend to lose access to the stable floor of contentment (if we had it in the first place), and instead rely more on elation. We have to defend our position to ensure that we keep feeling that positive emotion.

Also, what makes us feel elated one day becomes normal the next. If we got a buzz from getting ahead, then we may tire of that position after a while. We can feel bored or unfulfilled, and in order to feel elation again, we have to get ahead of more people. There will be times we feel elated, and times we don't.

Of course, some element of competition, and survival of the fittest, is in our nature. But that nature is also based on our lives being formed around contentment with occasional elation, rather than having our entire lives built around elation (which is how some people approach it these days).

Stoicism, 2000 years ago, encouraged people not to pursue highs, and to not overly desire money and success. It encouraged people not to give in to temptation, or to celebrate at the expense of others. This doesn't leave us devoid of emotion, nor even lacking in ambition. For example one of the most famous Stoic people was Marcus Aurelius, who was Emperor of Rome, and the most powerful person on Earth at the time. He was hailed as a just and fair leader, and was one of the "five good emperors". He wasn't perfect, but no-one is. He was Emperor, yet still tried to be virtuous, humble, and not chase elation and pleasure.

We can set out to be successful, but without the desire for excess elation. Our expectations can affect our subsequent experiences. Overall, this would create more harmonious and stable societies. Whilst everyone in a society *can* feel content at the same time, not everyone in society *can* feel elated at the same time. To focus more on contentment brings us closer in balance with our programming, which gives us greater chance for fulfilment as individuals.

Today, these values have somewhat fallen by the wayside. Children our encouraged to dream about what they could achieve, that they could be anything, that they can change the world, or to get to the very top. It's made to seem exciting and invigorating. Rich celebrities encourage us to be more like them. Social media encourages us to be boastful, to amass followers and "likes", and to get that short-term buzz.

Perhaps, instead, we should encourage children to remain humble and wary of excessive pleasure, so that they have a greater chance for contentment, and they can pass that on to other people.

Elation and its impact on others

Displaying elation can have an impact on our social relationships. After all, the amount of elation achievable is out of balance with our links to friends and family.

If what makes someone feel elated is something they share with someone else, then it can be a shared joy.

If what makes someone feel elated isn't something they share with someone else, then it can be uncomfortable to see someone else display elation.

For example if someone wins the lottery, and gets a huge rush, brags about it, and makes a big deal about it to their friends, this is more likely to sow resentment, and disrupt those bonds of friendship. The winner gets such a reward, because they see such significance to their elevation in wealth. Those around them may become more defensive or combative, to resist that change being cemented in the group's social dynamic.

Another example is if someone wins a race, and can't hide their elation and excitement. It signals to others that it means a lot to them, that winning is a high, and losing is a low. As a result, they may try to make those who they've beaten feel the low, whilst they are in the ascendancy.

Those who are more even tempered and happy with what they have are less likely to experience disruption of their social bonds through their life circumstances. We generally find them more trustworthy and stable, and an example of this is that leaders tend to be people that display this even temperament, rather than excessive emotion up and down.

Therefore elation is an indicator. It signals to others that we feel we have moved up. The strength of elation that we experience indicates the importance of the events to us. If we display excessive elation, then others may be wary of the impact on the relationship. We feel elated, but others may feel differently.

However, like with contentment, elation is quite a deep emotion, because it resides in our social relationships. If we do feel excessive elation, then it can be difficult to not feel elated, at something that makes us feel that way. It is less a choice we have, and more a representation of our circumstances. Sometimes, the more we lack something, or are oppressed, or made to feel less, the more we find elation at achieving the thing that we thought was unattainable. Nevertheless, understanding it, and how it makes others feel, can help our relationships.

Elation and empathy

The final point, on elation, is its relationship with empathy. *Elation cuts through empathy.*

When we feel elated, it tends to consume and fill us. As human beings, we only feel one emotion at any one time, so when we get that buzz of excitement, it leaves no room for empathising with others. The emotion is all about ourself, our achievements, and our success. We can't both feel elated for an experience we've just had, as well as sympathetic for someone else around us.

Another way to look at this is that if elation is an emotion we get when we advance our position, then in order for it to feel good, it *must* override empathy. After all, we have advanced our position over someone else. Someone else's position has worsened, yet we feel good. If we empathised with that person, then advancing our own position might be filled with guilt and regret, which it clearly isn't.

In most of life, this momentary lack of empathy is simply a side effect. I'm not suggesting those that win a race start trying to console those that they've beaten. We all accept that those that win the race feel good and can celebrate. And feeling elation also doesn't stop us being kind and caring. When we feel a buzz, we may feel enabled in helping others, which is a good thing, it's just that, at that time, our emotions aren't linked to the people we're helping.

Where this becomes more important is in our close interpersonal relationships. People tend to have personality traits based around contentment or elation. Some are steadier and more open; others are more excitable and up and down. This can trickle through to how we respond to our everyday activities. We obviously want partners, close friends and family to be happy, so seeing them elated may be good, and can lift us up, but it's a subtle point that when they're elated, they're not empathising with us. Most of the time this might not bother us, but sometimes it does.

Emotions

Where it might bother us the most is in our parents. As their children, we are tuned into wanting their time and attention, and wanting them to empathise with us. If they regularly display elation, or a buzz, from different activities they do, we know that at that moment, their emotions aren't linked to other people's. They aren't linked to our emotions, and we feel this. Often seeing our own parents feeling elated makes us a little uncomfortable. Not always – we want the best for them, but we can just find it a little frustrating, when they aren't tuned in to our emotions.

Also, seeing our parents display elation means they feel they have moved up in life a little, or are in the ascendancy. This affects our relationship with them. For example does their personality change when in this state? Is there more implicit pressure to succeed ourselves? Are we in a subtle (or obvious) power struggle with them, and now we have to ready ourselves against an emboldened person?

The reaction in the child, at seeing a parent elated, mirrors the nature of elation. Elation is rarely associated with friends, family and stability, so when it is displayed in a family environment, it tends to add distance.

When a child sees a parent elated, it often causes them to feel a little less valued. In turn, they may find that they have less access to contentment, and instead seek out greater elation of their own. In that way, eventually they may find that they have similar elation responses to their parents. This is one of the many ways that traits and characteristics flow from parent to child, and down generations in the parental cascade.

We can't change the way our parents react to different things, so we have to accept it, but perhaps it helps to know why things make us feel the way they do. Or, from the other side, to understand that just because we feel good, doesn't necessarily mean that others do too.

Managing elation may seem like an odd thing to do. We would effectively be trying to lessen the good feeling that success gives us, which at times seems counter intuitive. However, perhaps at times in our life, when that success is harder to maintain, we may find we want a little more steadiness, and more contentment, rather than elation. Therefore, the way to manage elation is to be cautious of it, and instead focus more on contentment.

Elation vs. contentment

Finally, on positive emotion, we can look at the relationship between elation and contentment.

Elation and contentment are yin and yang. Our personality tends to veer towards one rather than the other.

If we have access to contentment, through friends or family, then this tends to prevail. If not, or we find ourselves with great success, or the ability to advance our position relative to others, then we feel more elation.

The more diverged we are, the more we are likely to feel elated. Our identity: our acceptance in a group that subconsciously we look up to; results in feeling greater amounts of elation in our lives. The more diverged we are, the greater distance there is between us and our parents, so that we are more likely to lack contentment, and instead seek greater social comparisons.

The more self we have, the more contentment we feel. The more we are centred and grounded, aware of our impact on others, and how we come across, the more we are content with how things are, and we are more likely to be able to be secure in our social relationships.

Whether our personality develops more around elation or contentment is largely out of our control, and is more a representation of our circumstances. We simply have to live the circumstances we have, and whatever they are, we can make them work. After all, part of life is playing to our strengths, and turning our weaknesses into strengths. However, given elation is a little out of balance in our modern social environment, and can have unintended consequences, then if we have some spare capacity, we can try to steer ourselves towards contentment instead. Societies based around contentment, rather than elation, will allow more people to feel positive emotions.

In a world that is difficult enough already, perhaps we don't really care where the positive emotion comes from, we're just happy to have them. Nevertheless, the nature of each positive emotion has certain characteristics, and hopefully this section has at least provided a different viewpoint on the various types of positive emotion.

Negative feelings

This section is relatively short, and feel free to skip it if you don't want to read about negative emotions.

Negative emotions feel uncomfortable, and we'd rather not feel them. Sadness, anxiety, anger, fear, embarrassment, to name a few, are all feelings that we don't like. They all play a part in our programming; we are encouraged towards our evolutionary behaviours by the bad as well as the good. The problem, as mentioned before, is that our emotions, and the way they encourage us to act, are tuned for hunter-gatherer environments, not the one we find ourselves in. In our modern environment, there can be obstacles in the way.

Modern societies can produce such a vast range of circumstances that take us away from, or make it difficult to get, what we need. Also, negative emotion isn't shared out evenly in our societies, it works its way into some pockets and places more than others. As modern humans, we can be buffeted by negative emotions more than we should be.

There are two main types of negative emotions, the everyday emotions and the persistent ones.

The everyday emotions are part of the stresses of life, for example when in occasional (or regular) conflict with our friends, family, or colleagues, that play out on a daily basis.

On the other hand, the persistent negative emotions are ones that we associate with mental health. At the end of every day, once we've battled through the everyday emotions, in theory we should find some respite. But in the modern world, this often isn't the case. Low mood, anxiety or other negative emotions can persist.

Regarding the everyday emotions, there are normal stresses in any animals' life. Whether it's a field mouse avoiding a bird of prey, a cheetah needing its next meal, or a pack of wolves integrating a new member, there will be certain negative emotions encouraging certain behaviours. Those behaviours, in turn, help to resolve situations, and help the animals survive. The same is true of humans. There is a certain level of stress in the socialisation (and sometimes survivability) parts of our daily lives, which acts to try to guide us towards our evolutionary behaviours.

These everyday emotions tend to be short term. They are there to steer and guide us through the complexity of surviving, thriving and socialising. They pop up when difficulty needs to be resolved, or avoided.

Regarding persistent negative emotions, we can find that our environment just keeps throwing difficulty at us. We can find that our social relationships get out of hand, and end up in places where they are a jumble of knots, that are hard to unpick. We can find that we feel we know what we need to do, but we just can't do it, or we need a little extra strength to do it, and that is difficult to find. Persistent negative emotions can be an incredibly tough battle at times.

The two types of negative emotion, everyday and persistent ones, are linked. If our environment gives us too many different everyday challenges, our mood can lower more persistently. If we have more persistent difficulties, the everyday stresses become harder to battle.

We all feel this to a certain extent. We all have to weather more than our fair share of "normal stresses", because living in large, multi-layered societies is out of character compared to our evolutionary environment. We all face difficult emotions at some point in our lives.

The more persistent negative emotions (that we associate with mental health) are a difficult topic to define or write about concisely. There can be such a range of circumstances that cause them, for example people, activities, or environments.

A good definition is the World Health Organisation's definition of mental health[28]. It states that "Mental health is a state of well-being in which an individual realizes his or her own abilities, can cope with the normal stresses of life, can work productively and is able to make a contribution to his or her community".

The WHO definition generally holds. Whatever our circumstances, then, on balance, if we are lucky enough to realise our abilities, and feel secure in the position in society, then we can weather those "normal stresses", without feeling more persistent difficulty.

Perhaps the more difficult our circumstances, the harder it is to realise our abilities, but if we do, then according to that theory, we have good mental health.

Methods to help

It is always good to talk to someone (friends, family, colleagues, a counsellor, or anyone we have available) if we're finding difficulty with negative emotions. We are social beings, and are interlinked with others, and there is a powerful impact on ourselves by simply getting something off our chest.

If we need a little more help still, then in terms of some of the most widely used techniques, they can sound a little impersonal, but they're really just full of useful behaviours and understanding. Person-centred therapy aims to provide a supportive soundboard to allow someone to work through their own thoughts. Cognitive behavioural therapy simply helps us separate out the different aspects of negative emotion (the thoughts, physical sensations, and the way it affects our actions). These different aspects of negative emotion can work together, and our brain is quite good at inventing things that will annoy us the most.

All of these are helping us to make sense of a situation, when it is very difficult to do so, when fighting on the front line. Writing also does this. Writing things down tends to have a self-affirming effect on us, and using it can allow us to reinforce positive messages in ourselves, as well as see the wood for the trees.

There are also many small things we can do, such as exercise, getting into nature, medication, calming pursuits, or changing our routine, and different things work for different people.

The cause of persistent negative emotions

As mentioned, the source of mental health difficulty can be varied.

The WHO definition starts by referring to "realising our abilities". This is similar to saying that we feel good when we use behaviours that make us feel "us", and are treated how we want. We absorb and copy behaviours from those around us, in order to create integrated groups, and then using those behaviours gives us a positive reward. How we want to be treated is linked to our identity level, the maximum status we've attained in our lives, and when we've established, and are behaving according to our identity level, we feel good.

If we are prevented from behaving how we'd like, perhaps over an extended period of time, due to a person or environment, we may just not feel ourselves. If we are prevented from attaining our identity level, or not treated according to it, we can feel negative emotions. If we find that our behaviours, or our identity level, aren't a good fit for where we find ourselves in life, then it can be a source of difficulty.

For example, sometimes we can get stuck between who we need to be (based on previous successes), and where we find ourselves in the present. Perhaps, in the present, we don't have the good fortune, momentum, or support that got us our successes in the first place. Sometimes we can find that there are difficulties in two or more of: our family; our friends; the behaviours we need to use to feel most ourselves; and the social environment we find ourselves in. Perhaps we can deal with difficulty on one of those fronts, but if it's more than one, then problems can arise. Sometimes we can get stuck due to problems compounding problems compounding problems. Then we can find conflict in our social relationships, that becomes chicken-and-egg, and it can be difficult to unpick it all, and see the wood for the trees.

Another way to look at mental health is in relation to the giant interlinked web of society. Each person has their own personal web within this, and as we looked at earlier, each group can prop up other groups, a bit like a house of cards. It generally doesn't all fall down, and the bias in society is towards helping each other feel good, and maintain their social links, but it can fall down occasionally. When the one or two key groups, that make us feel most ourself, have difficulty in them, then this can affect more than just those groups, due to the way it may be propping them up.

Then there are parents. There can be all sorts of nuanced difficulty and conflict there that can cause mental health problems. They are generally the source of it all, but that doesn't mean that mental health is necessarily solved there. We all experience transference, from our parents onto society, and perhaps the more we transfer, the more difficulty is pushed under the rug, and the more we rely on our social lives away from them. Often it is better to rebuild our house of cards, rather than tackle parents head on. However, since parents underly our social lives, sometimes making some small wins, and improvements, with our parents, can change our perceptions of our social relationships. Each situation is different.

Finally, there is the prevailing societal environment. With everyone being diverged, we all feel greater headwinds to being our identity. If the societal environment gets harder, then people will feel greater headwinds, and the everyday stresses become greater. People's hunter-gatherer brains will be working overtime to try to find fulfilment in themselves, and social groups need to work harder to mediate and positively solve the difficulty, rather than give in to less constructive behaviours. Social media is one example of something that makes a societal environment harder, but there are many others too.

Difficulty multiplier

One final thing to say on negative emotions is that it is not a linear scale. If our circumstances are twice as hard, our negative emotions may be more than twice as hard.

Part of the reason for this is that we battle modern life on more than one front. In our web, we have our family, friends and work. Our webs are a little like a house of cards, with each group propping up the others, to some extent. Therefore if we have difficulty in one group, it can affect another, which in turn affects others.

The point to note is simply that the way we experience hardship may be very difficult to others. We only really have our own circumstances to understand emotions by, and it's so hard to appreciate how someone else can feel so differently, compared to how we do.

When someone faces difficulty, it is not just an issue they're facing, it's how that issue affects their whole picture: for example the totality of their social relationships, or the situations and environments that they interact in. Perhaps if we faced a similar issue, if we didn't have difficulty somewhere else in our lives too, then we may not appreciate the multiplying effect.

Sometimes we think "why don't they just...", because, to us, what we feel the other person needs to do, seems straightforward. We can't empathise with them, and understand why it's many times harder for someone else to do that than us, even when appearing to face the same issue. Sometimes we can be right, and the person just needs to break through a personal barrier, but at other times there is a much greater difficulty to appreciate.

Everyone is facing a different fight, and we should never judge a person until we've walked a mile in their shoes.

Negative emotions summary

Negative emotions are undesirable. We all experience them, whether everyday ones, or more persistent ones. When there is difficulty in society, it will filter into people's emotions, through our interconnected webs, one way or another. The more stretched society is, the more people chase elation and glory, then the more there will also be the opposite. Excessive positive emotion and negative emotion are yin and yang. Hopefully the world is moving to a place where our societies are shaped so that each person can feel fulfilled, and content, and negative emotions are felt less and less.

14

Family & Parents

Moving on to discuss family: they say we can choose our friends, but we can't choose our family, and never a truer thing was spoken.

When family works, it can be amazing, but when not, it can be very, very difficult. Yet, whether we have a family that works, or not, is largely out of our control.

Families were once very different. For hunter-gatherers, they would be the people we spent the majority of our lives with, the people who taught us how to hunt and survive, and the people we relax and socialise with, each evening around a campfire. There wouldn't have been a large range of circumstances that would have disrupted these bonds, and so they would have (generally) been secure, and a good basis for our programming. A family would have offered comfortable constraint, compared to the modern arrangement, which is often restraint, against the perceived freedom available outside of the family unit.

Imagine your actual family. The difference between it working perfectly, and what actually faces us, is what living in large, multi-layered societies does to the Homo Sapien family relationships. Our modern social environment can provide many varied circumstances that can disrupt the parent-child dynamic, or the sibling dynamic.

Despite the fact that family is often less-than-ideal, we still have all the aspects of our programming trying to encourage us towards resolving it, as if it could be ideal. Our brain is trying to be a hunter-gatherer, and encourage us to achieve what a hunter-gatherer could in their social environment, but against the backdrop of a different, modern set of circumstances.

This chapter is split into two main parts. The first three sections focus mainly on parents, and the second three sections look at development, siblings and emotions within families.

On parents, the first section looks at the basis of the parent-child dynamic. The second looks at how levels muddy the dynamic, effectively providing two competing forces: the dynamic within the family, and the dynamic of the parent's social position vs. the child's. The third section looks at parents as authority figures, and how our modern environment makes it so difficult to get the right amount of authority.

In the second half of this chapter, the fourth section looks at our development in our family. The fifth looks at siblings: the dynamic, and what is really driving, or causing behaviours; and the sixth looks at some common, and often confused, emotional conflict or projections within families.

As mentioned earlier, in this book "child" can refer to a child of any age, youthful or adult, and is simply used to refer to someone with respect to their parent. Hopefully it is clear from the context in each case whether what is said is more applicable to a young child or an adult child.

Family & Parents

The parent-child dynamic

A key example of our brains trying to feel like they would as hunter-gatherers occurs in the modern Homo Sapien parent.

We all want to be good parents. In fact, it's very important to us that we consider ourselves good parents. Even some very bad parents still believe they're good. It's an instinct within us. The problem is that often we find, when it comes down to it, that we aren't limited by who we *want* to be, but by the powerful forces defining what we can and can't do. Our brains then work a little harder to ignore all those things we can't do, and try to feel like good parents regardless.

Perhaps we want to act in certain ways as a parent, but find we can't. We don't like the idea we're a bad parent, so instead we change our definition of what a good parent is, until it fits our situation. We have good intentions; we just can't act on them. This is because of forces out of our control: our modern environment, and our own particular circumstances.

Changing our definition of a "good parent", until it fits our situation, may seem like an innocent thing to do, but its impact on the parent-child relationship is as big as the difference between a society of millions, and a small tribe. It is something we can't avoid doing, and almost *has* to happen, but it is an example of the way our brain shapes our perceptions of the world based on what is achievable for a hunter-gatherer (since that is what our programming is urging us towards), rather than what is achievable in our actual circumstances. When it shapes them in strange ways, it can work fine for the individual, but for others, they notice inconsistencies. In this case, the inconsistencies are perhaps noticed most by the child. They may see a parent trying to feel like a "complete parent" (and perhaps projecting that they are), without actually feeling the effects of a complete parent.

In any species it's important that parents want to be good parents. Parenting is such a crucial part of life across the animal kingdom. The desire to want to be a good parent is deeply engrained in us. It's just what's layered over the top of that, which is often the problem.

This is obviously frustrating for children, especially when young. As young children we are programmed to want and need everything. A child cannot appreciate the forces preventing the parent giving them things, that, on the surface, seem so easy to give.

As children grow, in the modern world, they can often pull away from the parents, or head off into different directions. The more the parent tries to impose on them, the more they shy away. The more the parent tries to rein them in, the more they frustrate them. Often a balance is reached, but it can often be a fragile or frustrating balance.

As a child, perhaps we think that when we're a parent, we'll be different. We'll be a great parent. We'll do all the things our parent didn't do, but we wanted. Well, unfortunately, often we find we can't. Not always, and good intentions and communication go a long way, but given how many difficult parent-child relationships there are in the world, and how many people find frustration in that from time to time, it's clear that something trumps our good will.

We've been in our large societies and civilisations for roughly 12,000 years. In 2009, Malcolm Gladwell stated that if we spend 10,000 hours (~a year) doing something, we can become an expert[29]. Whilst this is meant for skills such as learning a sport, or musical instrument, if we apply it to parenthood, it's clear that we are far from being perfect parents. In fact, we may not have improved all that much in 12,000 years.

Therefore, however good a parent we want to be, and however much our children mean everything to us, there are clearly forces at work that are more powerful than our intentions. Those forces create barriers, so that when we want to do something for our children, or say something important, there is just something in the way stopping us, or making it difficult. If there wasn't, then over 12,000 years, we would have mastered parenthood in large societies.

In fact, there is still very little out there telling us what to do, and how to be a good parent. People tell us their own styles, and there are many books on the subject, but often our situation can be so unique that we just have to throw out the rulebook, and go with our instincts, and do what we feel is best.

Part of the problem are those walls and barriers. It is not our will, or instinct that makes it hard. We instinctively know how to be a good parent, every animal on Earth does. Not knowing what to do isn't the problem, it's what's blocking us doing it, and how that all resolves (not to mention the complex and unusual circumstances that our family might find themselves in).

This can all create difficult, confusing and hard to resolve parent-child dynamics. This section shall explore this dynamic further, to unpick its nature a little. The two aspects discussed here are the cascade, and the unyielding nature that is present in families.

The cascade

The first thing to say is to look at the dynamic between a parent and child (of any age). Who is being driven by what? And what does each party really want?

What is driving the child is clear, it's the parents. We have an inbuilt need for certain things from our parents: time, attention, care, love, support. That is what a child really wants

A Theory of Everyone

in this relationship, even as an adult. Of course, it gets diverted and intermixed with their social lives, and influences from society can play a big part in conflict between parent and child, but underneath that all, a very strong driver is to get things from their parent.

What is driving the parent is less clear. Whilst the child has one focus, the parent doesn't. The reason for this is that the parent has their own parents, and is in-between their parents and their children.

Like their child, they want things from *their* parents, mainly those core needs. What they want from their children is different. As a parent, we want love and approval from our children, but not in a core way. Part of a parent wants their children to be a *reflection* of them, or how they see themselves.

The bond a child feels towards their parent, is different to the bond a parent feels towards their child.

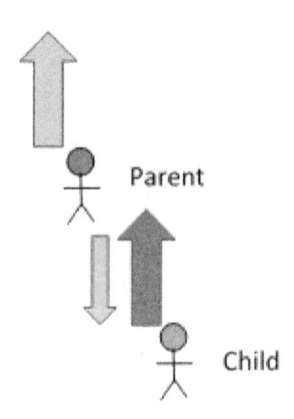

This causes influences from previous generations to affect the relationship in front of us. It also causes circumstances to flow down generations in a cascade.

Family & Parents

The result of the cascade is that the dynamic between parent and child, especially when the child reaches adulthood, is actually quite strange. For example, from the child's point of view, it is like playing a chess match against someone (our parent), and feeling like the other person is as invested in the match as we are, when in actual fact the other person is playing a different match in their minds (against their own parents), that is more important to them, and one we can't see.

The harder we fight, the harder we make our opponent's other invisible fight (i.e. our parent's fight against their *own* parent), and the more they push back because of that.

To the child, it feels like a direct conflict. To the parent, it feels like a conflict that just makes their own, other, conflicts more difficult (that being said, sometimes parents try to forget about all their other conflicts and focus entirely on the conflict with their child, one that is easier to win, and thereby causing more direct cascade of their personality and difficulties).

This dynamic means that, whilst conflict between a parent and child can go back and forth, and lead to entrenched positions on both sides, it is often difficult for the child to actually "win". And when the child pushes up against the parent and pressures them, especially on a really core issue, the parent will be pushed up against their own parent (our grandparent). In turn, they will be pushed up against their own parent (our great grandparent) and so on.

This is the process of the cascade.

We are like pools of water in a slowly trickling waterfall. We have our own shape, and fill our own space, and we are fed by the rain, but we are also fed by our parent's pool above us. They are fed by their parent's pool and so on.

Alternatively, we are like the front carriage of a steam train. Each generation of our family is a carriage behind us, and we are trying to find our way along the tracks whilst being pushed by each of those, and each of those is being pushed by the ones behind them: members of our family line going back generations.

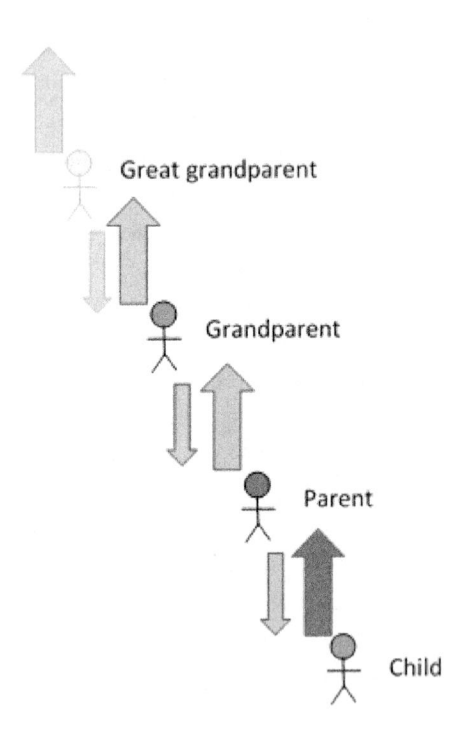

The cascade means that, one way or another, some of our parents' peculiarities, difficulties and personalities get passed to us.

This is obviously frustrating. We want to be free, and for them to give us everything we want. We can't see their invisible fight, so it seems so simple, why don't they just do it? Why do they act the way they do? How could they?

Family & Parents

The cascade plays the role of passing, and mediating, a range of traits, behaviours and emotions down generations. From an evolutionary point of view, this allows us to follow similar paths to our parents. Theoretically, this is a good thing. For our ancestors, it meant that they don't have to figure everything out from scratch. It would be helpful and beneficial to have similar traits and characteristics to our parents (with minor deviations), and to follow similar directions in life.

In the modern world, we are still interlinked with our parents on many fronts, for example through levels, or how our web was formed, or the type of group we use as our main definition, or how much self we have. As a result, we can gravitate towards similar lives (though this can of course be resisted where necessary, and everyone will be resisting this a little). The problem is that there is such a huge range of circumstances and difficulties, that the mechanism of the cascade isn't always beneficial. Instead of passing us helpful things, giving us an evolutionary advantage, the cascade instead passes us some of the difficulties of modern life (and those difficulties aren't spread out evenly).

In the modern world, the cascade happens slightly differently to how it would have done for our hunter-gatherer ancestors. For us, it happens in a more sly, disguised way. In hunter-gatherers, who spend the majority of their lives with their parents, the cascade would be much more obvious and direct (A to B). In the modern world, it still happens one way or the other, but often indirectly. Often it isn't A to B, it is instead A to X to B.

For example, difficulty with a parent leads to difficult social interactions. Those social interactions consume our focus, and are in the foreground of our daily lives, whilst our parents are in the background. Then, when we become a parent, and have our own children, we find that a lot of the pressures of parenthood is felt through those social interactions: competition; and the pressures of groups we are a part of. But our social interactions were formed against the backdrop of our parents. Therefore, instead of our parent's influence being direct (A to B), it is instead indirect (A to X to B, where X is our social web).

The cascade then looks like this:

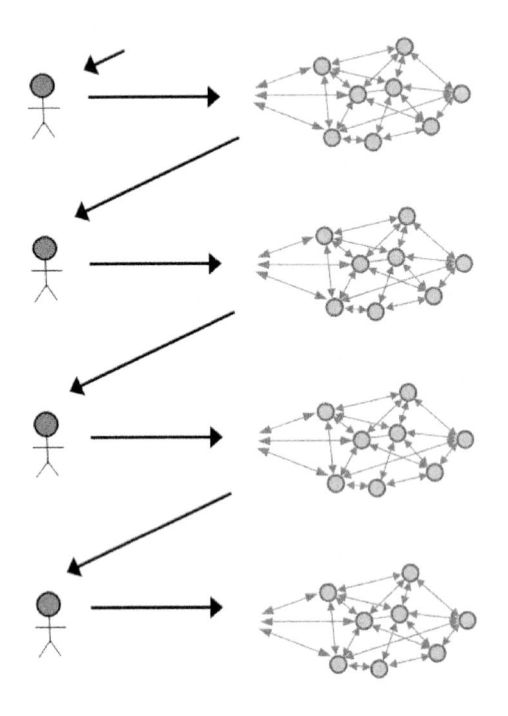

A person finds frustration or difficulty with their parent and deepens their social links. Difficulty with their parent gets transferred into those social relationships. Those social relationships then dictate how we act as a parent to our children. Our children find frustration or difficulty, and imprint their circumstances onto their own part of society, and so on.

Because of this indirect nature of the cascade, much of it happens without us even noticing. However, just like the five generations of Marcus' Roman family that we looked at earlier, to understand what is driving ourselves, and others around us, we have to consider family history to some extent, even when it is almost certainly not at the forefront of our minds, when interacting with the people around us.

Unyielding

The parent also has a need to *be* the parent. They cannot relinquish their control of the dynamic to the child.

In their minds they always are. Whatever the circumstances, the parent feels an urge not to yield the control of the dynamic.

This is for many reasons. One is a gut feeling of what would happen if the position was yielded, or reversed, so that the child is in the ascendency. Other factors include social pressures, and those from our own parents.

Mostly however, it is just a primal instinct. The parent held us as a baby, and watched us grow into an adult. They feel like the parent. They want us to be a reflection of them.

However it happens, the parent always feels the need to have the upper hand in the dynamic.

The unyielding nature of the parent is most visible when the child is an adult, when there is more equal conflict, and perhaps a more direct power struggle. There is a much closer match between the adult child and the parent, so the parent is pushed harder to maintain at least a small upper hand. However, the unyielding nature starts even when the child is young, even when the parent is an adult, and the child is small and very dependent on them. This is actually an important part of how an inherited level is passed from parent to child.

When children are very young, for example as a baby or young child, they see the world through innocence. They are more of a blank canvas, unaware of weird structure of society they will grow into. In some ways, this makes them quite judgemental! Not because of logic or defensiveness, but instead because they see things how they are. We get a sense of this, that they might see right through out defences, even as a baby. We sense that they have an unbiased view of the world, a sense of freedom.

And this can be truly scary. What if they see our insecurities? What if they grow into something more than ourselves, and make us feel judged and small? We don't have the freedom they do, we've been battered and bruised through life, to fit in to the society we grew into. We now have biases and defences, grudges and rivalries.

So, whilst we want the best for them, we can't help but keep their development in check. We socialise with them in ways that make *us* comfortable, rather than in ways that encourage them to the fullest. We may not like this idea, but when it comes to it, we feel we don't have a choice, we feel compelled to be unyielding.

Don't get me wrong, we can still do a huge amount for them, and believe we are good parents. It's just that we have the end destination in the back of our minds.

Through these early interactions, inherited and identity levels start to be transferred from parent to child.

As children grow into teenagers they change in many ways. Throughout the teenage years, a child will be trying out and learning new behaviours. In the modern world, we tend to learn behaviours through copying and trial and error, rather than by really understanding what behaviour is appropriate, or

Family & Parents

appreciating how others are receiving our behaviours. We test those around us, including our parents, in order to find boundaries. If we get away with something, we tend to believe that it's ok, rather than having an instinctual moral foundation.

This part of a child's development causes them to push up against the parent, possibly with very obtrusive behaviours, that the child doesn't appreciate the impact of. This is an important part the parent-child relationship, because it forces a dynamic one way or another. The emotional reaction of the parent, in these exchanges, informs the emotions of the child. Occasionally, the parent may find they have to choose between distancing themselves from the child (whilst maintaining the upper hand), and causing frustration, or imposing themselves on the child, causing frustration.

Again, this forces the transfer of inherited and identity levels. It also forces the cascade, since the child will now be more deeply testing the parent, pushing the parent up against their own difficulties in life, and causing the parent to transfer some of that difficulty to the child, as the parent faces both fronts.

The parent-child dynamic during these teenage years is often a reflection of a child, who is going through the process of fitting into an imperfect world, and a parent, who has (theoretically) already fitted into an imperfect world.

As the child becomes independent and an adult, and goes off away from the parent, living their own, separate life, the parent is still unyielding. Our unyielding nature persists, despite the fact the child and parent are now both adults. It's just the way it is.

It can be frustrating to be the child in this dynamic. Effectively part of the difficulty of our modern societies is transmitted to us through our parents, just as we will do the same to our children. The child's perspective is not one of understanding. Even if we understand, we're still left with the frustration. We feel what we *could be*, how our parents *could act*. We don't feel tied to our parents, at times we just feel constrained by them. There is often therefore a difference between how the child feels about the relationship, and what the dynamic of the relationship is. Even if, at times, we consciously understand what is going on, our emotions may not, and those emotions can cause us to lose sight of what is actually going on.

Unyielding is a strong and deep response in the parent. It can't be easily subverted. It is instinct or reflex, one that we don't consciously think of, but simple happens. It is because the parent will always see themselves as having, or needing, the upper hand, no matter the actual circumstances. This deep response of unyielding will cause the parent to, perhaps, do whatever is necessary in order to feel like they are in charge. Couple this with the need to feel like a good parent, and the parent sometimes does what (they feel) they need to, whilst believing they are doing the right thing, even if they know (in the back of their mind) that perhaps they aren't. This may seem illogical, but it's been happening for 12,000 years.

Parents and levels

A parent's unyielding nature comes into direct conflict with levels.

We have a driver to maximise our value in society, to be the wealthiest, most adored or exalted. Or, at least progress a little, and move forwards rather than backwards. But we also have the link to our parents, who are in a more fixed place.

Therefore, the child is trying to maximise their value, whilst the parent is trying to be unyielding, from the place they have settled in in life.

Family & Parents

To understand this, and the way that parental instincts conflict with modern circumstances, we can consider the situation whereby the child can "out-value" the parents. Then, like we saw in Marcus' Roman scenario, difficulty can ensue, and the parent-child relationship can be disrupted.

Sometimes children, as a child or adult, find greater position in society than their parents. They effectively "out-value" their parents. The parents will undoubtably be proud, and they will be pleased for the child, although they may not show it. The child's success reflects well on them as a parent, and they may find their social status improved a little with their friends and web, because of their child's success.

However, there is now two very different things going on.

One is the family dynamic, where the parent is unyielding, and needs the upper hand. The other is levels. On levels, the parent and child have found acceptance in different parts of society. Each feels a reflection of, and views the world from, their levels. If the child's level is higher, then the child will view the parent as less than them, based on levels. The parent may feel a little intimidated by the child's higher identity level.

On the family dynamic, the parent still needs to be unyielding, and the child still wants the parent's approval.

This conflict, between the family dynamic, and the level dynamic, is very difficult to resolve. Once the child has gained acceptance at the higher level, they will start to behave according to someone of that level. What was initially good for both parties, becomes a source of conflict, as the dynamic between parent and child changes.

The child's acceptance at a higher level causes the child to want the parent to both be proud of them, but also treat them in a way that recognises their higher level. The parent wants to approve of the child, but can't yield position, and perhaps doesn't feel right praising someone who is part of a higher-level group than them. Perhaps they just get a sense that it wouldn't come across as they want. All of this can cause an uncomfortable dynamic.

This creates a paradox for the parent. How can the parent be unyielding, and feel above the child, if the child has exceeded the parent in society? Luckily, for parents, our brains are very good at finding some way of resolving this. As human beings we tend to do this in one of three ways:

1. The parent simply reduces the child. They undermine them, or act in a derogatory way towards them. Or, perhaps they withhold approval or support, or frustrate the child by taking full credit for the child's success, and wait for a negative reaction, which they then focus on as the child being unreasonable and difficult. The situation can become chicken-and-egg, with the cause of difficulty hidden behind levels. This is very upsetting for the child. They cannot let go of their identity level, so the dynamic is simply hurtful. However, perhaps the parent feels it is all they can do, because they are between a rock and a hard place.

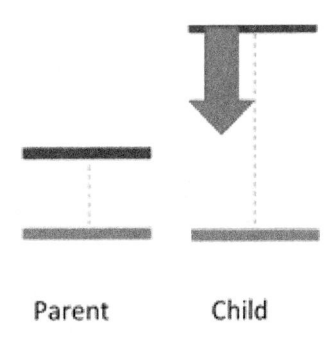

Family & Parents

2. The parent keeps setting the bar higher and higher. Whatever the child achieves, the parent encourages them to seek more. This is a way of not allowing the child to feel approval, or comfortable, at their identity level, without actively reducing the child. It is easy to justify as it appears to be "encouraging" or "just wanting the best for the child". However, in reality, it is frustrating for the child, as they are never allowed to feel good enough, despite their achievements exceeding their parent's. They may also feel lacking in support from the parent, since there will be distance between the parent and child, that is being masked over by this apparent supportiveness, to achieve the next success.

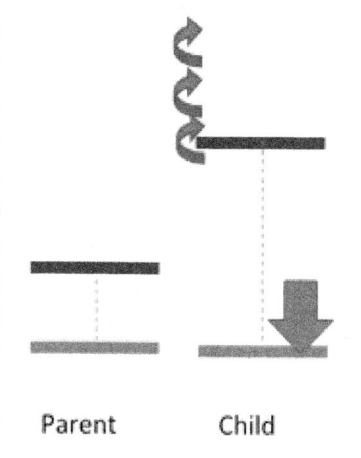

3. The parent raises themself through the child. The parent finds a way to associate themselves with the level the child has achieved. Perhaps this is through mixing with the parents of their child's friends, or

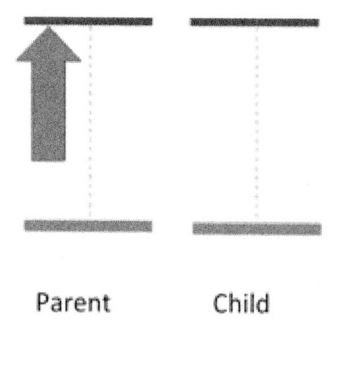

through joining the child on their endeavours. Once the parent feels acceptance at the child's level, then don't feel challenged by the child. They believe they have attained the same level too. This might seem like the best arrangement, and perhaps it is, but there are some unusual side effects. Both are now diverged. Both see themselves according to their identity level, but the other according to their inherited level. This can cause competitiveness and cross-conflict. When a parent and child are both diverged, there is emotional distance. The child may want support from time to time, as they try to maintain their identity level, but if they turn to the parent, the parent simply projects that they themselves comfortably achieve the identity level, perhaps at the expense of the child. Both are facing further to fall. The parent may feel greater strain on their own previous social relationships, now that they have "jumped up" too, and so distances themselves from the child to hide this, and instead merely projects security at the higher level. The relationship becomes purely about the social status, rather than more based in family. Perhaps more than that though, the child is still denied really feeling rewarded for what they have achieved. They have effectively "out-valued" the parent, but the parent will never yield position, and allow them to fully enjoy it, or live in it comfortably.

Ultimately, however the parent responds to the child achieving a higher identity level than them, this situation is very difficult to resolve. Both parties are being driven by such core drivers, that are pulling in different directions. The child cannot give up their successes, just like the parent cannot admit, and fully appreciate the child's successes. It is the conflict of the family dynamic versus the level dynamic.

As a child, we don't really appreciate how a parent may view our level, if we've "out-valued" them. Because of that, we aren't aware of the emotions the parent feels, when faced with us (not least because the parent will try to hide those emotions). Perhaps we can consider how we perceived our identity level before we achieved it, or how we perceive a higher identity level still, and imagine what we'd do if our own child achieved that.

There are solutions, and any relationship can be improved. However each relationship is so unique, that it takes a lot to achieve resolutions. Perhaps compromise, recognition, self-pride and openness are some of the paths that can be taken, but every situation is different.

Parents and authority

On the third topic on parents, we can consider parental authority.

Authority as a parent is very difficult for modern humans. Are we imposing ourselves too much, or too little? How do we know we are providing just the right amount of authority? When modern humans often struggle to know how they're really coming across, this can be doubly difficult. Plus, we also have to balance the authority of being a parent, with the authority of our successes and achievements in society: our family vs. levels. Then, very few people have natural authority in modern societies, and so often we have to learn new behaviours when parenthood comes around.

This section explores these ideas further, both looking at the dynamic, and also how it affects us as human beings growing up.

It's important to remember that much of this is out of our control, and our parents' control, although effort and goodwill go a long way. The cascade, going back generations, and our circumstances (the parent's levels vs. the child's), mean we are more limited in how the dynamic turns out than anyone would like.

Unconstrained

To start with, we shall consider one of the extremes: the dynamic where too little authority is applied, and the child actually becomes unconstrained.

This is often caused by levels. Sometimes the difference in levels between the child and parent is so great that the parent loses the ability to impose themselves, for example in one of the three ways mentioned in the last section.

Without the parent imposing themselves, the child actually has a certain amount of freedom.

However, this freedom is a double-edged sword, and often not permanent. Our tie to our parents is more than just how they behave towards us. Even if they aren't actively imposing themselves on us, we can't escape the fact that we absorb inherited positions similar to theirs. For example, we may have freedom at our identity level, but we still need to bridge the gap between our inherited level and our identity level. More than that though, we need some level of love and approval from our parents. The further we are away from our parent's levels, the harder that is.

This is effectively the options we have; we are either constrained by our parents, and have to put up with their (possibly uncomfortable) levels, or we become unconstrained, and feel distant from them, and lacking in love and support. Given how important parents are to human programming, it's often abiding by them that is the lesser of two less-than-perfect

Family & Parents

options, but each situation is unique. The choices we have will depend so much on the circumstances, whether we were unconstrained during adolescence, and what support we have elsewhere in our life.

In reality, becoming unconstrained is quite rare. It takes quite unusual circumstances, because of how strong the parent's need to be unyielding is.

This can happen when the child achieves or associates with something that is of very high standing, at least from the perspective of the parent, so that the parent feels unable to limit the child in a way that passes on levels and core needs. Alternatively, it can occur if the parent is facing great difficulty in their own life, and are weakened by that, so that they cannot behave how they would like towards the child. Perhaps they start to emotionally rely on the child for support, and a reverse relationship occurs. Neither situation is a reflection of the parent or child, it is likely simply down to circumstance: we all try to do the best we can, in our situation.

This can be difficult for both sides. The parent feels a little helpless, angry, or stressed. The child is deeply frustrated, and sees the parent as weak. The parent may find that, because of the large gap between them, if they tried to impose themselves in the present, they may have to be very harsh or obtrusive, which hurts both parties.

There is often a period, long or short, where the child does have a certain amount of freedom, perhaps enjoying their success, feeling unconstrained, and unaware of the situation. During this time, the child may have more freedom to fantasize about what they could achieve, as everyone else appears to be being held back a little, by something which they aren't. They may also have an inflated, or unusual, self-image. They will have rejected the idea they are similar to their parents, disregarding any similarities they do have, in favour of a self-image they simply want. This may at times leave them a little conflicted. They will find that they are very diverged, with strong role behaviours, such as a deep focus on work, and having adopted many of the behaviours and values of the subculture they associate with.

However, when the child faces difficulty in life, which everyone does at times, they will feel difficulty in turning to the parent, for fear of the parent being able to reverse the dynamic. Despite the *actual* dynamic, the parent still feels the need to be unyielding, and their programming will be going into overdrive to resolve the paradox, of levels versus family. Given half a chance, the parent could try to return the dynamic to one where they are in control, which would be very hurtful for the child, given their relative identity levels in society.

The unconstrained child, whether an adult or adolescent, may be a bit of a loose cannon. Because they aren't being constrained by their parent, they reject the constraint of others in society, struggle to fit into hierarchies, and may have deep rivalries. Those rivalries include a lot of transference, effectively including a lot of the frustration of their unconstrained situation. They feel they both want to be constrained by something, but also feel they don't want to be constrained by anything. Others may get a sense that they don't know where the unconstrained person will go, without a comfortable position in life, that the person feels content with.

Sometimes difficulty is never uncovered, but sometimes it is. If it is, it can be a very difficult situation to resolve. It can result in a deep power struggle between parent and child, as neither the parent nor the child wishes the other to have the upper hand. The levels can't be given up, but nor can the family dynamic. And, even if the parent-child relationship is solved, the child then still has to interact at the higher level against a certain headwind, which the parent is unlikely to be able to help with. Nevertheless, every situation can be so unique.

Too constrained

The opposite of unconstrained is too constrained. In this situation, the parent's behaviours are overly strong or dominant, which can be uncomfortable for the child.

This can happen in a number of ways. The parent can be strongly reducing of the child. Or, the parent can be distant but restrictive. Or, the parent can be overly supportive and defining of their child, in an obtrusive way. However it happens, the child feels too constrained, and finds it harder to pursue, and develop, their own individuality.

There are many situations where the parent probably feels like they are trying to lead or teach their children, without realising they are being overly restrictive on the child developing their own path in life, but each situation is unique. There are other situations where the parent is simply too constrained themselves, and this then cascades into their own parenting style, as they try to remain unyielding to their children, against their own headwinds.

In terms of how a person deals with being too constrained, it can actually be similar to how someone deals with being unconstrained.

This is because despite being opposites (unconstrained vs. too constrained), the common factor is that comfortable parental authority is lacking. Without that (and depending on their personality and circumstances), a person will either try to find comfortable authority elsewhere in society, or prevent anyone having authority over them, and defend it at all cost. Unconstrained or too constrained people can deal with it in the same way.

Therefore we can actually consider this more generally, and look at the idea that we have a space in our programming for an "authority need".

The authority need

On average, in society, parent-child relationships will be slightly more "too constrained" than "unconstrained". This is representative of the fact that parents have to provide a little extra restraint, to prevent their children being too comfortable in different sub-cultures to the one the parent is comfortable in, or to prevent the child "out-valuing" them. This causes the social delta that we looked at earlier in the book. The social delta causes the majority of us to be diverged, due to parents having to work harder to maintain authority. The social delta causes everyone's inherited levels (including those of our parents and their parents etc) to be lower and more inconvenient than each person would like.

As a side note, whether a parent wishes to be an "over constraining" type parent, an "under constraining" parent, or get it just right, is largely out of their control, although good intentions certainly help (good intentions = get the amount of constraint just right). Through the myriad of interactions that the parent and child have over the years, the dynamic is likely to simply develop not based on will, but on the unique circumstances, and the parent's own position in life. Therefore even with the best intentions, these situations may still occur.

We have a required part of our programming reserved for an authority.

It is something our programming expects, and needs to have, when we enter the world, but how it is fulfilled is more flexible.

If our parents comfortably fulfil this need, i.e. we look up to them, and accept their authority, then we feel most at ease.

Family & Parents

We can even resist strong authorities from society, because our authority need is already fulfilled, and so we are less affected by them.

If our parents don't fulfil this need, then we may find we are susceptible to other people trying to fulfil it. To cope with this, perhaps we find someone in society we really look up to, and who fulfils the need comfortably, or perhaps we simply defend this need, and prevent anyone taking a position of authority against us.

If our parents fulfil the need too strongly, then we need to find someone, or something else to counteract that. Often this will be alignment with a greater authority in society, who we use to fulfil our authority need, and keep our parent's uncomfortable impositions at bay.

Another way people can deal with a difficulty in their authority need, is to be authoritarian over others. This can be for many purposes, for example to have control over others (that can be exercised when they feel weaker), or to make others feel like they do, or to simply have an outlet for their emotions. Occasionally, people can become dominant over others in undesired way, which can be deeply uncomfortable.

The more equal society is, then the more, on average, parents can get just the right amount of authority and respect.

Parents as leaders

Looking at the authority need from the other way round, from the parent's perspective, this means that the parent has to *have* authority.

This can be difficult to achieve. We have natural instincts to be parents, but in the modern world we don't necessarily have natural authority. There are many reasons why this is the case. For hunter-gatherers, who travel around in small family-based units, each tribe will have natural leaders. Each tribe will have leadership skills and behaviours passed down from many, many generations before, and naturally embedded into people. Each parent will have more authority, and each child, growing up, will learn more natural authority, from copying the parent.

When we started to form settlements, people tended to split into leaders and followers. As settlements grew into civilisations (and the larger and more unequal society becomes), the smaller the number of leaders there are, and the greater number of followers there are. It becomes much less likely that natural authority is felt, and passed down family lines.

Also, the larger and more unequal society becomes, then levels have greater prominence in the parent-child relationship. We looked earlier at how a child's levels are generally biased towards the levels of the parent's:

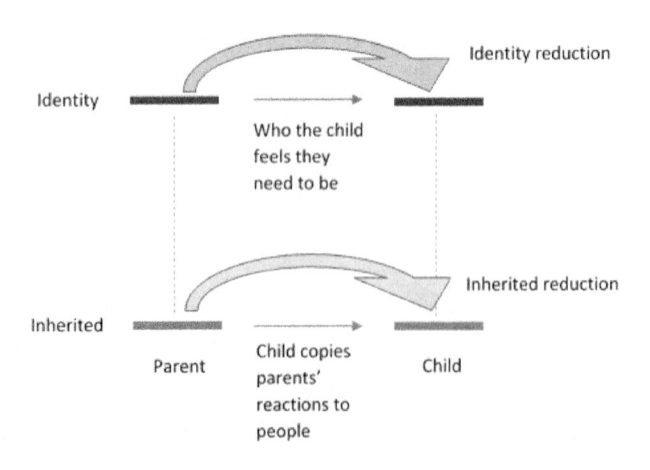

Identity — Identity reduction
Who the child feels they need to be

Inherited — Inherited reduction
Parent — Child copies parents' reactions to people — Child

Against all this, authority can be a difficult prospect. As these factors influence each parent-child relationship

Family & Parents

(influenced by the generations before, and the difficult social environment we find ourselves in), it will be common for some to veer towards "too much" authority, and some to veer towards "too little".

There is further difficulty in getting the right amount of authority: leadership has changed.

Leadership in big societies becomes more about large scale organisation, directing and managing subordinates, and impressing power and authority over others, so they do what you say. Leadership becomes less about leading a family, and more about climbing above others and telling them what to do. Leadership becomes less about leading a small group to survive in the wilderness, and instead more about leading people through a complex social environment, where everyone is behaving in an organisational type way.

These two types of leadership: family leadership vs. organisational leadership; are very different. Only a small proportion of people are able to do both naturally, and come across as the modern version of natural authority.

Family leadership of course requires some element of organisation. We have to lead our family, and are in charge of our children. There is often no-one above us to guide us, or to step in and help: the buck stops with us. We have to make decisions, and provide guidance and support. However, family leadership is more about the natural bonds between parent and child, that follows a similar process throughout nature. It is a finely tuned process that, through millions of years of evolution, is simply the way that offspring are nurtured into being adults.

Organisational leadership often has to be learnt. For example, if we take on a leadership role at work, or in our social clubs, then often it takes time to get used to that position. We learn behaviours that fit our roles, and learn how to act and inspire confidence. Often this requires copying leadership behaviours from those in similar positions. Businesses often send employees on management training courses, to teach them teamwork and leadership.

Whilst this is often successfully achieved, it is learnt behaviours not natural behaviours. We are learning to play a role, rather than changing our natural authority.

With so much organisational leadership around us, as well as so little opportunity to simply be natural family leaders (and a social structure that is stacked against parents, due to everyone being diverged), natural authority in a family falls by the wayside somewhat.

We grow up without learning natural leadership, and instead are faced with everyone behaving organisationally. The behaviours we do learn, mostly from in and around our close friends, often aren't applicable to parenthood. If we become a parent, we have to learn new parenting behaviours, that are often more organisational. We copy other parent's behaviours, and feel pressure to replicate their apparent successes. Instead of following natural processes and instincts, parenting follows fads and trends.

Natural parental leadership is where things are in balance, whereas in the modern world we can find that the set of behaviours we have (upon reaching adulthood) aren't applicable to parenting, or we become an organisational leader, and lead without the interpersonal connection.

All this means that getting the right amount of authority as a parent can be very difficult. Even if we want to impose a balanced amount of authority, we may not have the tools to successfully achieve it. A balance is often reached, and the emotions still guide families towards reasonable dynamics, but it is perhaps like a car veering down a road from side to side, rather than just driving in a straight line. Nevertheless, with it being so difficult, and there being variation from one family to another, it is perhaps no surprise that situations can occur where too much, or too little constraint is felt by the child.

In isolated tribes, the leadership will be more equally shared. Parents are then more natural leaders, and more comfortably fulfil the authority need of the children.

The same is true of more equal societies. There, we can step out of the rat race more easily, and be natural parents more of the time.

Parents summary

Essentially, being a modern human parent is fraught with difficulty. Our instincts are there, but they're often hidden, or not quite applicable to the situation in front of us.

For example, we need to balance our family dynamic with the dynamics that come from the various different societal positions of the family members. We feel an urge to limit our children more than we should, in order that they don't "out-value" us, or in order that they don't behave too strongly in ways that are very different to our own behaviours. We want to encourage them, but getting the right amount of authority is very difficult.

We may be diverged, and not have a strong idea of how we come across, or how our actions are received. We may have difficult parents of our own, and occasionally feel pushed up against them, between a rock and a hard place. But, we feel pressure and instinct to be a good parent regardless, and perhaps find ourselves trying to mentally shape the situation in front of us, into one where we are a good parent. We do this partly because it tends not to be our intentions, or our instincts, that prevent us being a good parent, but what is layered over the top, as well as the unusual circumstances and obstacles that modern societies put in our way. However, it leads to a split, whereby the children see a parent trying to project "completeness", but perhaps not feeling it. The child can, at times, feel lacking, whilst the parent is unyielding, and defensive of any lack of parenting skill. The child may then transfer some of their core emotions onto their friends and work instead.

The parent is being urged and pressured to be (and feel like) a well-rounded (hunter-gatherer) parent, in an environment where it isn't always possible.

On becoming a parent, we may not feel we have natural parental behaviours, and have to learn new ones, and adapt our personality. Instead of simply following behaviours that come naturally to us, instead we use more organisational ones. They are more impersonal, but necessary to guide our children through the modern social environment.

Being a modern parent is a difficult task, even at the best of times. Our environment makes it hard, just like it has done for every other modern human, whether in the last 5000 years of civilisation, or ever since 10,000 BC, when we gave up our natural hunter-gatherer lifestyle.

Our development and our family

In the second half of this chapter, we shall move on from the parent-child relationship to look at families more broadly. We will first look at adolescence, and how we change and grow in our families during this time. Then we shall look at siblings, before looking at the emotions and types of conflicts that come up in families.

Adolescence and becoming an adult

Roughly a quarter of our lives are spent growing into an adult. During this time, our environment, our emotions, and our circumstances can change a lot. All this is leading towards us becoming an adult, when the dust settles, and we have (theoretically) grown into the person we are.

There is a huge amount to learn and experience. As we do learn, and experience, our view of the world changes. Our view of the social landscape around us can be different depending on our age. That perception of the social landscape is important, because it is against that that we are interpreting our experiences.

Looking at *how* our view of the world differs, depending on our age, we can start with the psychology of young children, and then discuss how it changes as we grow into an adult. Important factors are how we view other people, and how the fundamental nature of our emotions change.

Young children are taking in the world for the very first time. This affects how they view other people. A good example of this is the "Sally-Anne test"[30].

In the test, a child is shown two people, Sally and Anne, and two baskets. Anne sees Sally put an item in one basket. Anne then leaves. Without Anne seeing, Sally switches the item to the second basket.

Anne then comes back. The child is then asked which basket Anne would look in first, after she's come back, in order to find the item. In their first few years, a child often says the second basket. The *child* saw Sally switch the item to the second basket, but can't appreciate that *Anne* didn't. It is difficult for the child to put themselves in Anne's shoes, and understand that Anne didn't see Sally switch the item to the second basket.

This shows how young children often experience the world only through their eyes and their emotions, rather than being able to understand other people's points of view. When someone upsets a young child, often explaining the complex reasoning of why someone might behave like that doesn't help, and instead the person that upset the child simply has to be decried as bad. Similarly, we live in an imperfect world, and whilst this is readily apparent to an adult, it is not to a child. When our imperfect world causes bad things to happen around the young child, they often don't understand, and they can even think that they might be causing it, and have to be reassured that they are not.

Even at the start of teenage years, emotions are still difficult to understand. The film Inside Out, other than being a fantastic film, shows this well. The different emotions: joy, sadness, anger and disgust, are separated out into different characters, and their interactions shown. The moral of the story is that each plays its part, and that being able to separate out the different emotions and talk about them can help. If emotions are a swirling pallet of colours, then they can be doubly so when we're experiencing them for the first time (whilst also having a huge range of new experiences). Each emotion, good or bad, raises new questions, doubts and unknowns, and takes a while to get used to, and learn where they go. Separating them out, and learning about them, can help a growing teen.

A person at the start of their teenage years may still struggle somewhat to understand other people's views. This is because it is difficult to appreciate an emotion, and how it affects our behaviour, if we have never experienced it ourselves. In the words of Confucius: I hear and I forget; I see and I remember; I *do* and I *understand*. Childhood experiences tend not to be too varied, so it can often be hard for a child to fully appreciate other people's points of view, simply because they haven't had the breadth of experiences to feel different emotions. As we grow and have different experiences, we slowly piece together the world, and why people act the way they do.

On the other side of this, when interacting with a growing person who hasn't experienced a particular emotion yet, it can be difficult to understand *their* point of view. Once we've learnt something, or experienced it, it can be very difficult to remember what it was like to *not* have known it, or to *not* have experienced it yet. We can't appreciate what the landscape looks like to someone who has a less full perception of it.

In terms of the traits of our teenage years, these are often quite distinct and strange in themselves. Perhaps the reason for this is less down to a natural teenage development, and more down to how our modern world changes that part of our development.

Modern teenagers are often lethargic and less energetic. Modern adults often don't feel like an adult. Hunter-gatherer teenagers are learning survival skills, and don't have the luxury of a lie in. Hunter-gatherer adults are proud beasts of nature. It's possible that the traits of modern human teenagers are representative of a subconscious curb on their growth as a human, without something proud and "adult" to grow into, with rites of passage that truly feel fulfilling against our programming.

In terms of the development of our levels during adolescence, each person's inherited position grows throughout that time, generally mimicking the parent's with respect to the age group around us. As we become an adult, it should roughly line up with the parent's. There are perhaps some situations where the growth of the inherited position is stunted (even if the identity level can be high in society), but generally the transfer of levels from parent to child is quite robust, through the dynamic they have. Through countless interactions, then questions are implicitly answered, behaviours are kept in check (with approval and disapproval), and some level of emotional connection is there.

When we're in our late teens or early 20s, our social lives are still more flexible than they will be as adults. We're still taking in the world: different people and different experiences. Whilst, as an adult, our social lives, position in life, and our core bonds become more concrete, before then, they aren't.

Our social bonds are yet to fully solidify. Who will become our main source of comparison? Who will be our rivalry, our support, or the people we feel most ourselves with? We can find that we become part of a new group, that we feel better reflects who we are, and that new group becomes an important part of us. We can still find new groups as an adult of course, but as an adult that group will be built on previous groups, who our thoughts return to, whereas as an adolescent this can become part of the foundation, and we can largely forget about previous groups. Of course this all varies from person to person, and depends hugely on the individual circumstances.

The result of this is that our emotions are more adaptable in our late teens, or early 20s. Our emotions are more cloudy, and less attributed to specific sources. We can be affected by some things happening near us, good and bad, and then forget about them. In contrast, as we become an adult, the dust settles, and it is harder to move around.

At the end of adolescence many things become more set: for example our comparisons, primary friendships, behaviours, our sources of comfort and elation, and our self-belief. These tend to persist throughout adulthood (unless we put effort into changing them). How we see the world at the end of adolescence forms part of our blueprint, and is often how we want, or need, to see the world throughout adulthood.

Of course we adapt, and the world changes, but there are some things within us that don't.

This creates a slight difference between the emotional responses to socialisation between adults and children. In the children the implications are often more fluid, but in the adult they are more concrete. This is reflective of the fact that, as human beings, as described throughout this book, our parents are our social anchor. We can deviate from them, and be different from them, but the further away from them we are, often the more difficult it becomes. In order to be an anchor, their position, behaviours and perceptions need to be more concrete. If the child is to learn from the adult as a reference point, then the adult must be more fixed. Sexual maturity and adulthood therefore go hand in hand.

This also creates a difference in perception between adolescents and adults. Adolescents are often more open, free-willed, and righteous, whereas adults tend to be more realistic, constrained and directed. As an adult's programming becomes less changeable, they are more likely to (as a collective) represent how society is at that current time.

There is also a nuanced side effect of this, for modern humans. Because there is so much variety in society (and experiences of that society vary so much from person to person), we can often find that our friends, views, behaviours, and bonds, harden up a little before we fully understand them. Sometimes, things that seem fine around the time of early adulthood, become more permanent before we realise they do, and come back to bite us later, at which point it is much harder to change them. It is a paradox, because even if someone told us that was going to happen, we might not believe them. We only really appreciate emotions when we've been on the receiving end of them.

By the end of adolescence, we are modern human adults. We have gone from a fresh-faced new-born, to understanding and trying to fit into our large modern societies. Through each experience, we develop behaviours, beliefs, and defences. We develop many layers as each experience resolves. Occasionally, we might try to take a layer off, but then we are reminded of a previous experience, and reform that layer with the associated behaviours, beliefs and defences.

Sometimes, all we can do is take life as it comes. It is what it is. We can plan, but then things change. We can try to head in a certain direction, only to find that we actually would have preferred to go in a different direction. Some things we wish had turned out differently. Some things that we desire, turn out to be things we don't actually want. Such is the trials of being a modern human.

Perhaps we are flowing down a river, only able to make minor changes to our speed or direction. Perhaps everything is predefined, and we are simply living out an already-finished story. Perhaps we, like everyone else, are facing the great unknown: the future; and trying to shape it as best we can (hopefully working together to make it better for everyone).

Attributes

Before moving on to the section on siblings, we can briefly consider our attributes, and how they affect our lives. Attributes can have some of the biggest impacts on our life, but their influence can often be elusive to unpick.

Attributes can include a large range of things, from our look, shape, size, abilities, strength, intelligence, skill, the way we sound, the loudness of our voice, or the way we move, to name but a few. Most are things that we can't change, but nevertheless they can impact our lives, good and bad.

Family & Parents

How our attributes affect our social lives is more obvious. They may affect how our friendships form, our interests, and our profession. In this short section we will briefly look at the more subtle impact of our attributes, which is how they compare to our parent's.

How our attributes compare to our parent's attributes can have a big impact on the parent-child dynamic.

Sometimes being similar to our parents is a detriment. If our parents fulfil a particular niche social role, based on their attributes, then we can then encroach onto that. Life can be tough at the best of times, and one way to deal with that is to find something that you're the best at, or a role that you can own, and build your life around that. When a child comes along, who is very like you, it can threaten your coping strategy for modern life.

On the other hand, sometimes being different from our parents is a detriment. We have less in common, or we have an attribute that our parents find threatening or difficult. People develop all sorts of defence mechanisms (and biases) based on their random experiences in life, for example with people that are tall, short, loud, quiet, overweight, skinny, attractive, or unattractive, to name a tiny fraction of possible attributes. If the parent then finds those attributes, that they've perhaps had a negative experience of, in their children, then it can be a cause of difficulty.

How our attributes compare to our parent's attributes can also have a big impact on our self-image.

Sometimes being similar to our parents can impact our self-image. For example there may be things about our parents that we don't like, that we then find difficult to accept in ourselves. Sometimes being different can impact our self-image, because we draw some of our self-image from how we see our parents. If we do differ from them, then we can feel we come across one way, similar to our parents, but actually we come across differently.

How our attributes, good and bad, compare to our parents can be important and even defining. But, unfortunately, there is little we can do about that, good or bad. We are who we are.

Nevertheless, the difference, and its impact, is often simple, and obvious to other people, but not us. That is because it gets hidden behind everything else in this book.

The more social freedom, and space, each person has, the less our children's attributes will affect the relationship. They can be more attractive than us, taller, more sociable, more intelligent, and it wouldn't matter. Similarly, they can be less, and it wouldn't matter. Our desire to maximise our value works best when it is about small increments, in step with friends and family, rather than in unequal societies, where it is drawn to heights of possibility, and can make large leaps. When we are less driven by our desire to maximise our value, then our children's attributes, good and bad, will have less of an effect on the dynamic.

When friends and family take greater prominence, and there is less competition in our core relationships, our lives are generally more comfortable.

Siblings

Sibling relationships are complicated! There are such strong emotions involved.

There is often a lot of conflicted emotions between siblings, as with any family dynamic. There is love, and a deep bond of shared (or similar) experiences. They are the people on the planet who we may have the greatest similarity with, even if we don't want to admit it (and, mostly, we don't). But at the same time, there can be deep rivalries, and bitter conflict.

Siblings can be great. We can be similar, work together, share our experiences, and learn from one another. Having siblings can often be a good source of learning social skills for a child. Or, siblings can be terrible, and be the bane of our lives, or the manifestation of our difficulties.

The defining aspect of siblings is equality. Every sibling wants to not be less than their other siblings. To be less than another sibling is deeply hurtful, frustrating and uncomfortable.

On the other side, each person is probably happy to be more than their other siblings.

Equality is a difficult prospect between siblings, because siblings will always be different. It's unlikely that they will have similar achievements, or follow the same path in life. Society values different things (although most are rooted in money and status). Therefore, siblings will naturally achieve different levels in society, have different friends, feel most themselves in different sub-cultures, and have different wealth.

In the sibling with the upper hand, the feelings are less strong. There is perhaps a little freedom in that position. But, there is also often a lack of understanding. They simply can't relate to feelings of difficulty in other siblings, or perhaps aren't even aware that their successes are causing difficulty for their siblings. After all there is little they can do about it. They can't undo their successes, so they may be forced, to avoid guilt, to believe that they are simply better, or the victor, and that the result is right. Yet, one thing is for sure, they certainly don't want to give up their position. Yielding even a little bit of the upper hand is very difficult for siblings. How can they trust each other, on a more equal playing field? What if there are hidden agendas? The emotions driving siblings are deep and strong after all. And, like any equality, for the sibling that doesn't have the upper hand, there is perhaps a small part of

A Theory of Everyone

them that wants to reverse the dynamic, and feel in ascendancy themselves. As a result, the sibling with the upper hand becomes unyielding.

To not have the upper hand puts a sibling in a double bind. They may want a little more in life, to equal their sibling at least, but the people they want to turn to (to help them with their frustration): their family; is instead a reminder that they have less.

They can find that it's very difficult to even talk about sibling hierarchies in families. To acknowledge it, is to admit a reality very difficult to change, and that is something that humans find very difficult. Even if they did air their grievances, others can't give them success on a platter, to meet their sibling's achievements, so the result is that often positive intention is said, but not communicated, and family conflicts become obscured.

Luckily, in the modern world, if they need to, there are many ways for a sibling to get their own back. The nature of sibling competition often changes throughout the course of their lives. Perhaps first of all it is about friends, then education, then money and jobs, then partners. Then perhaps it becomes about having children, and then how good a parent we are. Then, when both/all siblings realise that none of us are brilliant parents, it goes back to money and status. Sometimes later in life siblings forget why they were competing, and sometimes it goes on until the bitter end.

The antidote to all this is the parents.

Technically, the parents have the power to mediate and apply equal value. At the core of the matter, siblings are really just competing over parental approval. If the parents simply expressed that they valued their children equally, siblings can become bearable to us.

Family & Parents

However, as with everything, it gets very complicated. Everything is entangled. Parents are the solution, but may be the cause. They may be the cause simply because of their own parents, and the cascade.

And, in unequal societies, parenting can become very difficult.

For example, firstly, the two drivers, to be equal siblings in the family unit, and to be equal siblings in their successes in society, are both real and valid. How does the parent effectively communicate equal value, when they perhaps do not even appreciate the way each child feels valued by society? Or, if one child has found greater success than the parent, or the parent is diverged, there will be a deep hesitation before making a child feel warm and comfortable at their identity level.

The parent then has a balancing act. They have to balance sibling equality in the family unit, with diverse successes outside of the family unit. They have to try to make the children feel fulfilled in the family unit, but not more fulfilled than the parent themselves, otherwise unyielding becomes harder. They need to balance rewarding the child, and showing pride in their achievements, without showing a lack of pride in the individual.

This is often very difficult, hence why there are so many difficult sibling relationships out there. When we live in large societies, with value out there greater than the value we can get from our parents, parents can find themselves a referee between two teams playing a game they don't recognise, and each playing it differently.

Parents can achieve comfortable control. It is a balancing act but it can be achieved in some circumstances. External successes can be recognised, but without affecting the family dynamic. We then live two lives, one inside the family unit, and one outside. This can work, after all there are many, many situations where modern humans have to be two things at once. (as a side note, social media makes all our links stronger and tighter, so being two things at once is harder when we have much more regular contact with each side of the coin).

However, sometimes (or perhaps very often), comfortable control can't be wholly achieved.

As mentioned, if the parent is insecure in their identity level, which is very common, then they will find some mental block in being able to make their children feel comfortable in theirs. If the parent cannot make each sibling feel comfortable in their identity level, then siblings become more insecure, and the sibling dynamic is more influenced by external factors.

When the parent doesn't have the authority or capability to apply equal value to the children, or they have their own difficulty they're struggling against, that limits their behaviour, then they tend to do one of two things.

Sibling rivalries become established, that the parent doesn't resolve; or, the parent subconsciously creates rivalries by favouring one child.

The reason they do this is distance. To hide their own, perhaps slightly fragile identity, or their own difficulty, they use sibling rivalry. If the children are consumed with each other, they aren't paying attention to the parent. By allowing, or even encouraging a certain level of rivalry, the parent finds it easier to maintain their own identity.

You might think that the children should gang up on the parent, but unfortunately this is fraught with difficulty. For example, the parent is probably doing it because they have to, rather than any conscious thought. It would be a source of guilt and regret for a parent not to see each child develop to their fullest, so it would only be done when the parent feels inhibited. Also, the greater inequality that exists, the less trust is available between siblings, especially given what is at stake. And, not least, the more the children push up against the parent, the more the parent is pushed up against their own parents, and the more the parent may respond by subversively encouraging more competition.

The answer, as much as possible, is to value the children for who they are, not what they do: unconditional love and support. If the child is valued as a person, then their successes are something to simply enjoy, rather than covet and chase. However perhaps this is easier said than done.

Siblings can be very difficult. There is so much at stake, that it's so hard to be truly honest and open, and to really trust our siblings, or know what they're thinking. When it works, it can be great. When it doesn't, it can be very difficult. But, even when the sibling dynamic goes wrong, there is a bond between them always.

Our emotions and our family

There are many emotions in family, good and bad, that are often a result of the topics discussed earlier in this chapter. This section looks at some of the unusual implications of those topics.

The three aspects in this section are: our *parental projections*, where humans project emotions related to their parents onto others; *conflicted emotions*, where we often feel two things at once; and *obscured conflict*, where the heart of the matter can't be addressed, so conflict is driven by that matter, but manifests itself in a different topic.

Parental projection and annoyances

There was the simple rule that we looked at earlier, that is quite a generalisation, but nevertheless largely holds in most cases:

that everything we do represents some aspect of our relationship with our parents.

We often don't feel it, it is instead perhaps the mess under the carpet, that occasionally peeks through. However, in certain circumstances, some of the difficulty gets transferred over. It tends to be low level, and simply gets swept up in our personality, but it is there nonetheless.

It's likely that there are many annoying things that our parents do.

We can't really help it as human beings. These could be small, like mannerisms that get on our nerves, or something they repeatedly do, even though we've asked them not to, or expressed frustration at.

Often, we project these annoyances onto others. When other people do things that are similar, we find that annoying. It can't be helped, and we try to tolerate it, but at times it can be difficult, especially in our closer relationships.

These frustrations and annoyances then become part of the inwards and outwards forces in group dynamics. They are an outwards pull, that is preventing us forming an independent, wholly close group of friends, separate from our parents. Each person will bring their own set of things that annoy and frustrate them into a social group.

The annoyances from our parents appear to be minor, but often actually represent quite deep things. The emotional kernel, or what is under the carpet, are things we don't really want to get involved in, unless we have to, so instead our brain diverts and suppresses any deep difficulty, and they tend to pop up as these apparently minor traits.

Often the things that annoy us in our parents are to do with the fact that they are diverged (as every modern human is). For example, we get annoyed at their inconsistencies. They may project one thing, a level or persona, that they appear to fully believe, but then they don't always fulfil it. We see a broad range of their lives, as their children, and need a certain level of closeness, as well as needing to follow and learn from them (to some extent), and so the inconsistencies are more apparent to us. They disregard the differences. As their children, we find that annoying. It is implicit pressure to achieve something without the full arsenal to do it, and to disregard the differences ourselves.

Whilst parental annoyances can therefore be deep rooted, it's probably best to keep them that way, and just deal with the consequences. On reaching adulthood, it may be difficult to change what we find frustrating and annoying, but, sometimes we have to try, and find compromises.

Conflicted emotions

Life as modern humans involves conflicted emotions. This is not least because we have many aspects of duality, for example our identity level vs. our inherited level, or our family vs. our social life, or our internal self vs. our external self.

This is no truer than our emotions towards our parents.

The modern parental relationship is an ill-fitting glove. It's such an important relationship for a human being, but often there are issues and difficulties with it, in the modern world. We feel emotions, such as anger, frustration and guilt, at the same time as love and empathy.

The anger, or frustration, can be representative of the way we can feel the difficulty of modern society through our relationships with our parents. The guilt, on the other hand, is representative of the side that wants to help the parent, because we care about them, and want the best for them (deep down). The love and empathy are representative of the bond we share.

All of these emotions are wrapped up in the dynamic we have with them.

Perhaps the most conflicted emotion we feel is the guilt. This is because there will often be, even in "normal" modern parental relationships, some frustrations, restrictions, an unyielding nature, and a small element of control. Part of the child wants to resist this, but part of them can't. The part that can't is, in turn, partly because it hurts the parent not to be able to do those unyielding, slightly controlling, frustrating behaviours. We then feel guilt in preventing the parent doing things that restrict us.

This minor control can take many forms. Some even seem, on the surface, to be positive, like encouraging the child to placate the parent, for example as a mummy's boy or daddy's girl. Others can involve overly restrictive rules, or not allowing the child to quite enjoy their lives more than the parent enjoys theirs. Often the parent does things to prevent the child expressing their anger or frustration at the parent-child dynamic, or preventing criticism or free thought, in case they turn that on the parent themselves.

A lot of this has to go on because of levels. The parent is unyielding, from the more restrictive societal position that they have found themselves in. They also have to apply the social delta, due to our spread-out social lives, and the possibility the child can "out-value" them.

Sometimes the parent just has to loosen the reins a little, but at other times they are coming up against an immovable obstacle. Either way, if the child fights the parent's authority, they may actually cause the parent difficulty. The parent feels difficulty because it pushes them up against their own social links, testing their other relationships, and their relationship with their own parents. They can feel judged as a parent, or hurt from additional difficulties on top of an already challenging situation. The child then has the double-bind of feeling the need to fight the parent, but also feeling guilt for doing so.

It also gives the parent a conflict, between needing to feel like a good parent on one hand, but being restrictive and limiting (in what they feel they have to do as a modern parent) on the other. They know they are causing frustration and hurt, but (sometimes) feel they have no option.

As a child, at times we might feel we have to fight that bond, and deal with the guilt and distance, and other times we have to concede a little. Communication can help, and often a balance is eventually found with compromise.

Guilt is therefore an emotion that ties us to our parents. We can't pull away too far, else we may hurt the parent and feel guilty for it, even if they may be hurting us with restrictions, and frustrations, if we don't pull away.

There are many other examples of conflicted emotions. Essentially our modern world, which our programming isn't entirely set up for, creates mismatches and duality. Our emotions, good and bad, are encouraging us towards certain behaviours. However, as modern humans, we can't reach the hunter-gatherer shaped destination, and so we are left with those emotions, that are often multi-pronged, and conflicted. Sometimes they can urge us away from things we don't wholly want, towards things we don't wholly want. Such is the nature of modern life.

Obscured conflict

The final aspect in this section is on obscured conflict.

When there is conflict in a family, it can be big. It's difficult to completely avoid conflict in modern families, and when it happens it can often escalate. The problem is that the emotions involved are so deep and important.

Because the emotions in families are so deep, often we can't talk about any real issues we have, for example when it comes down to our core needs such as love, pride and support, or conflict between siblings. When it comes down to our social levels in society, it becomes very difficult to discuss them, because they are difficult to change or talk around. No one wants to admit that a family member has a "higher" social position than them for example. It can be terrifying and brave to be open with a family member, because trust can be hard to come by, or there is so much at stake if it goes wrong.

Instead, we have to make it about something else. In this way, the arguments often become obscured and difficult to deal with.

Whilst the conflict can then become about anything, the actual form of arguments tends to follow certain directions.

Arguments can move around. One minute we're in conflict on one thing, then a topic comes up, and one person latches onto that topic, and diverts the conflict in a different direction. That issue then becomes the focus, and the real issue is obscured further.

Arguments can involve positive projection. This involves saying one thing, that's good, but in such a way that a different message is actually conveyed. In families especially, we often need to appear reasonable, with positive intentions. The parents want to be good parents. Siblings can better further their aims by appearing to be helpful and supportive. The negative conflict can then be hidden behind these projected intentions. We can stir up or partake in conflict without appearing to.

Arguments can involve consolidation. When there is conflict, if we get the upper hand, we then stop fighting and pretend all is normal. Then, the other person in the conflict, who still feels compelled to fight, looks unreasonable, and can be labelled as the instigator. The person with the upper hand tries to solidify their position. The other person is painted into a corner where if they react strongly, they look like the aggressor.

Arguments can involve provocation focus. We rile the other person up, wait for them to get annoyed, and then focus on that reaction, rather than the real issue.

People generally only use obscured conflict when they have to. It's best not to use it unless you actually have to, as it often gets situations muddled, and often comes back to bite.

The main place obscured conflict occurs is in families, because of the deep, very difficult, or impossible, to resolve emotions. The modern family often can't operate in a way that fulfils each person's programming. When difficulty exists, we simply have to make conflict about something else.

However, obscured conflict does occasionally spill out into our social lives too.

For example, when our social situations involve conflict based around levels, the conflict may also become obscured. Inherited levels often simply can't be admitted, and instead the individual has to bridge the gap between their inherited level and their identity level by being a little obtrusive. One way to do that is with obscured conflict, that gets those around them tied up in conflicts that are difficult to unpick. The more obscured conflict there is in society in general, the greater an indication there is that levels are colliding, and difficult parent-child relationships exist.

In the modern world, social media often causes more obscured conflict. The disproportionate interactions, combined with the ease at which we can project ourselves positively, lends itself to conflicts becoming obscured.

Obscured conflict comes from a place of deep hurt, for example if our circumstances don't allow our needs to be

A Theory of Everyone

fulfilled, but there is no open conflict to pin it on: the hurt is happening in a disguised way. When used on others, it replicates this in them, by saying one thing but conveying something else, to tie them up in knots, and pass on hurt without appearing unreasonable. It leaves someone else with hurt, but also frustration at not being able to easily respond.

Then, we may not be able to see and understand motives, because we're always having to resolve what is said first. If what our conscious mind has to resolve (i.e. the words and meaning of challenges), differs from what our emotions need us to do (i.e. actions that represent the overall dynamic), we can't move forwards. We want to tackle the dynamic of the relationship (the emotions involved), but we can't, because the focus is being strongly drawn to a particular issue, that isn't what the conflict is really about.

There is likely a lot of obscured conflict in any modern parent-child relationship. Perhaps this comes down to the conflicting drivers: parents feel love, and a need for children to respect them, and be their reflection, but also a need to reduce and maintain control, against the backdrop of our imperfect societies. They do one thing but say another, to a greater or lesser extent. This is why parents are often a no-go area. Perhaps this whole book is about navigating that obscured conflict with a parent. However, when we're in the midst of it, it becomes very hard to make sense of it all.

There are likely many other ways obscured conflict can occur. The common theme is that challenges are being made to obscure the real issues. The real issues are rooted in the fact that our underlying programming is that of a hunter-gatherer, but we find ourselves living in a modern environment (a fact which can't be changed), and so the difficulty manifests itself in an obscured way.

Family & parents summary

There are many things that are difficult, and will always be difficult in families, and with our parents specifically. In life, we have to do what we need to do. However, understanding where we are, why we are there, and where we're going, can help. In some situations, going closer to our parents and families helps, and in other situations pulling away helps. Circumstances are so nuanced, and it is always helpful to talk to others, to try to unpick our own landscape in life.

15

Core Needs

The last chapter of Part VI looks at our core needs.

They drive most of what we do. Yet most of the time, we are unaware of them. As modern humans, they get buried and diverted, imprinted and transferred.

Those core needs are our emotional basics. They are our inner self, if you strip away the modern world: full of the need to get ahead, the anger of being behind, the frustration of being limited, and the glory of wealth and status.

However, with the modern world, our inner self gets hidden and diverted, transferred and imprinted.

This can cause some of the aspects of duality that we've looked at in this book. For example, there are the two levels: our inherited level (our anchor) and our identity level (our associations). Then there is our self: what we see in the mirror vs. how we feel we come across. Then there are our emotions: how they can transfer, and leave us feeling two things at once. Then there is our family: how we have to balance the family dynamic, with the social levels of different family members, and the need to balance parental authority with social authority.

Core Needs

We often barely notice this duality. Part of the reason for this is that our brain tries to resolve it all by making things simple, and focussing on one side of the coin. To us, we are only *one* thing.

We *are* our identity level. We want to *know* how we come across with surety. We only feel ourself in certain environments, and when behaving in certain ways. A parent, or child, generally feels the parent-child dynamic should be based on *one* set of criteria.

Nevertheless, the duality is still there, it's just that we've shaped our perceptions and beliefs about the world to make it all fit together.

Our programming has a core, but it is also flexible to fit to different environments. We are part fixed; part flexible. We transfer our core onto the world we grow into, and whilst the things that then fulfil us may be very different to what our programming was expecting, we can still feel ourselves, and feel largely fulfilled. However, perhaps the further we get away from that core, the harder it is.

We have duality, borne from the transference of our core needs onto our strange modern circumstances, but it often goes unnoticed in the way our brains can resolve it all.

Hunter-gatherers lived in an environment where that core can be fulfilled at their source, and there was little around them that caused the core to be buried or imprinted. In contrast, our modern environments very rarely allow the core to be fulfilled in isolation, and in the most part there is large transference onto the society around us. This transference causes our duality. The core is still there, if a little buried. We build a house of cards over it. Sometimes we react according to the transferred bits, and sometimes we react according to the core bits.

The more unequal a society, the more this happens. This is because our need to maximise our value is also strong, and competes, and conflicts, with our core needs. Do we want fame and glory, or do we want stable, comfortable, supportive friends and a loving family? Both can feel very good, but in different ways.

To provide an analogy: we are like racing cars. We are both the car (the engine and outer shell), and the driver behind the wheel.

It is the outer shell that everyone else sees. We can even feel that our identity is based around the outer shell. We can form friendships with people with similar outer shells. Some people are attracted to us because of our outer shell, and we can take pride in it. When we meet new people, we project that we are the outer shell, and we then take part in the race of life.

We jostle with others, sometimes ahead, sometimes behind. We want to get forwards. Those at the front look like they're having a great time, and are adored and exalted, and this seems good. Or, even if we don't particularly like racing, sometimes we find we have to race a little regardless, because if we don't, someone else will get in front of us.

Sometimes we might find ourself near the front of the race, but just not feel that we deserve to be there. Sometimes we're behind where we feel we need to be, and dislike the fact we have to race against people that we consider ourselves above.

Sometimes we find our environment isn't suited to us. Perhaps we are best on asphalt, but the current terrain is muddy, and we are overtaken by people with greater tread on their tyres. We have to wait until we're back on a smooth road, before our slick tyres allow us to make up ground.

Sometimes we enjoy the jostling and the racing, but sometimes it's too much, and we get disillusioned with it. We feel hurt, and we become just the driver, with many questions

Core Needs

that generally start with "why do" and "how could". We forget we are in a race, and at that point it doesn't matter how powerful our car is.

Inside that car is the driver, just us, as a human being. All we want is fairly basic things: love, family, security, belonging, support, children and close friends. However, most of these things get wrapped up, confused, and interlinked, with the racing around us.

There are times in life where the racing slows down around us, and we can step out of the car, and just be ourself. Sometimes this is good, and we can feel and express our core needs. Sometimes it isn't, and we feel very exposed, and we feel some of what is under the clouds. All we can do then, is to get back in the car, start racing again, and transfer some of those feelings onto our racing style.

The more unequal society is, and the further the distance between the first place and last place, the faster people have to race: there is more to gain and more to lose. The more the racing slows down, then the less people focus on racing, and the more, at times, people can get out of their cars, and just be themselves. They can make others feel good for just being themselves, rather than for how good their car is.

Our core needs are a mix of love, value, dependency, belonging and togetherness. We principally need them from our parents and groups, i.e. our modern-day version of our tribe.

Our core needs include everything that a hunter-gatherer would get so easily in their environment, from their social bonds. Anything additional to this, that our modern world throws at us (principally our spread-out social lives, inequality, and, these days, social media), gets layered over the top of those core needs. We imprint and transfer our core needs onto the circumstances we come across in life. Our core needs are still there, but they are now a little buried. They're fulfilled by what we come across, rather than in the place they're most suited to.

We then end up with aspects of duality, and strange beliefs borne from how our brains try to resolve that duality onto a more singular outlook. That singular outlook allows us to act purposefully in the modern world. That singular outlook also allows our programming to make us feel closer to how we want to as human beings: complete, fulfilled, comfortable and content. We'd feel that way much more easily in a tribe, where our core needs are met at their source. That feeling is therefore the hunter-gatherer shaped destination, that our emotions are urging us towards.

However, in our modern environment, we can't fully get to that hunter-gatherer destination.

In the modern world, with everyone racing, our parents can end up valuing us for our car, and only provide dependency to help us drive faster. Our groups can be about where we are in the race, and we find ourselves competing more with the people in those groups, as people jostle and move around, and our lives develop in different directions. And with all that, our desire to maximise our value (the third key driver) takes greater prominence, and becomes consumed by the race, fully believing we are a car, and focussing entirely on getting ahead. Our core needs can transfer onto things that head in different directions, and leave us stretched. We seek fulfilment in the race, rather than friends and family, and, when the racing is faster, we are then seeking fulfilment from something that is less secure, and fickler.

The more our environment differs from our evolutionary one, the more transference and imprinting occurs, and we are no longer being fulfilled by something that is the exact fit for our programming. Our environment no longer gives us a

Core Needs

square peg for a square hole, and a round peg for a round hole. Whilst this can (if we're lucky) be unnoticeable to an individual, there are some side effects, as described in this book.

Our core needs are incredibly strong. Every human being, no matter the state of the world they are born into, has them. They are the human being inside the race car.

There may be times, or even whole lifetimes, where we never feel our core needs are lacking. At other times we might feel they are. If we feel they are lacking, we can provide them for ourself, but it is much harder.

Our core needs are drawn from some of our more fixed nature as human beings. However, if our core needs are lacking (which they will be in every modern human being from time to time, to one extent or another) then, luckily, we are also part flexible. Whilst are core needs are there, often we have to do the best with what we have, and there is no harm in relying on that flexibility in our programming, when we need to.

The more equal the world is, the easier it will be for our core needs to be fulfilled.

16

Modern Life

In 12,000 years, since we gave up our hunter-gatherer lifestyle, our environment has changed a lot: from small farmsteads, to Neolithic settlements, to cities and civilisations, and to the modern world of globalisation and technology.

Yet we still have a psychology that is suited to hunter-gatherer tribes. That hunter-gatherer environment matches our programming, and allows it to be fulfilled. When this psychology is applied to large, interconnected societies, with complex, spread-out social lives, it works, but not perfectly. We end up with loose ends, with some parts that sort-of work, and other parts that are out of balance. We find conflict with others, as we each try to replicate the feeling of being a hunter-gatherer. We try to feel like we would if we had a hunter-gatherer tribe: surrounded by a close, supportive group, that replicates our needs, and makes us feel ourself.

We live alongside people with completely different views, perspectives, experiences and behaviours, many of which are unfathomable to ourselves. We find it hard to truly empathise with others, and people's reactions can be an unknown, and often surprise us.

Modern Life

Add in inequality, and things get much more difficult. The more society is stretched, the more we are stretched as individuals.

There are natural restoring forces to inequality, for example the side of our humanity that rejects, and becomes angry at being treated as less. Or, for example, the social instincts trying to draw stretched social groups together, or the forces drawing us towards our parents when that relationship becomes more distant. But real change in society takes time, and perhaps only happens over generations.

Our modern social environment leads to our duality. We take our core needs, our fundamentals, and we find they aren't met at the source, so we transfer them onto society. We end up with duality of status (in our divergence), duality of self (between who we think we are vs. how we come across), duality of emotions (between our emotional kernel, and our emotional fingerprint), and duality between our family dynamic and our social-level dynamic within our family.

As we grow through adolescence and early adulthood, this duality happens naturally, as our influences spread out over our social links, without us even realising. Our brain tries it's best to resolve it all onto our programming, and to us, we are one, we are our identity. Nevertheless, when we view others, we sometimes see two, and think "who do they think they are", and perhaps notice differences between how someone acts, and how they think they come across.

Despite all the complexity, for the most part, our societies just about work.

However, it only works when you consider the average of our vast societies. Within that, some will experience the good, some the bad. The difficulty of the environment isn't shared out equally. Until we have much closer monetary equality, the difficulty will continue to be distributed more randomly, and work its way into pockets of society. Greater equality will take time. Monetary equality can't be achieved until global equality is, since each country needs to compete with others. The world won't be equal, where we can truly and meaningfully work together (or just enjoy life), for perhaps a few hundred years.

Where does this leave us as an individual?

Since we have duality, often this means we must be two things at once. We must fight for what we believe in, but find acceptance with what we have. We must strive for individual success, but integrate with our friends and family. We must fight to be our identity, and be treated how we like, whilst recognising why that isn't always possible, and managing that through our social web. We must find certainty in knowing who we are, whilst also accepting the that we will never truly know how others perceive us. We must be a parent, or child, whilst being independent, and following our own path and destiny.

We can try to be two things at once, but it is hard, and it's likely we won't ever truly fulfil both sides of the coin. In fact, often, especially when we're socialising in groups, and our focus is drawn onto those around us, it's almost impossible to be two things at once. Instead, we may find that we have to be *one*. We have to instead change our beliefs, in order for the events around is to make sense, and fit with who we are. Being two things at once can, at times, be almost impossible, and so we shape our views of the world around us in order to resolve it all into something that works for us. Once we've done that, we can be *one* thing, and act with certainty and purpose.

Yet we still have that duality.

This causes difficulty in being an individual, as well as in having self, and being centred and grounded in the modern world. We can certainly improve our individuality and self, but

Modern Life

it takes some effort and energy to achieve, though it can be worthwhile to do so.

We are catapulted out of adolescence with an approach to life very influenced by our parents, our friends, and the world around us, good and bad. Many people find they are lucky and their approach to life works, and what they have allows them to pursue what they want. Sometimes we get what we want for a bit, but then it all falls apart, or we need to temper and change our approach to life a little.

Sometimes we have to battle down our own path. Sometimes we have to find someone who understands us, represents us, or inspires us, and learn from them. We have to find what works for us, when facing our present circumstances.

However we approach life, there is one thing we all have in common. We're all just human beings, finding our way in life in a modern environment, that differs from our evolutionary one. There are many forces that guide or buffer us, but, slow as it may seem, the world is slowly improving.

"Difficulties are just things to overcome, after all." - Ernest Shackleton.

"Fall seven times and stand up eight." - Japanese Proverb.

"You may encounter many defeats, but you must not be defeated. In fact, it may be necessary to encounter the defeats, so you can know who you are, what you can rise from, how you can still come out of it." - Maya Angelou.

"I will prepare and some day my chance will come." - Abraham Lincoln.

"Our greatest glory is not in never failing, but in rising every time we fail." - Confucius.

"One does not always do the best there is. One does the best one can." - Catherine the Great.

Notes

1 For the history of Charles Darwin, and *The Origin of Species*, see *Voyage of the Beagle*, first published in 1905, which details his journal during the voyage. Also see www.nhm.ac.uk/discover/charles-darwin-most-famous-biologist.html. For the history of London's air pollution, including during the industrial revolution, see https://ourworldindata.org/london-air-pollution and https://www.historic-uk.com/HistoryUK/HistoryofBritain/Timeline-Industrial-Revolution/.

2 Throughout this book, discussion of early man (and historical dates in general), taken from Richard Overy *The Times Complete History of the World* (Times Books; Eighth edition, 2010), as well as Andrew Marr *A History of the World* (Pan Books, 2013) and Yuval Noah Harari *Sapiens: A Brief History of Humankind* (Vintage, 2015).

3 See Emily E. Groopman, Rachel N. Carmody and Richard W. Wrangham "Cooking increases net energy gain from a lipid-rich food" *Am J Phys Anthropol* (January 2015), 156(1): 11-18, which also discusses other food groups, and https://www.acsedu.co.uk/uploads/Food/Lesson%201%20and%20Assignment%201%20Sample%20Human%20Nutrition%20II.pdf.

4 Estimated from Google Maps, for example a walking trip from Cairo to Singapore takes 2290 hrs non-stop (a year has 8760 hours).

5 See https://en.wikipedia.org/wiki/Estimates_of_historical_world_population, which summarises the key studies that estimate population size between 10,000 BC and 3000 BC.

6 Richard H. Wilkinson *The Complete Gods and Goddesses of Ancient Egypt* (Thames and Hudson Ltd, May 2003).

7 https://www.ancient.eu/Utu-Shamash (Joshua J. Mark, 31 January 2017).

8 https://www.thoughtco.com/ancient-maya-astronomy-2136314 (Dr. Christopher Minster, 24 July 2019). I have applied some liberty in attributing later Maya beliefs to the early development of the

civilisation, however, few records exist of that early time, and I feel it is a fair assumption to make, at least to illustrate the point made.

9 https://www.universetoday.com/22570/venus-the-morning-star/.

10 Littleton, C. Scott *Gods, Goddesses, and Mythology* (Benchmark Books; New, 2005).

11 https://blog.britishmuseum.org/solar-eclipses-then-and-now/ (Jonathan Taylor, Curator, Middle East, 21 August 2017).

12 Kevin Leloux "The Battle of the Eclipse (May 28, 585 BC): a discussion of the Lydo-Median treaty and the Halys border" *Polemos* (December 2016) Vol 19-2, 31-54. Available here: https://www.academia.edu/32406140/The_Battle_Of_The_Eclipse _May_28_585_BC_A_Discussion_Of_The_Lydo_Median_Treaty _And_The_Halys_Border_Polemos_19_2_2016_p_31_54.

13 https://penelope.uchicago.edu/Thayer/E/Gazetteer/Topics/astronomy/_Texts/secondary/journals/The_Observatory/Eclipse_of_Pericles*.html.

14 Dicks, D. R *Early Greek astronomy to Aristotle* (Ithaca, N.Y.: Cornell University Press, 1970).

15 Henry C King *The History of the Telescope* (Dover Publications, 01 September 2003).

16 Jerome J. Langford *Galileo, Science, and the Church* (University of Michigan Press, 31 October 1992).

17 https://science.nasa.gov/science-news/science-at-nasa/2014/23jul_superstorm.

18 https://trove.nla.gov.au/newspaper/article/77351480.

19 https://oceana.org/marine-life/sea-turtles-reptiles/leatherback-turtle.

20 Sunquist, M.; Sunquist, F. *Wild Cats of the World* (Chicago: University of Chicago Press, 2002).

21 Prof. Mary Beard *SQPR: A History of Ancient Rome* (Profile Books, 20 October 2015), and the BBC documentary *Julius Caesar Revealed* (also by Prof. Mary Beard).

22 http://uttpalthewebbro.weebly.com/history.html.

23 Jay M Enoch "History of Mirrors Dating Back 8000 Years" *Optometry and Vision Science* (Nov. 2006) 83(10):775-81.

Notes

24 https://www.indiatimes.com/trending/human-interest/meet-the-real-life-mowgli-dina-sanichar-who-was-raised-by-a-pack-of-wolves-358296.html.

25 Carl Rogers *Client-Centered Therapy* (Constable, 1951).

26 https://en.wikipedia.org/wiki/Timeline_of_social_media.

27 See *Meditations* by Marcus Aurelius, or Massimo Pigliucci *How to Be a Stoic: Using Ancient Philosophy to Live a Modern Life* (Basic Books, 08 May 2018).

28 https://www.who.int/news-room/fact-sheets/detail/mental-health-strengthening-our-response (30 March 2018).

29 Malcolm Gladwell *Outliers: The Story of Success* (Penguin, 24 June 2009).

30 Wimmer, Heinz; Perner, Josef "Beliefs about beliefs: Representation and constraining function of wrong beliefs in young children's understanding" *Cognition* (1983) 13: 103–128.

All websites noted here reference their version on 02 March 2021 (accessible via https://archive.org/web/, should they have changed since).

About the author

John Almeryn was born in London. He studied Engineering at Christ's College, Cambridge University, before becoming a Chartered Engineer. Later in his career, he qualified as a Patent Attorney. He lives in Derby.